The Joy of Fatherhood

The First Twelve Months

EXPANDED 2ND EDITION

Marcus Jacob Goldman, M.D.

THREE RIVERS PRESS • NEW YORK

THREE RIVERS PRESS and the Tugboat design are registered trademarks of Random House, Inc.

Originally published in the United States by Prima Publishing, a division of Random House, Inc., Roseville, California, in 2001.

All products mentioned in this book are trademarks of their respective companies.

Interior photos copyright © PhotoDisc (pages 2, 28, 54, 102, 124, 144, 184, 206, 222, 242), copyright © Lorna Eby (page 80), copyright © Erin Upchurch (page 166), and copyright © Vanessa Perez (page 262).

Library of Congress Cataloging-in-Publication Data

Goldman, Marcus Jacob.
    The joy of fatherhood : the first twelve months / Marcus Jacob Goldman.—Exp. 2nd Ed.
    Includes index.
    1. Fatherhood. 2. Fathers. I. Title.

HQ756.G582 2000
306.874'2—dc21   00-035977
                                                                          CIP

ISBN 0-7615-2424-X

Printed in the United States of America

10 9 8 7 6

Second Edition

To my parents, without whom being a father would be impossible.

To my wife, Lori, without whom being a father would be unthinkable.

To Alex Benjamin, Zachary Evan, Jacob Lewis, Brett Daniel, and Dylan Shane, without whom being a father would be meaningless.

Contents

Acknowledgments

I've come to realize that writing a book, like learning to be a father, is necessarily the result of listening to and living through the experiences of life. The following people have selflessly stopped along the way to help me learn, grow, and develop. To these people, I'm forever indebted.

To Thomas G. Gutheil, M.D., who gave me my start in writing and taught me to "never worry alone." To Victoria Alexander, who, with kindness and enthusiasm, encouraged me to express myself through the written word. To Ed Carp, who taught me self-respect.

I am also indebted to those who lovingly care for my children: Martin Luloff, M.D., and the other doctors and nurses at Main Street Pediatrics, for helping out me and my wife by looking after our increasing number of children. To the doctors, nurses, and aides at the Metro West Medical Center and Children's Hospital of Boston for saving our baby. I would also like to thank Tommi Murphy for her love, affection, and friendship over the past two years. She has been, is, and always will be a member of our family.

I would also like to thank Dave Wasserman, C.P.A., for crunching numbers, and William Land, M.D., for having another baby recently just to keep me company. A special thanks goes out to my friends Steve and Renée Marcus, Bev Reed, and the entire cast at New England Geriatrics—I appreciate the faith you place in me. I am also grateful to my agent, Jackie Simenauer, for her help, support, and cruise tips. A big thank you is also due to Michael E. Knight, for his much appreciated help in making this book simply the best it can be, and to Chad Caruthers, for his patience and guidance on this project.

Finally, a special thanks to Lori—my wife and the mother of my four children—for her love, support, and patience.

Introduction

The Beginning of the Journey

Welcome to the world of fatherhood! Whether you're an expectant dad or already have a new baby, one thing is certain—your life will never be the same. Mine sure isn't. I soon discovered that the births of my children turned my previously right-side-up world upside-down and sideways. Being a new dad was disorienting to say the least. It would be a while before I learned that having a baby—becoming a new dad—takes getting used to.

I clearly wasn't *used* to *anything* in the delivery room. My newborn baby peered up at me through the seemingly dozens of receiving blankets we fledgling parents had twisted him into. I held my baby up so that we were nose to nose—his tiny, new one to my big, older one. We stared at each other. The object of his intensely curious gaze must surely have been the look of stark lunacy indelibly scribbled on my face. I wasn't ready to be his father. I wasn't ready to be anyone's father. Confused with my role, my paternal uncertainty grew, leading to greater levels of discomfort. I didn't realize that being a good dad took time and experience. There didn't seem to be any good way to ease into the job and unfortunately, few, if any, resources were available to help me learn.

As a father, the changes in my life would be far-reaching. Although I didn't know it at the time, sometime in the near future my children would challenge my patience and humanity by assaulting the calm and quiet that should accompany sleep, rolling repeatedly into the filthy fireplace, eating my favorite books, and coming exceedingly close to falling down the cellar stairs. They would also thrill me and fill me with unparalleled joy by being charming, playful, funny, and loving. As a result of the new dynamics of my family, my relationship with my wife would also change. How nice it would have been to have been a bit familiar with some of these possibilities before I became a father. *The Joy of Fatherhood,* a book written by a man for men, aims to provide you with information on some of the possible emotions, thoughts, and behaviors that new fathers and their families may experience.

What's in This Book?

While I've included a great many definitions, techniques, and important clinical and scientific information, I've tried to avoid making this book overly technical. *The Joy of Fatherhood* is designed to help you explore and better understand your new role as a father. Child-care books sometimes inadvertently shy away from the emotional realities of raising a baby. I've tried to address not only the basics—what to expect each month, how to interact with your baby—but also the conflicting emotions you, as a man, might be experiencing and the complexities of maintaining a healthy relationship with your partner.

How Is This Book Organized?

The Joy of Fatherhood consists of thirteen chapters, and two appendixes: One on common childhood ailments, the other a resource section designed to provide you with some additional sources to help you become a better father. With the exception of the first chapter, which is designed to get you through labor and delivery and the postpartum period, each chapter covers one month of the first year of your baby's life. Each chapter is organized to help you learn the basics of growing with your baby, partner, and family. To ensure consistency and ease of reading, each chapter is similarly organized and usually contains the following sections:

What's New with Your Baby?: This section contains important information about your baby's physical and emotional growth, health, and development.

Focuses: These shaded sections contain practical information, useful "how-to" instructions, questions and answers, essential clinical information, and concrete advice on topics of particular concern to new dads.

What's New with Mom?: As you'll soon discover, your baby will demand love, attention, and guidance from both you and your partner. How is your partner coping with these new experiences? This section will focus on her feelings and ways to help maintain a healthy relationship with her.

What's New with Dad?: *The Joy of Fatherhood* was written to help new dads cope with the monumental changes that invariably accompany the birth of a baby. This section will help identify the various, often contradictory feelings frequently experienced by new dads.

Being There for Your Baby: How can you stay involved with your baby? Why is it important? What can you do to remain close to your baby? How can you take care of your own physical and emotional health? This section will help new dads learn to be there for their babies, to negotiate difficult feelings, and, just as important, to use their knowledge and experience to maintain a healthy relationship with themselves.

Growing Together: This section briefly summarizes the chapter's important points and touches upon what's next, with an emphasis on learning and growing together with your new family.

Bonding with Baby: As your baby grows and develops, the types of activities in which the two of you can participate change. This section offers some ideas to help you get to know your baby better and develop the bonds of trust and love through play. Many of the suggestions will also help your baby learn important skills needed for later stages of development.

Also included throughout the book are helpful tips, definitions, and updates on essential information. Dads' "real-life" experiences and thoughts are used throughout the book to emphasize key issues and to make difficult-to-talk-about subjects a bit easier to understand.

The Importance of Language

While it's not always possible to avoid offending everyone, I've tried hard to use terminology that most everyone can identify with. The word "partner" is used throughout the book to describe the mother of your baby. In addition, rather than using "he or she" to describe your baby, I've randomly alternated gender throughout the text. Finally, this book assumes that you're going through the first twelve months with a partner and not on your own.

Final Words

From our birth to adulthood, though we may struggle with our own identities as males, there is, within all of us, the possibility of fatherhood, however far from our minds at times. It starts with an awareness that, all other things being equal, we boys may one day become fathers. Our life experiences form the roots of fatherhood. These roots store in our memory everything we've lived through, good and bad. With any luck, the next generation of "roots" will use the enriched soil of our fathering to grow up healthy and strong.

You can make no more valuable an investment than to be a thoughtful, loving father to your baby and to learn and grow together with your child. It's my sincere hope that *The Joy of Fatherhood* will accompany you on your journey together and help prepare you for what lies ahead.

The Joy of Fatherhood

When that kid looks into your eyes and you know
it's yours, you know what it means to be alive.

—ANONYMOUS FATHER

CHAPTER 1

From Pregnancy to Parenthood

Just eight or nine months ago, it may have seemed unlikely that you'd be reading about becoming a father. How things have changed! As the months sped by, you've hopefully had the opportunity to "get ready"—perhaps you've joined your partner on her routine prenatal doctor visits, heard your baby's heartbeat, picked out names, and put the crib together (or tried to anyway). Have you done it all? There seems to be little left to do other than wait for the event.

Get ready for a surprise! As the abstraction of pregnancy quickly transforms into the concrete realities of a child (by the third trimester, you can actually see and feel parts of your baby as it moves around in your partner's abdomen), you'll need to do more than just sit around and wait. In fact, the last few months of your partner's pregnancy should be an emotionally active and stimulating time. Are you ready? What are you feeling?

You'll probably be relieved to learn that there are no wrong answers. Each dad-to-be has his own way of perceiving the entire phenomenon of fathering:

"I was shaking wildly with anticipation! I couldn't wait!"

"Everybody was talking about how magical it all is. I'm ashamed to say that I felt about as numb as you could feel. It's like my whole body went to the dentist and got Novocain."

TIP

As you begin your journey into the box containing crib parts, be cautiously optimistic, but not cocky. There are two long pieces of steel, each containing a kick bar (a spring-loaded device responsible for lowering the side rails). Attach these long metal pieces so that the spring-loaded bars point down toward the floor and push in toward the inside of the crib.

Invariably, during the month or two prior to the birth of your baby, you'll be filled with a variety of mixed feelings. You'll most certainly be joyous and eager to meet your little wonder, but at the same time, if you're like most dads, you may have some frightening thoughts or feelings as well:

"I have so many other things I want to do with my life. I'm concerned about my impending lack of freedom. I want to be a good dad, but, in order to be with my baby, I know I'll be unable to do a lot of things I used to do."

For sure, there'll be issues that need sorting out. Giving them consideration now, before your baby's grand entrance, gives you a time advantage you'll want to seize. Now that all the basics are taken care of—the name, the crib, the curtains—do yourself the service of welcoming this thought-provoking time.

What's New with the Dad-to-Be?

Being a dad is one of the oldest "professions" around. Men from all walks of life have been getting ready for, and have been both thrilled and confused by, fatherhood since the beginning of time.

You May Be Thinking About . . .

Your Dad or Other Male Role Models: It's very common for dads-to-be to think about fatherhood in terms of our own paternal role models. Some men are wary of their impending fatherhood, fearing that they may repeat mistakes made by their dads. You wouldn't be the first dad-to-be to consider these issues—in fact, every generation of men has tried to reconfigure the concept of fathering:

"I know, from experience, that my father tried, sometimes in vain, to redefine the way he fathered. He, like most everyone else, reacted strongly against many of the rearing practices of his father and, like most everyone else, ended up making many of the same mistakes. His father, he would tell me, was too hard on him. Believe it or not, my grandfather talked to me about the mistakes that he felt his father, my great-grandfather, made and told me that, lo and behold, he too repeated many of those mistakes."

Because the notion of "fatherhood" sometimes carries with it a history of "bad"—for example, the traits of infidelity or violence—for some men the thought of successfully fathering feels unrealistic. Conversely, other men are able to learn from their dads' mistakes and feel good about their fathering potential.

Of course, many men have had great experiences with their loving dads. Your preparation for fatherhood, for example, may be characterized by memories of kindness, purpose, and love:

"I'm excited about using a lot of the parenting skills I learned from my dad. He wasn't perfect, but he made me feel loved, needed, important, and worthwhile."

If you're like most men, you have a mixture of feelings about your dad— you hope to be as competent as your father but may fear emulating the parts that were not to your liking. Trying to incorporate into yourself those positive attributes shown to you by your dad while rejecting his negative traits is a challenging yet worthwhile goal. Recognizing your mixed feelings, trying to see your dad as a whole person (not just as all "good" or all "bad"), and sharing your feelings with your partner are some ways to cope with your uncertainty.

If possible, take some time to talk to your father about raising you. Share some of your anxiety about approaching fatherhood. It is likely your father felt some of the same feelings and fear that you are experiencing. Talk about both the good and the bad. As you do, your relationship with your father will grow, and he can become a good source to which you can turn later on. Just because the skills of a father are learned primarily on the job, it's still a good idea to learn from the experience of others. If you can't turn to your father, go to a grandfather, uncle, or other respected male in your life for advice and tips. You don't have to use what they tell you, but sometimes they may offer something you can use.

> "Mark Twain once said his father was the dumbest person he knew. However, after he left home and then came back for a visit, he was surprised at how much his father had learned in such a short amount of time. I used to think my father didn't know anything about being a good father. However, now that I am in that position, with children that act the way I did, I have a better understanding of what my father was going through at the time. The two of us discuss what worked with me and what didn't."

Your Lack of Fathering Experience: Apprehension strikes again! Don't worry—you'll soon be able to add "dad" to your resume:

> "It's certainly disconcerting to be expected to be a good father just as soon as my baby pops out. It was now my turn to step up to the plate, and I panicked. I hadn't practiced—the bat was too heavy. Here was the test, and I hadn't studied. I clearly had no fathering experience. Most certainly, I wouldn't want to be a member of a family that would have me as a father."

Join the club. Your lack of experience doesn't stop the instant your child is born—it's a lifelong learning process. My children, for example, always seem to know exactly what they want and when to demand it, while I, on the other hand, always seem to know nothing. In fact, the older I become, the less experienced I feel. Knowing nothing seems to propel me to greater, previously uncharted and unexplored heights of uncertainty. I always have questions and complaints; this is an integral part of fatherhood.

You learn the most by running enthusiastically—perhaps screaming wildly—toward the inexperience and uncertainty. Don't pressure yourself by thinking that you have to know everything. Believe it or not, you may discover that the greatest pleasures will come as a result of your confusion.

Pressure to Be a "Perfect" Dad: You may have some very real concerns about your ability to be a "perfect" dad, if such a thing exists:

"I wanted so much to be a good father, but I felt as though I had no road map. All I had was a preconceived notion of how the collective fathers of the past had done. I needed to do something now, before my son was born, to prepare for my baby."

Learning to be a "great" dad can't be done by reading a book or taking a course. If it could be done that way, we'd all be pretty boring, noncreative parents. There's really no way to practice, and it's improbable that you can completely prepare for what lies ahead. On the other hand, preparation for membership in the world of fatherhood begins as soon as we start to think. Preparation for fatherhood starts when we're first aware that we have a father, or someone like him, and understand that we too can become fathers:

"I never considered that the road to fatherhood might be rough and jagged, not smooth and straight."

Our journey into fatherhood begins long before we touch a woman or sponge off her sweat in the delivery room. The beginning of the journey pre-dates the quarts of water and ginger ale she'll consume after the birth and precedes our first try at changing a poop-packed diaper. The truth is that we prepare for it our entire lives. Putting pressure on yourself to be a "perfect" or "great" dad goes against the grain of experiences that really will make you a terrific dad. As we'll see, being a great dad has more to do with consistency, being there, and loving and supporting your baby and partner than any special skills or preparation—in fact, none are required!

Your Future Together with Your Baby: Some dads liken the impending birth of a child to the beginning of a great journey. Fatherhood, to many, is a long, emotional adventure:

"I had all these fantasies, even before my son was born. He and I traveled in time. We went back together, to the time I sat on my father's lap and listened to records. We went back even further, my boy and I, to the time my father looked at *my* new, naked, wet, shiny little body and thought about his father. Then my son and I went into the future together, where he told me he loved me, and then even farther into the future, where he spoke harshly to me, telling me that he hated me and that I had ruined his life. We then traveled back to the birthing room, somewhere in the middle of my time line and at the beginning of his . . ."

. . . while other dads are more concrete, but no less definitive, in their fantasies:

"I can't wait to play baseball with my kid!"

Allow yourself the luxury of fantasy. You may also find that you're not thinking about anything in particular. That's okay too. Don't forget that every man comes into the community of fathering with a different psychological dynamic—a result of the interplay between his nature and nurture. The end result? Each dad-to-be has his own "fingerprint" that distinguishes his actions and feelings from the next father.

Take a role in your baby's development even before birth. Talk to him, sing your favorite songs, or read stories. It not only helps your baby learn who you are but also helps you begin a relationship with him at the same time.

You May Be Feeling . . .

Pride, Joy, and Excitement: Despite the complicated mixture of feelings engendered by the impending birth, most dads-to-be can't avoid gushing with pride. Even your co-workers will notice your increased energy and enthusiasm. As the last month or two tick away, along with whatever ambivalent feelings you may have, joyous emotions are inevitable.

Boredom: Sometimes waiting can seem like forever—just ask your partner. Some dads express relief when the pregnancy is finally over.

Frustration with Your Partner's Physical Condition: It's not uncommon for dads to voice dismay over the appearance of their partners. After all, your partner has undergone some very impressive changes. She's gained weight, her face is probably fuller, her breasts may be engorged and tender, and she may be uncomfortable or even in pain. While some dads like the way their partners look, others may find it an adjustment:

"It's hard to get some sleep at night in the same bed as my wife. She's always moving around, snuggles giant pillows that take up half the bed, and wants me to rub this ache or that. If that wasn't bad enough, the dozen trips to the bathroom each night only add to the pouches under my eyes."

Try to put yourself in her place—how would you look and feel if you were walking around with a 30-pound sack of flour strapped to your abdomen all day? Try to remember that her physical changes are only temporary—she'll lose 25 pounds the moment the baby is delivered. However, don't expect your partner to instantly return to normal. It can take a few months for her to re-gain her pre-pregnancy figure.

Before you judge your partner, take a look in the mirror yourself. Many fa-thers gain weight during their partner's pregnancy. However, the father can't shed a lot of it instantly at birth.

Frustration with Her Emotional State: Your partner may be feeling irritable or depressed; she may be sick and tired of carrying the baby. If she's on an emo-tional roller coaster, try pampering her a little. Treat her to a romantic dinner somewhere special, buy her some flowers, or rub her aching feet.

Anxiety: The closer your partner gets to her due date, the more nervous and anxious fathers become, especially first-time fathers. You never know when the phone call at work will be your wife saying she's going into labor or if, going to bed at night, the sun will rise on the two of you at the hospital.

"One night my wife knocked over a glass and said 'I spilled my water.' Still asleep, I thought she said her water had broke. Instantly I was up, getting dressed, grabbing bags to take to the hospital, and heading for the car with my heart racing. Luckily, before I took off, my wife let me know I was mistaken."

What's New with Your Partner?

What's new? Just about everything! Your partner is ending a monumental period in her life and will soon be starting another. While her body has undergone impressive changes, her way of looking at the world has also been altered. As the final months approach, she'll experience a multitude of feelings and physical sensations.

Emotional—She May Feel . . .

Fear and Apprehension: As the birth experience becomes more imminent, your partner may be feeling fearful, panicked, or apprehensive. The thought of giving birth, coupled with everything she's heard from her mother or friends regarding the process of birth, whether by cesarean section or vaginally, may make her mighty nervous. She might not feel soothed by your statements of support, but reassure her that you'll be there with her nonetheless. It's tough, of course, for you to fully understand or identify with her feelings:

> "I don't know. The closest I can come to imagining the fear and pain of childbirth is to imagine myself at the dentist's office, naked, strapped to a chair, with teeth sticking out all over my body. The dentist comes in and says, 'They have to come out, and we're out of anesthetic.'"

> "I get down on my knees, in the middle of the bedroom, every day of my wife's pregnancy and give thanks that I'm not a pregnant woman. This behavior, of course, does little to reassure my wife, and she's asked me to give thanks somewhere else."

Many women may question their ability to mother and may fear the awesome responsibilities that accompany having a child. She may be mourning the loss of her job or may simply fear her loss of freedom. Since her fears probably sound familiar, you're in a unique position to offer her an ear.

Joy and Excitement: Along with feelings of apprehension come joy and excitement. Despite any misgivings she may have, she's likely to be thrilled!

> "My wife loved being pregnant and was incredibly excited about the delivery. It was hard for me to understand how her enthusiasm to see our baby overshadowed any fears she may have had about the birth process."

Impatience: By the end of the ninth month, regardless of their expectations, most women are truly ready to deliver. Tired of carrying around a backbreaking load, especially if she's had a high-risk pregnancy or been confined to bed, your partner may be anxious to "get it over with."

Exhaustion: As men, it's often hard for us to understand that pregnancy is an exhausting experience—emotionally and physically. By the end of the ninth month, your partner will be running out of steam. As a result of her biology, weight gain, and the obvious task of carrying the baby, her energy level will very likely be low.

Physical—She May Have . . .

Changes in Her Body: As you know, your partner's body has undergone multiple changes. Some of these changes may include significant weight gain; marks, lines, or spots on her skin; fullness in the face; swelling of the legs and ankles; and varicose veins or hemorrhoids. In anticipation of her body's need to nourish the baby, her breasts have become swollen and tender. You'll likely also notice a darkening of her nipples.

Pain: In the closing months of pregnancy, your partner will probably be quite uncomfortable at times. Your baby, almost fully developed, is twisting and turning and doing cartwheels and somersaults—proving that he means business! At the same time, however, as your baby continues to grow within your partner, there'll be little room left at the inn! He may be positioned against sensitive areas within the body, causing your partner significant pain or discomfort, especially at night.

Despite the negative aspects of pregnancy, most women welcome the opportunity to mother. How can you stay involved? Remember, as a dad-to-be and later on as a full-fledged dad, you'll discover that doing for each other ultimately helps everyone.

Being There for Your Partner and Baby

Even though your baby hasn't yet made its appearance, it's important to be as engaged with the process of pregnancy and birth as possible. After all, the "team" approach to pregnancy, birth, and raising your baby ensures that no one has to worry alone. While being there emotionally is essential, you'll also need to help in more concrete ways.

Before the Birth

Assist Your Partner: Ask her how you can help to lighten her considerable load. If she does the bulk of the shopping and laundry, help her with carrying or do it for her. Massage her back and neck. Be patient and supportive.

Make Decisions Together: Making decisions together will bring the two of you even closer together. Working together to get the nursery ready, choosing names, or attending childbirth classes will strengthen your resolve and ability to survive the first few months of your baby's life. Work on solidifying your alliance with your partner. Being involved with each other will also provide your baby with a loving and nurturing environment.

Prepare for the Birth with Her: Getting ready for your baby encompasses far more than just being familiar with "dad" things. Preparing also means that you'll need to be familiar with what your partner will be going through—during labor and afterward.

Don't assume that your partner is the only one who needs to learn about the process of labor and delivery. Remember, you're in this together—all of it. By the time labor comes along, it is helpful to be familiar with the common terms and procedures of childbirth.

Words and Phrases to Know

Labor and Delivery Terms

- **Fetal monitor:** A fetal monitor is a machine that measures the heart rate of your baby. It's strapped to your partner's abdomen.

- **Scalp monitor:** A scalp monitor is applied directly to your baby's head, by the obstetrician, through your partner's vagina. The monitor can closely track your baby's vital signs during labor.

- **IV:** An IV, or intravenous line, is a thin, flexible plastic tube temporarily inserted into your partner's vein via a thin needle. It's used to deliver fluids and medicines. Some doctors routinely use them. During a cesarean section, it will always be used.

- **Epidural:** An epidural is a form of anesthesia sometimes given during labor. It doesn't cause your partner to sleep. The anesthesiologist places a small, thin tube in your partner's spine via a thin needle. The doctor can then administer medication directly to the nerves responsible for labor pains. Epidurals can greatly relieve the pain and suffering that accompanies advanced labor and may be used during cesarean sections as well. Not all hospitals offer epidurals. Look into this in advance and see if there are any additional requirements in order to receive an epidural.

- **Catheter:** A urinary catheter is a flexible, soft, clear tube that is temporarily placed in the woman's urethra (opening where the urine comes out) and that allows urine to flow from the bladder. It'll be used only if your partner's anesthesia prevents her from emptying her bladder on her own.

- **Pitocin:** This drug, otherwise know as oxytocin, is given intravenously to induce labor or to accelerate a labor that is not progressing by causing the uterus to contract. It is often called "pit" by physicians.

TIPS

- During a prenatal visit, record your baby's heartbeat with a small tape recorder. Listen to it with your partner, late at night, while you're both in bed. You'll probably end up talking to each other about things you've never talked about before.

- Most hospitals offer a pre-birth visit. Do your best to go with your partner. While she will be interested in what the rooms are like, you should be scouting out for where the ice machine is located and if the delivery area has a pantry where you can get other items for your partner, such as Jell-O cups, juice or soda, and even crackers. Time your trip on the way down to the hospital so you know how long it takes. You should also try the drive at different times to see if rush hour traffic will cause problems. If that is the case, try to find an alternate route. The better prepared you are, the easier it will be.

- **Cord:** For nine months, your partner and baby have been linked together by the umbilical cord. Sometimes during labor, the obstetrician may detect, either through ultrasound, physical examination, or monitoring of the baby's vital signs, that the cord is wrapped around the baby's neck. In some cases, particularly if the baby is in distress, a cesarean section may result.

TIP

The father should now be knowledgeable in the process of childbirth. However, be careful not to be "Mr. Know-It-All" around your partner, especially when she is in pain. She may tell you where you can take your knowledge and what you can do with it when you get there.

- **Effacement:** Effacement refers to the degree of flattening of the woman's cervix during labor. The cervix must be completely flat, or effaced, for labor to proceed to birth.

- **Dilation:** This refers to the size of the cervical opening. It's detected by manual examination with gloved fingers. The final stage of labor finds the cervix completely dilated. Your partner must be dilated to 10 centimeters before the baby can be delivered.

- **Deceleration:** This refers to a decrease in the baby's heart rate while in the uterus. Although a certain amount and pattern of deceleration is acceptable, chronic or severe decelerations during labor could mean that the baby is in distress.

- **Ultrasound:** An ultrasound is a machine that can "see" your baby in the uterus by using sound waves. Among other things, it may be used during labor to assess the position of the baby.

- **Cesarean section:** A cesarean section, otherwise known as a c-section, is a procedure whereby the baby is surgically removed from your partner's abdomen. It's used in emergencies or may be planned. It has become quite controversial but is generally safe. Because her abdominal muscles have been cut, your partner's recovery time will be longer, and she may be sore for weeks.

- **Water:** The "water," or amniotic fluid, is the substance your baby has been floating in all these months and that has helped sustain and protect her. This substance is held inside your partner by membranes that may rupture on their own or be broken by the doctor to induce labor.

- **Meconium:** Meconium, usually confined to your baby's digestive system, is the waste he produces while in the uterus. Sometimes, when your partner's water breaks, the doctor may detect meconium in the fluid. During birth, when the baby starts to breathe, he may be at risk for inhaling or choking on meconium. The obstetrician may have a pediatrician in the room during birth or may take special precautions, such as carefully suctioning your baby as soon as his head is visible. However, meconium is generally not something to worry much about.

- **Placenta:** Just when you thought the delivery was over, watch for this large, slippery, bloody mass to pop out of your partner's vagina. Your obstetrician will examine it to make certain no pieces are left behind.

Newborn Terms

- **Apgar:** These are scores given to your baby by the nurse or pediatrician directly after birth. The scores (on a scale from zero to ten) are taken at one minute and five minutes after birth and measure a variety of important characteristics, such as your baby's appearance, breathing rate, muscular activity, reflexive movements, and heart rate.

- **Eye ointment:** Your baby will be given an antibiotic ointment or drops as a precaution against certain sexually transmitted diseases.

- **Blood test:** Your baby will have blood drawn to check for different illnesses.

- **Physical examination:** Your baby will undergo an extensive physical examination shortly after birth. The doctor will check your baby's size, strength, perceptive abilities, and reflexes. The doctor will also examine your baby's many organ systems, including excretory function and genitals.

- **Receiving blankets:** These small, soft blankets are used to wrap your baby in after birth.

- **Swaddle:** Swaddling is a technique used to snugly wrap your baby in her receiving blanket. While swaddling can soothe a tearful newborn, not all babies enjoy being bundled up. One of my babies loved to be wrapped up, another was indifferent, and another reacted against it ferociously. Learning to swaddle is not difficult. Watch your baby's nurse.

- **Layette:** This is a set of clothing for newborns.
- **Pacifier:** As you're probably aware, this is a small piece of rubber attached to a piece of plastic. When placed in your baby's mouth, it may stop him from crying. There are many variations, and they are known by many different terms—among them nuks, nipples, binkies, and suckers.

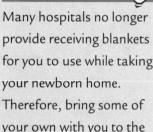

TIP

Many hospitals no longer provide receiving blankets for you to use while taking your newborn home. Therefore, bring some of your own with you to the hospital. In the past, pacifiers were also provided. However, as more hospitals are becoming "breast friendly," they will not be given because some fear that pacifiers make learning to feed from the breast more difficult for the baby.

- **Ounce:** An ounce is a unit of measurement generally used to describe how much your baby has had to drink. It's roughly equal to the amount of water you might gargle with in the morning.
- **Hepatitis vaccine:** While not universally given, this injection will protect your baby from contracting the hepatitis B virus, a potentially life-threatening infectious disease that attacks the liver. Be sure to discuss this injection with the pediatrician *before* the birth. Your baby will need two more injections to complete the series. While most shots are well tolerated, we'll discuss adverse and serious reactions on page 61.
- **Circumcision:** Circumcision involves the surgical removal of the foreskin of the penis. There has been great debate over the years as to the pluses and minuses of circumcision. You, your partner, and your pediatrician should discuss the procedure well in advance of the birth. Circumcision is not a difficult procedure. However, if you elect to have it done at the hospital, insist on the most qualified person to perform it.
- **Poop:** Get tough. Get used to it.
- **Postpartum:** A nonspecific time period beginning after delivery—for example, two weeks postpartum.

Breast-Feeding Terms

- **Breast shields:** These plastic objects (they look like flying saucers) help protect your partner's nipples from irritation. They're worn inside a bra.

- **Breast pads:** These can be either cloth or disposable. Breast pads absorb milk that leaks between feedings as well as during. They are worn inside the bra and help protect your partner's clothing.

- **Pump:** Your partner may pump milk from her breasts using an electric or hand pump. The milk can be frozen and stored for later use. The pump makes a great conversation piece.

- **Colostrum:** Your partner's breasts will not produce milk right away. Instead, your baby will drink a substance known as colostrum. This liquid is full of nutrients and carries within it special protective substances that help your baby's new immune system prepare to fight disease.

TIP

When in the hospital, don't be offended if you are asked who you are by hospital personnel—in fact, you may have to wear an ID bracelet. Many hospitals take these precautions to protect against baby abductions. Your baby may be fitted with an ID bracelet that sounds an alarm if she is removed from the nursery.

Taking Care of Yourself

Part of your preparation for childbirth entails caring for yourself. You'll need to remain healthy and energized for what lies ahead. Make certain, for example, that your stay at the hospital is as comfortable as possible. While you won't have every amenity of home, you can clearly bring a little bit of home with you. Remember, labor can take anywhere from minutes to two or three days. You may find yourself sitting in the hospital birthing room for a long time before anything happens!

FOCUS: BREAST FEEDING AND DADS

Preparing with your spouse means exploring things together that, on the surface, may not seem to involve you. Everyone knows, for example, that breast feeding is good for your baby—among other things, it protects your baby from infectious diseases via your partner's antibodies, which are present in breast milk. The question we'll focus on, however, is whether breast feeding is good for you. Why should you, a dad-to-be, discuss your feelings about breast feeding? Remember, everything you and your partner do, even separately, will have an impact on your lives as a whole. Both of you may have already discussed breast feeding and its implications. If not, however, now is as good a time as any.

While breast feeding can be a satisfying experience for both of you, it can also become tedious and stressful. Listed here are some of breast feeding's advantages and disadvantages as they apply to dads.

Breast-Feeding Advantages (from Dad's Perspective)

Convenient: Breast feeding is really convenient. Since you don't have to heat up a bottle, it may mean getting up less at night (some dads, however, will get the baby and bring it to their partners).

In some respects, the convenience of breast feeding also gives both you and your partner more freedom and flexibility. Since you don't have to carry baby formula and bottles, worry about the formula staying fresh, or warm it up, going out with the baby is made a bit simpler.

Soothing: Breast feeding has an almost instantaneous quieting and soothing effect on babies as well.

Inexpensive: Another nice aspect of breast feeding is that it's much cheaper than buying formula, bottles, and rubber nipples. You'll also not need to clean a lot of bottles.

Breast-Feeding Disadvantages (from Dad's Perspective)

Feeling Left Out: While some dads relish the thought of their baby's having a special closeness with their partners, other dads feel left out or even envious. With the baby at your partner's breast instead of in your arms with a bottle, you may feel less intimately involved. Ask your partner to pump milk so you can feed the baby breast milk with a bottle on occasion. He still gets the breast milk, your partner gets a break, and you get to bond with him.

Dealing with a Frustrated Partner: Your partner may also develop sore, swollen, or cracked nipples, which can be distressing and extremely painful. You'll hear about it, particularly if the baby has been fussy all day and done little but nursed. When this happens, it can be a good time to pump breast milk for one feeding and use a bottle so as to allow the nipples to heal.

Physical Turnoffs: Some men are turned off by breast milk, especially if their partner's breasts release milk during sexual activity. On occasion, in response to hearing a baby cry, your partner's breasts may release milk in a public place.

Other dads become annoyed with their partners for inadvertently revealing their breasts in public as they prepare to feed the baby—something that occurs occasionally even with the most cautious of mothers. To avoid this, dads should help their partners by holding a blanket while the baby latches on to the breast and your partner gets situated.

Less Freedom for Mom and Dad: While breast feeding gives you and your partner a certain flexibility when out together *with* the baby, you may find that getting out of the house together, *without* the baby, is more difficult:

> *"Not having the baby on a bottle was a pain. My wife would have to pump her breasts for the milk and then show the babysitter how to feed the baby. The baby*

(cont.)

FOCUS: BREAST FEEDING AND DADS

(continued)

never wanted the milk because it didn't come right out of the breast. We'd come home to find the sitter in tears and our baby screaming."

Breast feeding is a complicated issue. Hopefully, you and your partner will spend some time talking together about the pluses and minuses. If you're concerned about issues of your own personal intimacy with your baby, consider giving her a supplemental bottle in the evening. Be sure to discuss this with your partner in advance and don't just go ahead and do it while she's sleeping. While you may think you are helping, your partner may be upset for a number of different and not always rational reasons.

Growing Together: Your Baby Is Born

Well, the moment has arrived. If you're lucky, you'll be holding your little bundle just after the birth. What are you feeling? What's the experience like? The range of emotions is about as varied as one could imagine. There's plenty of room for a variety of feelings—sometimes all coexisting at the same time!

"It was just like I thought it would be—spiritual."

"That Placenta Monster was unbelievable! I wish we could take *that* thing home!!"

"My baby looked like some kind of alien. How am I going to learn to love that thing?"

"It was awesome, unforgettable, magical! I'm the luckiest guy in the universe!"

So, what are you feeling? Just a few of the many possibilities are listed here:

- **Overwhelmed:** It's not uncommon for dads to feel "wowed" by the process. You may feel bewildered, overwhelmed, or tearful—or all three at once. As in my experience, disorientation is not uncommon. It hit me when someone in the birthing room called me "dad." I was so dazed that I turned around to see if my dad had come in. As it turns out, I was the only father in the room!

- **Wonder:** A sense of wonder or awe is common:

"I just couldn't get over the whole thing. I mean just 10 minutes ago, my daughter was inside my partner! How can this be?"

- **Anticlimactic:** Some dads report feeling disappointed that the process has ended:

"It took us years to conceive and almost a year to carry the child. Now, before you know it, it's over. So, what happens next?"

TIPS

- Go out of your way to develop a good working relationship with your partner's birthing nurse. Treat the nurse with respect, and she will more than repay you with vital information and help throughout the birth process.

- If you have a conflict with your nurse that cannot be overcome, consider asking for a different nurse. It can make all the difference between a good or a bad experience.

- Get used to seeing countless strangers putting their fingers inside your partner's vagina during labor. They'll be checking for dilation and effacement.

- Don't hold anything your partner says while in labor against her. The intensity of her contractions and other labor pains, especially if your partner has opted for natural childbirth, can make even the mildest woman swear like a truck driver.

- Do not videotape the actual birth unless cleared by the obstetrician and your partner.

FOCUS: WHAT TO PACK IN YOUR HOSPITAL BAG

- **Change of clothing:** Labor and delivery is a messy business. Be prepared and bring a change of clothes. In addition, many hospitals now provide dads with a place to sleep. If your partner's labor is lengthy, you'll want to doze and refresh yourself upon awakening. A change of clothes can be great if you end up sleeping overnight in the hospital.

- **Soap, shampoo, toothbrush, and deodorant:** Most modern hospital rooms have showers. If you've slept over, you may want to freshen up a bit.

- **Small tape recorder:** I enjoyed capturing the sounds of the hospital room on tape—nurses, my comments and observations, my wife's comments and jokes, and the beeps of the machines. I turned the tape recorder on upon our arrival to the room and let it run until the birth. Also, since many physicians will not allow videotaping of the time immediately surrounding the birth, audiotaping is a nice alternative. If you want to capture that first cry, it's best to do it with your tape recorder. Don't forget to bring a cassette and batteries, and make sure you let everyone know that they're being taped.

- **Disgusted:** Some dads are nauseated by the entire birth process (but nonetheless go on to be loving dads).

- **Confused:** A great many things confuse a great many of us:

"Now, what exactly just happened?"

- **Pride:** Most dads express tremendous pride in this great achievement.

- **Euphoric:** New dads quite commonly feel as though they're sitting on top of the world.

- **Scared About Leaving the Hospital:** This feeling doesn't usually fully emerge until you pull up to your house. Since the hospital was so helpful, some dads may be concerned about the transition. After all, the hospital provided an environment rich in guidance and structure that vanished the instant you placed your baby in the car seat in the hospital

- **Still camera:** A must. Don't forget plenty of film. Make sure the flash is working properly. Change the batteries if necessary.

- **Video camera:** If you don't own one, then borrow or rent one. Make sure you have enough film and that the battery is charged. Bring the AC adapter with you just in case.

- **Distractions:** Hospital TV is generally worthless, and you may find yourself bored out of your mind. Since your time in the birthing room may go on for days, bring magazines, a book, your homework, or headphones for your cassette player. Try to get some rest, but have distractions on hand for those quiet times when you don't feel like napping.

- **Food:** Pack quick-energy, wholesome foods, like crackers, fruit, nuts, or yogurt. Don't pack or eat things that can cause bad breath such as garlic. Also, pack some breath mints. Your partner will not want you around if you smell like nacho cheese tortilla chips.

- **Birthing aides:** Bring your birth class crib notes, especially those related to breathing techniques. Also, bring a tennis ball in case your partner has back labor, a very painful type of labor that is sometimes made a bit easier by pressure applied to the back with a soft object.

parking lot. The exhaustion that comes with every new baby will now be shared only between you and your partner:

"As a new father, I can remember wanting to make room in the back of the car for the various nurses and aides that helped us care for our new daughter. It would have been nice to take them home for a year or two."

Most of the time, dads will feel a combination of all these feelings, and more. Don't worry too much if you notice other feelings or if the entire experience was unpleasant for you. There's more—much more—to a baby than its birth, and there are some things you can do right away to bring yourself closer to your new baby.

Holding your new baby, while appearing to be a basic, simple action, is not that easy for first-time dads. Nonetheless, learning to hold your baby is impor-

FOCUS: HOW TO HOLD YOUR NEW BABY

- **Overcome barriers:** Some dads stop themselves from holding a newborn for a variety of reasons. They're full of "gook," they're frail or fragile appearing, or they seem too tiny. Convince yourself that they're none of these things.

- **Be cautious but confident:** Newborns are small and weak, and you'll have to adjust yourself to accommodate them, but they won't break when picked up. In fact, they *love* to be carried around.

- **Attend to your baby's neck:** This is really the only thing you'll need to worry about. Always support it one way or another.

- **Wrap your baby:** There are numerous ways to pick up and carry a baby, and with time and practice, you'll learn them all. The easiest way to learn is with a swaddled baby. The birthing nurse can teach you how to swad-dle. Picking up a swaddled baby is easier because the baby is now more like a little package or bundle.

"No matter how easy it looks for others to swaddle a baby, it is tough to get it right. After several tries, I just let my wife do it. Otherwise, the blanket would come undone very easily or a limb would be sticking out."

- **Pick up your baby:** If the baby's head is to your left, place your right hand behind the baby's neck (on the right side of the baby). Place your left hand under the baby's bottom. Pick the baby up, making certain not to let his head flop backward. The baby should be perpendicular to your chest. Holding your left hand still, guide the baby to the left with your right hand so that the baby comes to rest on your left forearm. The baby's neck will now be supported by your left arm and steadied by the right. Feel free to coo, stroke, and cuddle.

tant and will bring you closer, immediately, to your little bundle. The following Focus describes the proper technique.

Bonding with Baby

Throughout the first year of a baby's life, it's important for the father to bond with his baby. At the end of each chapter, this book will discuss ways of growing closer to your child at the various stages of development. While most would consider this best to start in the chapter about the first month, bonding can and should begin while the baby is still in the womb.

Fathers can bond with their unborn baby by simply talking to him. If you know the gender of the baby and have already decided on a name, call him by name when you speak to him. If you can sing or play an instrument, introduce your baby to these sounds. Also, try reading stories. Whatever you do, the more you speak to your baby, the easier it will be for him to recognize your voice.

Your bonding need not be limited to voice or sounds. Also, include touch. Feel the baby through your partner's stomach. You can even play games by tapping your partner's stomach or speaking on one side then the other to see if your baby will move to follow the sound of your voice or your touch.

"I enjoyed playing with my daughter before she was born. I would tap on one side of my wife and talk to her. Then I would do the same on the other side. Sometimes she would turn inside the womb in response to the change in the location of the tapping. As the baby grew, the game

TIPS

• After she has been examined by the nurse, share an intimate moment with your baby. Set your video camera on a counter and film yourself welcoming your baby to the world. You can show it to her when she's older—she'll love it.

• Congratulate your partner for a job well done. While you're at it, don't forget to congratulate yourself!

FOCUS: CIRCUMCISION

If you have a boy, this is one of the decisions that must be made. While most men don't like to think about a sharp instrument around that part of their anatomy, it is important for you to be involved. While some religions take a stand one way or the other on this issue, it is usually the decision of the parents whether to circumcise their son. If you are unsure, talk to a few pediatricians. While some may be militantly for or against, a good doctor should provide the pros and cons and then let you decide.

If you decide to circumcise your son, be sure to listen to the doctor or nurse as they explain how to care for your son's circumcision. It's also a good idea to go with your son for his circumcision if possible, as it allows a time for the two of you to bond.

"When I took my son to be circumcised while we were at the hospital, there were two other fathers doing the same. The nurse led all three pairs of fathers pushing their sons in the little bassinets across to the other side of the postpartum area. I'm sure it was clear to anyone watching us where we were headed."

became less comfortable for my wife, who had to endure the motion inside her."

Once the baby is outside of the womb, continue bonding immediately. While the doctor will usually give the baby to your partner to hold, be right there beside her so you can take part in the baby's first extra-womb experience. Talk to the baby. He will know your voice if he heard it through the womb. While your partner will want to hold him, take any opportunity to hold your baby during your stay at the hospital. When you hold your first child for the first time, you may experience a feeling like nothing you have ever felt before.

"When my daughter was just born, I called her name, and she looked at me with recognition. She knew the sound of my voice. I was thrilled and felt like I was on cloud nine."

"After my first child was born, the doctor had to do some reconstruction on my wife. For over a half an hour, my child and I got to bond and be very close as I held her tightly. I will never forget that moment."

Bonding immediately after the birth of your child will consist mainly of holding him. However, anytime the baby must leave for tests or other things, go with him. While you may just be an observer, your baby will know you will be there for him.

Growing Together

As we'll see, the birth process is merely the beginning of a marvelous, but often bumpy, journey. It's a journey you'll take together—you, your partner, and your baby. As a new father, you'll likely have questions or concerns about that journey. How will you be as a dad? Can you deliver the love and attention your baby needs in order to flourish? Can you find the time? How will you talk to your baby? Will you be able to relate to him? Will you be able to unconditionally love him?

Most of us will drive up to the house with our partners and new child with a healthy combination of joy, fear, love, apprehension, and pride. Each time I pulled into the driveway with a brand new baby, I felt triumphant because of my pride at having had a beautiful, healthy child and terrified because I didn't know what to expect next. As I soon found out, for many reasons, the first few weeks at home with a newborn, regardless of how many you've had, are unlike any other. Let's find out why!

As one child psychologist friend of mine explains it with
tongue in cheek, your baby only needs a lot of light at night
if he's reading or he's entertaining guests.

—LAWRENCE KUTNER

2

The First Month

Congratulations! You and your family have made it home. In looking back, you're probably a bit dazed and overwhelmed by everything that's happened thus far. Now that your baby is here, though, you're probably trying to manage your worries and anxieties about how you'll do as a dad. As you journey through the first month, you'll be greeted by new physical and emotional challenges. New dads have lots of questions and concerns. How will you get along with your partner? Will your baby like you? Will you be involved? Will you be able to be as involved as you'd like? What sacrifices will you need to make?

"I wasn't ready for all the excitement. I mean, for the longest time, it was just me and my wife. Now, all of a sudden, there's three of us . . . and one of us isn't very cooperative! I had to quickly get ready for the adventure of a lifetime. What a roller coaster!"

With the exception of the first week or two—when some newborns (not mine) spend much of their time sleeping—your new home life will definitely be like nothing you've ever experienced . . .

What's New with Your Baby?

Even at the tender age of a few days, your baby is already developing and growing. You may be tempted to distance yourself, even flee, from your newborn's day-to-day routine—choosing instead to defer such care to your partner. However, since this stage finds your baby literally changing before your eyes, this important time in her life isn't to be missed!

Developmental Milestones

While the rewards of caring for someone so completely helpless are not immediately obvious, careful observation reveals that the newborn already possesses a variety of moves, behaviors, and reflexes that are sure to wow and dazzle the observant dad:

> "It was incredible. This baby, only a few days old, seemed to be taking in everything around her. I couldn't believe how active and stimulated she was. I mean she wasn't up walking around, but if you looked long and hard enough, you could see the drive and perseverance that'll one day propel her on her own!"

Motor Strength: Although your baby's neck is very fragile, he'll try to lift his head up a bit while lying on his stomach. In some cases, your baby may even be able to hold his head still while seated upright on your lap. You may also notice spontaneous flailing and moving of his arms and legs. His hands may be balled up into fists.

Reflexes and Adaptive Behaviors: Your baby should manifest a number of reflexive and adaptive behaviors. Newborns will, for example, put their fingers in their mouths and will grasp at objects placed in their hands. In an attempt to find the breast, they'll turn their heads toward an object stroking their cheeks (the rooting reflex) and, as discussed in this chapter, may also have a strong startle reflex. Even when fast asleep, newborns will suck.

Sensory Perception: Your baby may focus on an object placed in front of her visual field for brief periods of time and may even be able to briefly track the object as it moves. Your baby may also respond to noises by crying or becoming still or quiet. She will spend a lot of time looking at contrasting colors, such as black and white, or the dark area of objects and faces. Your baby may also begin to mimic your face. She may stick out her tongue when she sees you do the same.

Psychological: Your baby may have a very slight awareness of her primary caretaker as a separate person and may be responsive to and excited by her caretaker's face and voice. Your baby may become quiet when picked up. The primary psychological "mechanism" at this stage is sucking.

TIP

Consider videotaping each new milestone as you and your partner discover them. It takes only a few seconds. You'll be surprised how quickly they come and go!

While developmental milestones are an interesting and important set of behaviors and adaptations, it's important to note that the timeliness of such milestones is relative. There's great variability among babies, and the development of your child may not follow the usual path. One of my children, who's now an avid chatter bug, didn't speak until he was two years old. If you're concerned about the development of your baby, discuss it with your partner and feel free to consult with your pediatrician.

What Is Your Baby's Day Like?

Sleeping: Newborns generally spend great amounts of time sleeping—particularly for the first few days. Resist the urge to feel blessed with a "good-sleeping" baby. Conversely, don't worry if your baby sleeps very soundly for long periods of time. Have no fear! Your baby will soon awaken with a vigor:

> "I'll never forget the excitement and reassurance I felt as I observed my new son sleeping soundly in his bassinet. I commented to my wife that he seemed to be such a good sleeper. He wasn't very active, and so many of my worries faded. I felt as if I'd been given a bit of time to regroup and orient myself toward the pleasures of fathering. Little did I know!"

It seems amazing that during these first few days, your slumbering baby can be passed back and forth from relative to relative with nary a peep. Since the newborn baby sleeps so much, this is a good time to practice your holding techniques.

Feeding: Babies possess a great "orality." That is, they assess the world by putting it into their mouths. For your newborn, the breast or bottle *is* the world. When your baby isn't fast asleep, she will likely want to exercise her

Reprinted with Special Permission of King Feature Syndicate

orality by eating and sucking. As we'll see, some babies are easier to feed than others. Breast-fed babies may want to eat more frequently than bottle-fed babies.

Crying: To your newborn, crying is the preferred method of communication. She'll do it often and for many different reasons. This form of expression may be accompanied by vigorous movements of her arms and legs. In the absence of any obvious medical problems or other discomforts like hunger or a wet diaper, most crying newborns will respond to being held. Since a baby's cry can arouse a great many feelings in a new mom or dad, we'll return to it later in this chapter and in chapters three and four.

Excreting: As you may have heard, your baby will spend a great deal of time excreting. Since he doesn't yet possess the capacity to regulate his feeding schedule, there's no way to predict when he'll pee or poop. It's safe to say that the fluids will generally arrive at the least desirable time. The first few bowel movements may be greenish, and you may feel as if your baby is a little alien creature. Don't freak—it's normal. Breast-fed babies may have yellowish, almost liquid stools containing seedlike objects, while bottle-fed babies may have slightly a more solid brownish stool.

Mood Instability: Moodiness seems to be the hallmark of the newborn: calm, cooperative, and adorable one minute, enraged and screaming the next. This is completely normal and temporary.

Health Issues: First Visit to the Pediatrician

Most babies are born healthy, which is, of course, a tremendous relief to new parents. During the first month of life, with the exception of a rare cold, most

TIPS

• Feeding your baby is an excellent way to get to know him. It's also a fabulous way to make eye contact and to smile and talk to him. The newborn's field of vision is conveniently about the distance from the crook of your arm to your face. Just right.

• Once your baby has fallen asleep, lie down on your back and place him on your chest, making certain his head is turned to one side or the other. Now enjoy your free time together—watch TV, read, give your partner a break, or just watch your little bundle grow.

• Beware of what you say in the house when the baby monitor is on, particularly if the in-laws are visiting. A monitor is an amplification system and can easily detect conversations in other rooms.

will likely remain that way. Despite this fact, your newborn will need to see her doctor for a checkup.

Barring major medical problems, you won't have to visit your child's pediatrician much until several weeks after birth. As a dad, you should find this first visit fascinating and invaluable. Your child's pediatrician will be a source of reassurance and guidance for you, your partner, and your children for decades. Being involved with your family means being up-to-date with your baby's health—don't miss the first visit!

Measuring Height, Weight, and Head Circumference: At the first visit, the doctor or nurse will check your baby's height, weight, and head circumference. To help determine whether your baby is growing normally compared to other children, the doctor will assign a percentile to the figures, comparing the measurements to other same-age babies. Since all children develop and grow at different rates, don't be too alarmed if your baby seems "too big" or "too small" during this first office visit. Feel free to discuss any of your concerns about your baby's size with your pediatrician.

History: After the measurements, you'll be asked how things have been going and whether there have been any noticeable problems with your baby.

Your pediatrician will also want to know how your baby is feeding, sleeping, and acting. As a father, feel free to join your partner in describing life at home. Since two people living together may have differing views of how things are going, it's important for your pediatrician to obtain your perspective as well.

Physical Examination: Since your baby is likely to be nearly naked from being measured and is possibly hungry as well, he's probably screaming. You may marvel at the doctor's ability to hear your baby's heartbeat through all the crying. You can expect the doctor to perform a thorough examination. She'll check the heart for abnormal sounds or murmurs, the lungs for breathing sounds, the mouth and throat for any abnormalities, the eyes for reactivity and clarity, the ears for infection, and the nose for blockages. The doctor will also assess your baby's general well-being, neurological status, musculoskeletal system for tone and strength, abdomen for hernias, extremities, and genital and excretory systems. If your baby received her first hepatitis vaccine at birth, she may be given the second in the series during this visit. The pediatrician may discuss vitamins and fluoride treatments.

Most newborns pass their first examination with flying colors. As a dad, though, you may have special questions and concerns regarding your baby. No matter how seemingly trivial, take the time to discuss any of these issues with the pediatrician. While many dads choose not to accompany their partners on this first visit, the advantages are impressive:

> "I never thought that I'd be interested enough in someone else's health to actually want to go with them to see a doctor. I was also a little nervous about it because I felt like I just didn't know anything about babies and I didn't think I had anything of importance to talk about. The doctor was very understanding, though, and after a while, I felt comfortable discussing many of my concerns with her. I even asked her some questions about the way the baby looked. I'd been wanting to ask my wife about the baby but couldn't for some reason. It was a very positive experience."

While moms are often more concerned with "functional issues" such as bowel and feeding schedules, dads usually have questions concerning the appearance of their baby.

Q: *Why does my son have pimples all over his face and neck?*

A: Infant acne is a common and harmless condition. It's usually caused by maternal hormones circulating in your baby's bloodstream as well as incompletely developed skin pores. Washing the area with warm water can help cure this temporary condition, although it tends to disappear on its own without treatment.

Q: *Why is the top of my son's head peeling?*

A: It's not uncommon for a newborn to have a condition known as "cradle cap." This insignificant dryness of the scalp is treated with oil or a cleansing with mild dandruff shampoo.

Q: *Why is there a big, red, fuzzy "X" on the back of my daughter's neck?*

A: Birthmarks and rashes are common to the newborn but may be alarming to the new parent. The so-called stork bite present on the head or back of the neck will eventually fade and disappear. Some birthmarks may be more permanent but can be lightened or, in many cases, erased through laser surgery.

Q: *Is it normal for my daughter to be bald?*

A: Although it may feel embarrassing for dads to think of their little girls as bald, the amount of hair present during these early stages is not an indication of what's to come. In fact, the newborn's hair, whether copious or just fuzz, may soon fall out anyway and be replaced by more mature hair. However, some newborns just keep growing the hair with which they began life.

Q: *My son seems to jump and flail his arms whenever I pick him up. Will he be a nervous kid?*

A: The startle, or Moro, reflex is a normal behavior indicating that your baby's nervous system is working properly. Newborns use this reflex to steady themselves when fearful or when experiencing a falling sensation. This reflex will slowly disappear over the next few months.

Q: *Is it normal for my son to grunt and snore when he sleeps?*

A: You'll notice various breathing patterns, especially if you are using a baby monitor. The grunting and snoring may be the result of a particular stage of sleep called "rapid eye movement" (REM) sleep. REM sleep brings dreams and other physical and emotional manifestations and is very common during infancy. It's normally associated with heavy, irregular breathing. As your baby gets older, his percentage of REM sleep will diminish, as will his grunting and snoring.

Q: *My son seems so fragile. What happens if I accidentally touch the soft spot on my son's head? Can he break if I hold him the wrong way? If I forget to support his neck, will his head fall off?*

A: Your baby's head won't fall off. It's very common, though, for new dads to feel funny about holding their babies. With practice and experience, you'll soon learn that they're not that fragile. Since your baby isn't yet capable of doing this on his own, make sure to support his head and neck.

The soft spots on his head (fontanels) are the result of an incomplete closure of the forming bones that make up the skull. This membranous layer allows the head to expand to accommodate your baby's growing brain and allow the head to squeeze through the birth canal. Blood vessels located underneath the front fontanel will sometimes cause the membrane to pulsate. It's generally sturdy and may be safely touched (although doing so gives me the willies). The largest of the two areas, the membrane near the front of the head, will be completely closed by the time your child is about 18 months old.

Q: *My son's umbilical cord is still attached. It seems kind of gross. Will the umbilical cord area ever look normal?*

A: The umbilical cord may fall off soon after your newborn arrives home or may stay attached for several weeks. In short time, the remaining tissues will also scar and fall off, leaving a beautiful, kissable little belly button. To help speed up the drying process, be sure to apply rubbing alcohol to the cord remnant after every diaper change. Keep the cord uncovered by the diaper as well.

TIP

As you prepare to leave the pediatrician's office, make sure to write down his name and phone number. You may feel compelled to phone the office from time to time to seek advice or reassurance.

Q: *Why is my daughter's face so swollen and puffy? She doesn't seem like she'll be very attractive.*

A: Don't worry! While in the uterus, your baby was curled up into a little ball. The situation was made even more uncomfortable for her during her trip through the birth canal. As a result, it's quite common for a newborn's head, nose, forehead, and areas around the eyes and even ears to be mashed or flattened—even bent or malformed. In time, however, the puffiness, swelling, and strangely shaped organs will likely snap back into place.

Q: *My son has big breasts and sometimes milk comes out of them. Is this normal?*

A: This is normal in healthy newborns. Hormones circulating in the mother's bloodstream prior to birth can affect hormone levels in the newborn. Your baby's breast size will soon normalize, and the lactation (milk production) will cease.

Q: *My daughter's tongue looks like a road map. There are white lines and shapes all over it. What's going on here?*

A: A "geographic" tongue is of no clinical importance and may in time disappear. Babies can occasionally develop a fungal infection of the mouth known as candidiasis, or thrush. Check with your pediatrician if you're concerned.

What's New with Mom?

What's new with mom? Plenty! Much more, in fact, than she might let on. Having just been through the emotional and physical exhaustion of birth, she's now dealing with a rush of hormones circulating in her bloodstream. In addition, she too will have many of the same concerns and fears as you do.

Emotional—She May Feel . . .

Joyous: For some women, giving birth to a healthy baby may represent the culmination of a lifelong dream. While not true of all women, many experience childbirth as a wonderful and magical act that reinforces their sense of femininity and purpose. She may also feel special since her baby is the product of her relationship with you.

Concerned or Preoccupied with Her Body: Understandably, many women may marvel at and/or be horrified with the extent of change they and their bodies have undergone. Some women may become preoccupied with how their breasts are working or when or how they'll lose the weight they've gained.

Irritable: Rare for some, common for others:

> "Why does my wife snarl and act as though she wants to devour me? I'm afraid to go to bed at night for fear that I'll wake up to find her gnawing on one of my legs."

Reprinted with Special Permission of King Feature Syndicate

As a result of exhaustion, her circulating hormone levels, feelings of being overwhelmed, and lack of sleep (being up all night attending to the baby), your partner may see certain things—including you, your baby, or your in-laws—as unbearable. In time, this too shall pass.

Moody, Sad, or Tearful: Because of her recent experiences and traumas, as well as the biology of birth and the postpartum period, it's fairly typical for many new mothers to feel blue or sad. She may become tearful, have a diminished appetite, or have mood swings. This normal condition can last from days to weeks, and she'll benefit greatly from your support and encouragement.

More severe signs and symptoms of depression—not caring for herself or the baby, unable to sleep when the opportunity arises, self-loathing or suicidal feelings, inability to experience any sort of pleasure, bizarre behavior, or hostility toward or ruminations about the safety of the baby—signify a more serious condition. These signs and symptoms should be brought to the attention of your partner's physician immediately.

Overwhelmed and/or Scared: To be responsible for the life of another human being can be an awesome burden. New moms frequently feel overwhelmed and may feel frightened of running out of steam or fearful that they're simply not up to the task. These very common concerns are, unfortunately, infrequently discussed. Encourage her to share her feelings with you and acknowledge her strengths and efforts.

Capable *and* Inadequate: It's completely normal for mom to experience many different sets of opposing feelings. Babies make us all feel this way! Your partner will very likely have feelings of competence during certain times, alternating with feelings of complete inadequacy at others.

Physical—She May Have . . .

Tender Breasts: Even if your partner isn't nursing, the discomfort caused by engorged breasts can add to her stress. If she's nursing, her milk will come in soon after she arrives home from the hospital. Her nipples can crack and bleed, which can be very irritating and can contribute to her moodiness or irritability. On the other hand, she may find her ability to squirt milk from her breasts to be fascinating, while you may feel less than excited about this.

Vaginal Discharge: Your partner will have a blood-tinged vaginal discharge for weeks as her reproductive organs recuperate from the pregnancy and birth.

Fatigue: Even if she's not nursing around the clock, she'll be physically exhausted. It's not uncommon for a dad to awaken in the morning, only to find the baby firmly attached to his deeply sleeping partner. Her fatigue may impair her ability to recall how the baby ended up in bed!

Painful C-Section Incision: If your partner has had a c-section, she may have abdominal pain for weeks. As a result, she may have a difficult time performing such basic tasks as getting out of a chair or bed. Lifting the baby may also cause her great pain. Care must be taken with the suture line, and she mustn't exert herself or carry heavy objects. New mothers are often discharged from

TIPS

• Discuss with your partner how much company or family visitors the two of you want during the first month. Everyone wants to come and see the new baby. However, you should put yourselves first. You need time and privacy to get comfortable with your new baby and with being a family instead of just a couple. Also, offer to screen your partner's phone calls.

• Make sure your partner has a comfortable rocking chair. This will make nursing easier. A rocking ottoman, or even just a footstool so she can put her legs up, is also beneficial. Plus, when you're holding your newborn, you can use the chair too!

the hospital after only a brief recovery period. Watch her closely, and don't let her overexert herself.

What's New with Dad?

You've taken your baby to the doctor's office, have witnessed some developmental milestones, and can repeat the four basic newborn behaviors—peeing, pooping, eating, and sleeping. You've also been noticing your partner's emotional and physical changes. Good for you! These new experiences and observations bring you closer to your new family.

Reprinted with Special Permission of King Feature Syndicate

What are you noticing about yourself? How are you doing? What's expected of you? What do you want to be to your baby? Are you and your partner speaking the same language? Are you functioning as a team? Throwing yourself into your family's day-to-day routine will help you learn even more about yourself, your child, and your partner. The new skills and feelings you develop may surprise you.

The first month at home with your baby and partner can be greatly satisfying as well as disconcerting. You should allow yourself the luxury of having a mixture of feelings.

You May Feel . . .

Pride and Joy: Although not universally true, the birth of your baby may enhance your feelings of being a man. Many dads feel more masculine or "manly," and you may find that your self-esteem has risen a point or two. You may also feel proud to be seen carrying your baby in public—showing those around you that you're involved in caring for your baby, are capable of loving, and are a sexually potent person.

Fatigue and Exhaustion: Like your partner, you'll probably experience feelings of exhaustion or fatigue—particularly if you are helping to care for your baby at night or are helping to care for him upon your return home from a hard day's work.

Ambivalence: After a particularly horrible day or night with your baby, you may find yourself asking these questions: Do I really want to do this? Do I want to give up all my fun to care for someone who doesn't seem to appreciate me? How can I possibly move up in my career when I have to be home so much? Why does a trip to a distant country seem so appealing to me right about now?

Reprinted with Special Permission of King Feature Syndicate

Dads may also be bothered by feelings of guilt if they aren't getting up at night much with their partners or when they feel like running out of the house and not coming back:

> "I would squeal with childlike delight and stomp my feet on the pavement when the front door closed, leaving me outside of the house and on my way to work. I felt badly that my poor wife was stuck at home with the little monster. I couldn't stand the screaming . . ."

Your baby's moodiness—gleeful one minute, enraged the next—may be tough to handle:

"I feel uncomfortable with the randomness of my baby's moods. They're completely unpredictable."

Even when things seem intolerable, try to remember that each particular phase is time limited. The issues that are frustrating you—your baby's inability to sleep regularly and her screaming—will not last forever and will in fact be replaced by other more tolerable, even fabulous, behaviors. Try also to remember that your baby will grow quickly. Share your frustrations with your partner, and do your best to work through your misery. Try to identify at least one thing you enjoy about each stage of your baby's life.

Irritability, Anger, Depression: Your partner doesn't have a monopoly on exhaustion and postpartum depression. As her partner, you may be the unwitting recipient of her postpartum moodiness, which may result in some postpartum sadness of your own. Dads also need to grow accustomed to a variety of brand new baby behaviors. For instance, baby's body fluids can easily rattle a squeamish dad:

"I'll never forget the first time my newborn puked on me. I ran around the house like an idiot yelling, 'Get it off me! get it off me!' like someone had dripped battery acid on my shoulder and it was eating its way through my flesh. But times have changed, and I'm used to it. I wear it like a badge of courage now—a war decoration of sorts."

Sleep deprivation can accentuate an already tense situation, particularly during those nights when your baby refuses to go to bed or when he wakes up the instant he is put down. A baby who tortures parents all night can really get on the nerves of the parents. The key to coping with it is to realize they are not doing it to bother you on purpose. A newborn does not understand the concept of spite. Now, as they get older, this will change. If you start to get angry with your baby, give yourself a quick time-out. Go wash your face in the bathroom, take a walk through your house, or get a drink of water—anything that will give you time to cool down.

Love (Some of the Time): While many claim that they fell in love with their babies immediately, more often than not this isn't the case. There may be wonderment and pride, but love is an emotion that often takes practice and time:

"I'll never forget seeing my son for the first time. He was all wrinkled and gray. His head was pointy, and he was covered in slime. I felt so guilty because I didn't love him right away. I thought that he was probably the ugliest thing I had ever seen. But now, a year later, we're inseparable. I'm so in love with him that I can't stand being away."

While love at first sight is admirable, it's not always possible. Don't push yourself. You'll learn to deal with those moments when you "hate" your baby. When you do feel the emotion of love for your baby, though, whether it builds slowly over the first year or happens immediately, there's not a feeling in the world that can match it.

Resentment: Dads sometimes feel left out or even envious of mom's relationship with their baby.

When relatives visit, rather than asking how you're doing, they seem to be more interested in your baby or your partner. Also, since your partner is unable to have intercourse for the first six weeks after birth and may have a markedly diminished sex drive anyway, some dads feel sexually frustrated. This situation can further contribute to feelings of deprivation. Dads may also find that their partners are preoccupied with caring for themselves and the baby:

"My wife seemed much more interested in her own breasts than with anything I had to say. The three of them were all great friends—a complete love affair. They were inseparable."

The best way to cope with these feelings is through ongoing dialogue with your partner. Throughout this book, we'll look at ways in which you can relax, take care of yourself, and carve out special time for you and your baby.

Being There for Your Baby

Many dads express concern over their roles in the growth of their families. You may be feeling apprehensive about issues of bonding or love and may even feel compelled to do something drastic, like spending lots of money on large stuffed animals or toys your baby can't yet appreciate. Above all, you want to ensure your place in the life of your baby. If you work long hours and rarely see your baby, your concerns may be increased.

TIP

Don't worry about making mistakes. Babies are pretty forgiving.

The truth is that just helping to care for your newborn will endear you to your partner and baby and will instill within you a sense of pride and belonging. Your baby will grow up feeling loved and needed, and you won't need to go on any buying sprees.

Try to take off as much time as possible after the birth of your baby. Your partner will love having you around, and you'll benefit from being with your baby. Prepare for the birth and your absence from work by saving money. Use vacation time or discuss your planned absence with your boss. Some companies offer paternity leave. Check to see if your employer does.

The Crying Baby

For dads who are not accustomed to hearing shrieking and screaming, trying to soothe or comfort their tearful babe can be a challenge:

> "I spent the better part of one entire afternoon looking for the 'off' switch. I figured something that screamed this much must be powered by batteries."

Tears and crying (not yours) indicate that your baby is trying to communicate a need of some sort. Many babies who are otherwise healthy, dry, and fed will stop crying when they're picked up and held. Although you may feel as though you can't meet all of her needs, remember that by responding to your newborn with love and caring, she will learn to trust the world. Remember, to your newborn, you and your partner *are* the world. As you make your way through these difficult times, experiment with the available variables. Use common sense, creativity, and patience.

A baby's crying and screaming can give rise to feelings of rage or even disturbing fantasies. A crying baby should not, however, be allowed to "cry it out" until she's older—perhaps six months or so. Manipulating some of the previously listed variables may help to calm your screaming baby. There's no substitute, however, for working with your partner:

> "One night, we were unable to stop our baby from screaming. I had an exam the next day, and my wife was exhausted. We were both edgy and

CRYING CHECKLIST

✔ **Hunger:** Has it been a while since the last feeding? Often, a breast or warm bottle is enough to soothe a crying baby.

✔ **Gas or stomachache:** Babies respond to stomach cramps or gas by screaming or crying loudly. Often, cramps and gas are the result of the baby gulping air while he is feeding. Burping your baby frequently during feedings may be necessary. For the nursing baby, certain foods eaten by your partner may upset your baby's stomach. Sometimes cramps can be the result of a lactose intolerance or intolerance of certain baby formulas.

✔ **Diaper:** Is the baby's diaper wet or dirty? Many babies will need a diaper change during or just shortly after eating, while others may have only two or three poopy diapers in a day. Breast-fed babies tend to need more diaper changes, but almost all newborns need an average of eight diaper changes a day.

✔ **Clothing:** Is there something about your baby's clothing that might be bothering him? Is it too tight? Is the tag rubbing against his neck?

✔ **Temperature:** Many babies prefer to be bundled or swaddled, while others seem to favor being lightly dressed.

✔ **Fatigue:** Babies usually respond to their own fatigue by crying. If you suspect that your baby is tired, try rocking or walking her to sleep.

✔ **Medical problems:** Rarely, the newborn may develop a medical problem that causes discomfort. Ear infections, for example, lead to crying and increased irritability. A diaper rash or constipation can also be quite painful.

✔ **Colic:** There aren't any clear reasons for the kinds of behaviors that are evident when a baby is "colicky." We'll review the latest thinking on colic in the next chapter.

✔ **Position:** Many babies will cry if they feel vulnerable or placed in a physical position that leaves them feeling exposed, insecure, or uncomfortable.

✔ **Temperament:** All babies are born with a certain temperament, and some are more likely than others to respond to discomfort or a sense of displeasure with tears.

✔ **Noise level:** Some babies enjoy a background noise, be it TV, Vivaldi, or Led Zeppelin. Others sleep best with no noise at all and may be terrified by the lullaby on their music box.

✔ **No obvious reason:** Sometimes, the reason for a baby's tears are not diagnosable.

yelling at each other and even at our baby. I think what really saved us that night was the feeling that we were both in it together. I catnapped for 15 minutes or so while she walked the house with him. Then we switched. It wasn't perfect, but it was nice to have someone to hand my son over to."

> ## TIP
>
> To help soothe a crying baby, try running a vacuum cleaner, a hair dryer, or even a bathroom fan. The "white noise" can really help. Babies are used to a lot of noise. The womb is not a hall of silence. They constantly hear their mother's heartbeat, stomach gurgles, and other bodily noises. Therefore, complete silence can be frightening to a newborn.

Above all, try to be tolerant and creative. If you are at your wit's end, you can always put your baby down in a safe place and take a few minutes to compose yourself.

Changing Diapers

So you always wanted to be a detective? Here's your opportunity. Part of the "police work" of caring for a baby is detecting when a diaper change is needed. Once detected, you'll also need to actually change the dirty diaper:

> "How could I, someone who according to my wife is incapable of properly loading the dishwasher, be expected to correctly change the load in my baby's shorts?"

The key here is organization. Changing a wriggling baby is not easy, and he'll scoff at the notion of cooperation. Since you'll have undressed him, he'll likely be screaming. To make matters worse, there's a fairly reasonable chance that he'll pee on you.

> "I used to think that if a baby just filled his diaper, you had some time before he went again. Not true! One time while I was cleaning up my son, he pooped a stream for several feet, right off the changing table onto furniture and the carpet. Then, while I was occupied with trying to block this first attack, he ambushed me with pee in the face. I learned to keep the penis always covered."

Your baby should be changed whenever his diaper becomes very wet or when he has pooped. This is the best way to prevent a diaper rash. Be sure to wash your hands (and, if he got into the poop, your baby's hands as well) after changing your baby.

Sooner or later, you will experience the "blow-out." It is not the amount of stool that makes this such a terrible experience but, rather, where the stool goes. Often, it will leak out up the baby's back. However, it can also go out through the legs or up through the front of the diaper. For your first blowout, you may need your partner's help.

TIP

Diapers and babies—too loose they leak, too tight they shriek.

However, chances are she will be gone and you are on your own. The key is to remove the clothing without getting stool all over the baby, yourself, and the changing table. Then clean up the baby and re-diaper as quickly as possible. Sometimes giving the baby an impromptu bath in the sink is the easiest way to get him clean.

Feeding Your Baby

Since it brings the two of you closer and is soothing and comforting, feeding your baby should be considered a special event. Like other skills you're devel-

---

DIAPER CHANGING

- Since diaper wipes stick together and are hard to pull out of the container individually, set several out prior to undressing your baby.

- Don't throw ordinary diaper wipes into the toilet. They'll clog the septic system. You can purchase flushable wipes.

- Don't forget to thoroughly clean the space between the skin folds. By doing this, you'll help prevent a rash.

- A dry disposable diaper will crinkle when you poke at it, even through your baby's clothes. A wet one will be spongy and thick.

- Never leave your newborn unattended on a counter, bed, or changing table or near small children or pets.

FOCUS: HOW TO CHANGE A DIAPER

- **Detect:** Most newborn poop won't smell bad (although bottle-fed poops may have an odor), so you may not be able to detect it with your nose. Many moms will stick their fingers in the diaper and let the chips fall where they may. You may wish (as I've chosen to) to seek an alternative route. Pull the clothing to one side and take a visual peek instead.

- **Remove the clothing:** It's not possible to readily comprehend the physics of infant clothing. Hiding its snaps and zippers and secret hatches, most infant clothing (with the exception of two-piece outfits) doesn't want to be opened. Infant clothing seems to scream out, "Go away, I will not let you in." Keep in mind that you don't need to understand everything about infant clothing. Like eighth-grade math, just memorize it.

  Most one-piece outfits will have either snaps or a single zipper running from the inside of one leg across the groin area to the other leg. Some outfits will unsnap or unzip completely, while others stop at the cuff. Unzip or unsnap the outfit and pull the baby's legs out by gently bending each leg at the knee. Tuck the bottom portion of the outfit under the baby's back. You don't need to completely remove the outfit. If the baby is also wearing one-piece underclothing, unsnap and peel back.

oping, learning to feed your baby will take time and practice. You'll soon learn what positions, formulas, and rubber nipples please your baby. If your partner is nursing, you may still be able to feed your baby, either by giving a bottle of formula once or twice a day or by using pumped breast milk. Your baby won't yet have a particular feeding schedule, so you and your partner need to decide who'll get up when or for which feeding.

Hold your baby close to you so he feels secure. You'll want to smile and place the bottle gently in his mouth. Since a newborn can't really comfortably drink more than a few ounces at a time, he will need to be burped frequently. Hold your baby upright on your shoulder and pat gently in the middle of his back until he burps. Since each baby communicates differently, knowing when he is finished drinking may take some practice.

- **Remove the diaper:** If you're using disposable diapers, simply peel back the adhesive or Velcro strips and carefully pull the diaper off from front to back. To protect the changing table, you may wish to leave the baby lying on the diaper while you clean her. Or, even better, place a clean diaper under the old one in advance. If you're using cloth diapers with a diaper wrap, remove the wrap and then the diaper.

- **Wipe:** Using diaper wipes or a moist, warm cloth, gently wipe the area clean. You may need to steady your wiggling baby with one hand on his tummy while you wipe. For boys, make sure to wash under the scrotum. For girls, wipe from front to back to avoid getting stool in the vaginal area. If your baby's bottom appears red or inflamed, you may apply a balm as directed by your pharmacist or your baby's pediatrician.

- **Re-diaper:** Fan open the diaper (or, for cloth, place in diaper wrap), lift your baby's legs up together, slide the diaper under, put your baby's legs down, and apply the adhesive or Velcro strips. Leave enough room for at least two fingers to slide in. If you undertighten, your baby will pee or poop all over her clothing. If you overtighten, your baby will be uncomfortable and shriek. Put your baby's clothes back on.

Problems with Feeding

- **Reflux:** Some babies tend to regurgitate everything they drink. Consult your pediatrician if this develops.

- **Pyloric stenosis:** This is a serious but surgically curable problem that causes forceful, projectile vomiting.

- **Not latching on:** It may take your baby several days or even a week or two to learn to nurse correctly. Your partner may become irritated with him for not drinking properly. With practice, he will almost always learn the proper technique.

- **Other medical issues:** Any number of medical problems, such as facial or mouth abnormalities or formula intolerance, can result in problems

FEEDING

- *Don't* feed your baby cow's milk until approved of by your baby's pediatrician. (Cow's milk does not contain all the nutrients your newborn needs. In addition, the immature digestive system of many babies means they find cow's milk difficult to digest; it's often not approved until the baby is one year old.)

- Once your baby is done with a bottle, don't use that bottle again until it has been cleaned and sterilized. Also, don't forget to refrigerate all fresh bottles of formula or milk.

- If you insist on using the microwave to heat your baby's bottle, don't test the temperature of the formula until you have first shaken the bottle briskly. (Some studies have found that microwaving bottles of formula can destroy vitamins and nutrients. Be sure to discuss the microwave with your pediatrician.)

- If your baby won't burp, try rubbing the ball of your palm in a circle on her back.

- If your baby spits up frequently, instead of wearing a diaper on your shoulder, consider putting a bib on your baby and flopping it over your shoulder when you burp him. Never allow your baby to sleep in a bib, however.

with feeding. Diarrhea can quickly lead to dehydration, a serious problem for a newborn. If your baby's diaper remains dry for much of the day, if she appears pale, or if the lining of her mouth or tongue appears dry, you should alert your pediatrician.

Getting Your Baby to Sleep

Getting a baby to sleep is not difficult; getting a baby to sleep when you want him to is. You've probably noticed that your baby will sleep soundly through a rock concert on TV but will awaken easily at the slightest noise when you crawl into bed:

> "Why is it that this baby will sleep through heavy road construction, an air show, a test of the emergency broadcast system, and a violent thunderstorm, but if drool falls out of my mouth and hits my pillow, she wakes up?"

Sometimes rocking your baby, either in a cradle or in your arms, is a good way to help her sleep. A gentle up-and-down motion, even bouncing your bottom on the edge of a bed while holding her in your arms or on your shoulder, can do the trick.

Some parents bring the baby into bed in the early morning hours, while other parents try to induce sleep by taking the baby for a ride in the car or putting her on top of a gently whirling washing machine. You'll discover many tricks of your own through trial and error. Even as newborns, each of my three children had a vastly different ritual for going to sleep at night!

Washing Your Baby

Bathing your baby is a nice way to get to know him. For working dads, a bath can be a great bonding experience. Your baby may be washed in the sink or in a small plastic tub. Support his head and neck well. Wash gently with a soft cloth and warm water. I discuss bathing techniques in depth in the next chapter.

Loving Your Baby

Remember that everything you do with your baby will strengthen your bond and reinforce feelings of love between the two of you. Feel free to talk to your

TIPS

- If your newborn is unable to sleep in a bassinet or crib, consider placing him down, asleep, on his back in the pullout section of the car safety seat. Make certain the straps and belts are safely tucked away or are latched. Place your baby and the seat in the crib.

- To prevent suffocation, don't place your baby to sleep on her stomach or near stuffed animals, blankets, comforters, or pillows.

- Don't forget to photograph your baby's first bath.

baby, and tell her how you're feeling about things. Converse with your baby, feel the softness of her skin, and rub her chest and belly. Simply by spending loving time with your baby, you can't go wrong.

Bonding with Baby

The first month is when you as a father can really begin to physically bond with your new baby. The best thing you can do is just get involved. For many men, nurturing a baby does not come naturally. In fact, you may even be embarrassed by what you don't know about children. Don't let that stop you. What is important is that you have the desire to learn more and improve yourself. Remember, the only way to become a good father is through "on-the-job training."

Burp Your Baby

Since your partner will usually solely provide your baby's nourishment, especially if you decide to breast-feed him, you are often left out of an important bonding moment. However, if you can't feed, be there to burp. After he is done feeding, take your newborn from your partner and proceed to get the gas out of him. Put a cloth over your shoulder, then securely hold him against your shoulder while you pat or rub his back. Don't be concerned if he spits up. That

---

TIPS

• Through chaos comes creativity. Don't raise your baby from a textbook. Some of the best baby-care techniques come through trial and error.

• Eat when you can, sleep when you can, and don't wake a sleeping newborn unless you know there's a massive poop inside his shorts.

• Go out alone with your partner once a week for a meal or coffee. Now that you're parents, it's important to carve out quality time for just the two of you.

is common. This gives you an opportunity to get to know your baby. It also provides time for your partner to rest and relax.

Hold Your Baby

After burping him, or any other time, just hold him. You can do this while watching TV, surfing the Internet, reading a book, or doing a dozen other activities that require only one hand. Even when he goes to sleep, don't rush to put him down in the bassinet or cradle. Let him feel close to you. Try lying down on your back and placing the baby on your bare chest. He will feel your warmth. You may want to undress the baby so the two of you can feel the skin-to-skin contact similar to that of breast feeding. However, I recommend keeping the diaper on at all times.

Observe Your Baby

At this stage in his development, your baby will not be very active, and he will sleep a lot. However, take time to look at your baby. Observe his little hands and feet—how they are just like yours, but in miniature. Your baby is a product of your partner and you. Get to know him now. Before long, he will be much bigger. Babies are little only once. Don't let this time pass you by.

Growing Together

During the first several weeks postpartum, while your baby grows and develops, you'll likely undergo an equally significant transition—a growth spurt as a parent. As a father, you're growing, developing, and learning in ways that were previously unimaginable. Having a child gives rise to an interesting developmental process whereby you and your child can become a growing unit together.

Toward the end of the first month, your newborn will start to look like a person rather than a little wrinkled doll. Your baby's level of awareness and motor activity will increase. Along with this comes a marked increase in your family responsibilities. By facing the challenges to date, you're honoring your family and preparing for the next phase of your life together, when juggling work, play, and family becomes an even greater challenge.

[Fatherhood] is the single most creative, complicated, fulfilling, frustrating, engrossing, enriching, depleting endeavor of a man's adult life.

—KYLE D. PRUETT

3

The Second Month

The first month has come and gone. Thanks in part to your dedication and patience, your baby is growing and thriving. If you're like most new dads, you've probably lost track of some of the outside world and may be feeling a bit sensory deprived:

"I haven't read a newspaper in three weeks. What year is it anyway?"

If you've been paying attention to your baby, your knowledge of who's in first place in the National Hockey League has been replaced by your concerns over the rash on your baby's groin or your partner's cracked nipples. My, how times have changed. While news from the outside world may barely permeate your home, thus far you've survived the crying and carrying on—your own as well as your baby's. You may even be an expert at changing diapers! As you'll soon discover, the second month brings with it a variety of new challenges—some of which might be disorienting. Hopefully, though, you and your partner have been helping each other coast through the best of times and struggle together through the toughest.

Between your home responsibilities and work, you may feel stretched in a thousand different directions. While the intensity of your responsibilities at home will probably increase this month, those stresses will be offset by remarkable changes in your baby:

"My son changes every single day. It's astounding! We've had to start using larger diapers already! Pretty soon, his head's going to pop out of the roof."

What's New with Your Baby?

Your baby's a little growing machine. If you watch closely, you'll be rewarded! Staying involved will guarantee you a front-row seat for some truly amazing behaviors.

Developmental Milestones

While previously interested only in the basic necessities of life, during the second month your baby is quickly learning to become a social being.

Motor Strength: Your baby is improving upon his skills. With time and practice, he may be able to lift his head up to about a 45-degree angle. By the end of the second month, some babies may even be able to lift their heads to a 90-degree angle. Your baby will probably want to look around and may even be able to hold his head steady while on your lap. There's also a slight chance that he may be able to roll over. Your baby may be able to grasp and even hold onto objects and might be able to reach for something held in front of him. Your baby may also make various noises and will generally be more active.

Sensory Perception: Your baby will be better able to follow or track objects placed in her visual field and will seem more interested in her surroundings. She may also become more sensitive to noises and sounds.

Reprinted with Special Permission of King Feature Syndicate

Psychological: It's usually during the second month that your baby will do something truly wonderful for you:

> "I'll never, ever forget the first time my daughter smiled at me. She smiled at my wife first, probably because her voice is higher and because she's the primary caregiver and I was feeling a bit left out. One day, I finished changing her, and I smiled. She looked right into my eyes and smiled back. I was so excited that I almost dropped her poopy diaper! Her smile made me feel as though she knew who I was. I think she really loves me!"

TIP

Babies like to look at stark contrasts. Try placing a simple black-and-white picture in her view and watch. Your baby will usually stare intently at the picture, and you may wonder if she's hypnotized. It will also keep her occupied, and she may forget about crying for a while.

Nothing brings more delight (particularly since the rewards of caring for a crying baby night and day seem few at first) than a socially smiling baby. The social smile generally becomes apparent during the sixth to seventh week but may also take a bit longer. Although your baby may have smiled at an earlier stage, during sleep, for example, such smiling was more related to the developing nervous and muscular system, whereas the social smile is a direct response to you.

At this stage, your baby may also start to laugh at you as you make silly faces or gently tickle her. She is beginning to react to you and her environment.

What Is Your Baby's Day Like?

Since physical and emotional growth take a great deal of energy, your baby must prepare himself. It should come as no surprise, then, that the majority of your baby's time will still be spent doing what he does best . . .

Sleeping: The good news is that because your baby is developing normally, she will be spending fewer hours sleeping. The nature of her sleep is also changing, and your baby will be spending a bit less time in REM sleep. The bad news is that an awake and alert baby may be up doing other things, like crying or screaming:

"It was strange how our baby just sort of woke up one day. She's great to be around, but I sometimes wish she'd go back to sleep."

Crying: Everything about your baby will be bigger and stronger. In fact, you'll probably notice that concentrating on a football game or a movie is far more difficult because your baby's screams and cries are significantly louder. It may take extra effort to calm him. Since your baby is quickly learning about life's various options, he will also be better at "contacting" you:

"My son certainly packs a hell of a wallop, especially when he's cold. He used to have such a tiny little cry. Bigger lungs, more sound I guess. The great part is that I'm actually beginning to tell the difference between his hungry cry, wet cry, temperature cry, and tired cry."

Changing Moods: The moodiness of the newborn may well persist into the second month and, given the baby's increased energy level, may actually intensify. Depending on the comfort level of your baby, coupled with his innate temperament, this stage can be quite a challenge:

"Our baby is actually worse. He's cranky and miserable, and we can't soothe him. It's maddening. I called the hospital—they won't take him back. I used to be able to hold him while I was watching TV, but now I can't even do that. The house is very tense. I'm trying hard to love him, but he makes it tough."

Remember, no particular stage lasts forever. Hang in there. Things will soon get better. The next several months will prove to you that your baby is capable of much more than just screaming and crying.

Feeding: Since your baby is awake a bit more, she may demand to be fed more frequently. This can be tough on nursing moms and potentially stressful for the entire family. A supplemental bottle sometimes helps to solve this problem.

TIP

When carrying your baby, try carrying her upright and facing away from you. This will let her look around and explore the world. Watch how her head will scan left and right like a little radar receiver, trying to take everything in at once.

Excreting: The breast-fed baby will continue to produce soft yellowish poops, while the bottle-fed baby will produce slightly more solid poops. By this time, you've probably moved up a size or two in diapers. Bigger baby, bigger diapers. Bigger diapers, more poop. Changing the two-month-old is challenging since they have far more control over their bodies than newborns.

Being Curious: As a newborn, your baby's primary mission was to secure life-sustaining nourishment. You'll soon notice, however, that your growing baby will develop interests in other things as well. Because it gives parents the sense that there's more to their baby than just physical neediness, his new-found curiosity is an exciting development:

> "I was so used to seeing my son sleeping all the time that I was shocked when he started looking around. He seemed so much more human or at least a part of the family. He actually seems interested in me—even curious at times! To think that only a month or two ago he was still inside my wife. Boy, he's really come a long way! How much better can it get?"

TIP

Before you go to the doctor, sit down with your partner and write down any questions you may have. During the course of the visit, it's easy to forget some of the questions you had previously. If they are written down, you will be ready. Also, don't be afraid to ask what you may think are stupid questions, as the doctor most likely has heard them before. Remember, the only stupid question is the one that is not asked.

While your baby may not yet be able to ask questions, he seems to be thinking about it! Your child's developing curiosity is only one of what will be dozens of soon-to-come thrilling behaviors and characteristics.

Health Issues: Second-Month Pediatric Visit

During your baby's second visit to the pediatrician's office, the doctor will want to know how things are at home, whether your baby is sleeping and eating well, and how his general behavior has been. Your baby's measurements will be taken. With special attention to milestones and growth, the doctor will perform a physical examination on your squirming baby. Unless your child has a bad cold or other illness, it is also likely that she will be given some or all of the following immunizations:

- **DPT:** This protects your baby against some very serious infectious diseases—diphtheria, tetanus, and pertussis (whooping cough).

- **OPV:** This vaccine, given orally, immunizes your baby against polio, a debilitating muscle disease.

- **Hemophilus Influenza B:** This vaccine protects your baby against hemophilus influenza B bacteria, which can be fatal to small children.

Since your baby is bigger, physical defects or imperfections may be more easily noticeable. As always, if you have any questions about your baby, such as those below, be sure to ask.

Q: *I've noticed that my son's scrotum is getting bigger and bigger. Is he well endowed? If so, I'd like to think I had something to do with it.*

A: Don't flatter yourself. Swelling of the scrotum can be caused by a number of conditions, and problems with the genitourinary system are not uncommon. Fortunately, most aren't serious. One common cause of scrotal swelling is a *hydrocele,* which is caused by fluid that accumulates within the scrotum. Much of the time, it disappears on its own. On occasion, its correction requires a relatively minor surgical procedure. Very rarely, the scrotum may change in shape or size rapidly, or a small hardened area in the groin above the scrotum will develop. Should these changes occur, it might signal a more serious but surgically curable condition. Alert your doctor immediately.

Another common but reparable problem is a *hypospadias,* which occurs when the opening to the penis develops in the wrong place, such as under the penis.

Very rarely, a circumcision can become infected and require antibiotic treatment. If your child has a hydrocele or any other problem with his urinary system, your pediatrician will likely refer you to a pediatric urologist, a specialist who can follow your child's condition closely.

Q: *My son was born with a hernia. What is it?*

A: A hernia can develop as a result of a weakness in the wall of the abdominal cavity. Sometimes, the layers that comprise the walls can bulge outward, creating a balloon-like swelling or bulge in the groin, abdomen, umbilical area, or scrotum. Some hernias go away on their own, while others can easily be surgically repaired. Rarely, a loop of intestines can become caught in the balloon-like bulge, creating a potentially serious medical problem requiring emergency surgery.

Q: *What is an undescended testicle? Does this mean my son won't be able to have children?*

A: During your baby's development in the uterus, the testicles normally descend from inside the abdominal cavity—migrating southward to their home in the scrotum. Sometimes, the testicles' journey takes a bit longer. After birth, many undescended testicles will eventually drop down into the scrotum on their own, while some will require surgical intervention. Your pediatrician will be able to detect this condition and offer recommendations. Your son's fertility most likely won't be affected.

Q: *What kinds of reactions can I expect from my daughter's immunization shots? Are they serious?*

A: Reactions to shots are typically not serious and usually consist of fever, irritability, tenderness, or swelling near the injection site and vomiting. Rarely, certain shots can cause life-threatening problems characterized by very high fever, confusion, erratic behavior, seizures, or extreme fatigue or listlessness. Be sure to talk to your doctor in advance so you know what signs to look for. Should any of these develop, your child might be developing an infection of the brain or nervous system called *encephalitis*. Call your doctor immediately.

Q: *My daughter's like a camel—she spits up frequently. My partner and I are always covered with puke. What's going on here? Is this normal?*

A: Many babies, by their nature, spit up (regurgitate) frequently. As long as she doesn't become dehydrated (if your baby's diapers are generally wet and if the inside of her mouth is pink and moist, she is probably not dehydrated), there's no danger. On occasion, babies with a condition know as *gastric reflux* may regurgitate frequently. They may be cranky because of the irritation

> ## TIP
>
> If at all possible, make arrangements so you can go with your partner to your baby's doctor appointments. The second-month visit is very important since your baby likely will be given a number of vaccinations. Holding the baby while he gets shots can be difficult for your partner. (Not that it will be easy for you.) However, your support will be greatly appreciated by your partner.

caused by repeated spitting up and may also be hungry since they find it so difficult to keep milk or formula down. These babies may require a formula change or may need to be placed on medication temporarily. On the other hand, pyloric stenosis (forceful, projectile vomiting) is a serious problem that requires surgical intervention. Discuss any concerns with the pediatrician.

Q: *My daughter hiccups all the time. Are the hiccups dangerous?*

A: No. Nobody seems to have the definitive answer for why people hiccup. Most babies hiccup frequently during the first few months, especially after feeding. While it may signal a need to burp, most of the time there's little that needs to be done.

TIP

Always keep a burp cloth handy. I tuck it into one of my pants pockets and walk around the house like a quarterback with a rag to wipe his hands. While you may rarely need it while carrying it, the moment you don't have it, your baby will decide to return his last meal. Be warned.

Q: *My baby likes to sleep on his stomach. Is that OK?*

A: Until your baby is able to control his head, it's advisable to have him sleep either on his side or back. A baby whose head gets stuck face down on a soft surface runs the risk of suffocation.

Q: *What is SIDS?*

A: SIDS (sudden infant death syndrome), also know as crib death, while relatively rare, is nevertheless responsible for the deaths of thousands of infants each year. Typically affecting babies up to the age of 12 months, the causes of SIDS are not yet clear. Many babies who do succumb to this sudden cessation of breathing may have some preexisting medical problems or may have been exposed to illicit drugs or alcohol while in the uterus. There's also recent evidence implicating maternal smoking during pregnancy. For some babies, however, there's no good explanation. Soft items placed near the baby's mouth, such as lambskins, comforters, pillows, or very soft or spongy mattresses, may be contributory, particularly if the baby is on her stomach and can only breath in air that she has just exhaled. For babies with respiratory problems, special monitoring equipment is available.

Q: *Is there anything wrong with using a pacifier to help my baby get to sleep? My poor wife has such sore nipples that she can't take the constant sucking anymore.*

A: When used for brief periods, during strategically important times, pacifiers can really be quite useful. There are, however, many differing points of view regarding this little piece of rubber. Some experts maintain that the baby must learn to sleep without the help of such oral aids, while others feel that there's nothing wrong with a five-year-old walking around with one hanging out of her mouth.

Some experts feel that the use of a pacifier prevents thumb sucking, while others fear its potentially deleterious effects on the child's teeth. One practical disadvantage of a pacifier is that it frequently falls out of the baby's mouth in the middle of the night and awakens him and then you. On the other hand, they can be lifesaving to the sore mom. They're tough to keep clean, however, and are often used in an attempt to quiet a baby who might be distressed about something unrelated to sleeping or sucking. You'll need to weigh the pluses and minuses and consult with your partner and pediatrician to help you decide what's best for your baby.

 TIP

After you've weathered three or four days of colic, try to anticipate the evening's activities. Build it into your schedule. That way, it won't come as a surprise. For example . . . "Home from work, eat, watch the news, carry the screaming baby around for two hours, read in bed, sleep a bit."

What's New with Mom?

Some of the physical and emotional conditions present during the first month may be lingering, but she may also have new issues.

Emotional—She May Feel . . .

Frustrated: Your partner may feel frustrated for any number of reasons. If she's home with the baby while you've gone back to work, she may resent your ability to leave the house while she's left to care for a screaming baby. She may also feel frustrated if the baby's not nursing well or is cranky during the day:

> "I came home from work to find my wife in tears. She said that our baby had screamed all day long. She had to carry him around all day, he wouldn't nap, and he puked up everything she fed him."

FOCUS: COLIC

All babies cry, and there's a wide range of infant behaviors and traits that can be considered normal. Some babies, for example, hardly fuss and cry, while others are "high maintenance" and require constant soothing. "Colic" describes something quite different, although nobody really knows what it is!

Q: What is colic?

A: The term "colic" is used to describe a particular behavior in infants who cry far more intensively at a given time of the day—generally late afternoon or evening—and are unable to be soothed. The crying is vigorous and accompanied by heightened motor activity. Often pulling her knees up to her stomach, your baby will seem very agitated.

Although "colic" sounds like an objective medical phrase, it actually has no diagnosable cause and doesn't represent any specific medical problem. Many theories have been advanced, but the reasons for colic are unknown. Physical examination reveals no abnormalities that might account for the behavior.

Q: How can it be stopped?

A: Mother nature started it, and only she can stop it. Although largely inconsolable, your baby may stop crying for a minute or two in response to being held, rocked, or fed. Temperature changes, baths, and antigas drops may be helpful but usually aren't. For the most part, your baby will continue to scream for hours no matter what you do. He will then abruptly stop and fall asleep. Your baby will suffer no long-term effects from these episodes (which will generally cease within a month or two), but you may feel as if you will.

Q: What can my partner and I do with our distress?

A: It's unfortunate that colic comes on the heels of a long, exhausting workday for both you and your partner:

"My son would typically start in just as my wife and I were ready to drop from exhaustion. It was the end of the day, and we'd both be so on edge. I remember once having to take him from my wife. He kept smashing his face into hers and would scream and shake. It was scary, and I didn't know what to do to help. She said that she felt like losing it, and I was in better control that night, so I took him for an hour while my wife took a long shower. She felt better afterward, and I gave him back to her while I did some work on my car. By that time, my wife had managed to nurse him to sleep."

The colicky baby can drive even the most level-headed parent wild. Anger and feelings of violence toward the baby aren't uncommon. What can you do to help each other cope?

- **Talk:** You must be willing to talk with each other about the stress of the situation. Partners who do so and who feel that they're not alone almost always come out better from the experience.

- **Trade:** Trade your baby back and forth to allow your partner to unwind and get her hearing back.

- **Joke:** Keep a sense of humor. Try to look at the lighter side of the crisis. Maybe your baby will become a great orator, or perhaps you could prop him up outside to scare away the crows.

- **Enlist relatives:** Enlist trustworthy friends or relatives to be with you during these difficult few months.

- **Shower or bathe:** Give the baby to your partner and take a relaxing hot shower or bath.

- **Wait:** This too shall pass. Don't give up on your baby. Some research reveals that colicky babies grow up to be more engaged with those around them.

- **Don't blame your baby:** Try to show your baby love and admiration even though you feel like tossing her through the window. Colic is nobody's fault.

(cont.)

FOCUS: COLIC

(continued)

- **Call your pediatrician:** Call your pediatrician for suggestions or support. The doctor may want to see your baby just to make certain there are no medical reasons for his apparent discomfort. She'll probably reassure you that this stage won't last forever.

- **Seek professional help:** If your feelings of hopelessness, rage, depression, or violence become more than simply a passing thought, seek mental health counseling or discuss the problem with the pediatrician. If you're alone and feel that you're unable to control your anger, put the baby in a safe place and take a few minutes to compose yourself. Consider asking a trusted friend or relative to watch the baby for a while so you can regroup.

Her self-image may be suffering as well, particularly if she's nursing and is still carrying some extra weight. She may also be realizing that she's given up a substantial portion of her free time, work, or hobbies to raise the baby:

> "I think my partner resents the fact that she isn't working right now. I mean she's working in the home caring for our daughter, but she doesn't see it as the same thing."

Overwhelmed and Emotionally Drained: If your partner has traditionally been the one to take care of the house, she may be exhausted by the 24-hour job of caring for you and the baby, keeping herself together, and wondering if she's doing a good job. She may also feel as if she is spread too thin.

Now is the time to pitch in and do your bit to help out (see the suggestions in "Being There for Your Baby and Your Partner" later in this chapter). Surveys have shown that even when both partners work outside the home full time, men do significantly less housework than their female partners do.

Protective: As we'll see, you and your partner may develop any number of hostile feelings toward each other for many different reasons:

> "My wife thinks that she knows how to do everything best. The truth is that there are some things I'm better at. She gets so darned protective—she won't give him up sometimes!"

Happy: Above all, in the minutes between the hours of confusion and crying or feeding or pooping, your wife may well be satisfied with her new role. She may take pride in her abilities as a mom and may feel pleasure, peace, and happiness with the new baby.

Uninterested in Sex: Your partner's sexual desire will slowly return. By about the end of the second month, her body will probably have healed from the labor and delivery (remember, though, that some women take longer to heal than others), and she may again be interested in having sex (presumably with you). However, exhaustion (see the following discussion) and frustration (see the previous discussion) can dampen anyone's sex drive.

Remember to be patient and take it slowly. Postpartum intercourse can be painful for your partner so ease into it. It also can help to time your love fest for a period when you know your baby will be fast asleep.

Physical—She May Have . . .

An Exhausted Body: This may well be one of the hallmarks of life in the second month. Not only is her body still recovering from delivery, but she's up all day and night. If you've gone back to work, she may be alone for much of the day. Despite your involvement, chances are that she's doing the bulk of the work. In addition, shopping and traveling with the baby can be stressful and exhausting.

Sore Breasts: If your breast-fed baby is a frequent feeder or regurgitates and needs to feed frequently,

TIPS

• If your partner needs a break, take the baby for a while.

• Cook dinner once in a while or bring it home.

• Hold your baby in the evening to give your frazzled partner a break.

your partner may develop sore nipples. She also may become frustrated, even angry or tearful, because of the stress associated with the constant nursing.

Extra Weight: She may be having trouble taking off the extra weight she put on during pregnancy. This may or may not be a source of stress for her. Always try to be positive for your partner. If she wants to work out, do it with her. Walking is a great source of exercise, and it is easy to do together. Either carry the baby in a sling or push him in a stroller. This is a good time to talk to your partner about the day and discuss your experiences as parents.

What's New with Dad?

You May Feel . . .

Tired: If you're not the kind of person who can easily get back to sleep, you're in for some trouble:

> "I was so exhausted. I remember being woken up at the crack of dawn every day and being unable to get back to sleep. I felt like my body was bleeding fatigue. Sometimes I'd just get up at 4 A.M. and go to the local donut shop to join the silently brooding brotherhood of other exhausted fathers. There we would all sit, eating fat-filled donuts and staring at each other. How much *better* can it get?"

If the baby is nursing, you stand a reasonable chance of being woken up every few hours. Often, the baby won't want to go back to sleep. Your fatigue will also be the result of an active mind as well. The fact that you may be supporting your family, juggling work and home, and trying to be a good partner and loving dad may catch up with you, leaving you drained and tired.

Competitive: You and your partner may find yourselves competing for "who knows best." Competition may also develop around the issue of who works harder or who gets up most or who is more tired:

> "I guess my wife and I really need to talk more. I get home at the end of a horrible day, and there's my wife, hoisting the baby onto me. We argue about who's worked the hardest or who's more exhausted.

Sometimes I forget that she's had a tough day, but she doesn't seem to appreciate my lousy day either."

Turned Off to Your Partner: Sometimes what is arousing to your partner may have the opposite effect on you:

"One night, while we were in bed, my wife thought it would be cute if she squirted breast milk in my general direction. She thought it was cool, but it nauseated me. Maybe she can go on *Letterman*. I try to be happy for her because I know that her body is doing some amazing things, but I just don't feel like touching her. I feel pretty guilty about the whole thing."

These feelings, along with sexual frustration and feeling left out, may sometimes produce feelings for other women:

"I was shocked to discover how badly people misinterpreted my relationship with a female co-worker. The rumor was that I was having an affair. I didn't, although I was attracted to her and we spent lots of time together. I guess in retrospect I can understand why people thought I slept with her."

Some dads make the terrible mistake of acting on their sexual impulses. Issues of sexuality demand discussion. Try to deal with your feelings not through neglect or action but through dialogue with your partner or, if necessary, with a counselor.

Irritable: Because of intense sleep deprivation and/or emotional conflict, you may be feeling irritable. You've had to part with many of the things you used to enjoy—going out, watching TV, goofing off, eating, sleeping, and so on. Tension between you and your partner and the general lack of privacy in your new lifestyle may also contribute to this state.

Pushed to Be More/Less Involved: You may feel pushed to be more or less involved. Sometimes dads can feel both of these conflicting emotions:

"I'm so tired when I get home from work and there's my wife standing at the door, greeting me with our baby, who is screaming. Actually, they're both screaming. She wants me to take him for an hour or two so she can go do something. I feel like it's not fair. Then again, she's had him all day. Sometimes we argue because we've both had bad days."

Love and Admiration for Your Baby: Even though you may feel angry with your situation or even a bit depressed, it's hard not to love your newly alert and responsive baby and want to spend time with her.

Being There for Your Baby and Your Partner

While still completely helpless and relatively immobile (the baby, not you), your baby will nonetheless be more active, engaged, and energetic. He will likely be more demanding as well. As a result, you'll be called upon to become even more involved in day-to-day care issues. This is a great time to learn new skills and to polish up on your older ones!

The Sleepless Baby

Some babies sleep soundly and delightfully from 7 P.M. to 7 A.M. without a peep. Moms and dads can regroup a bit and get some much needed rest. Most of the rest of us, however, learn to tolerate far less sleep.

You've probably been through it dozens of times already. After having carried your grumpy baby around for hours, you gently put her down in her crib. You try to fool her by leaving your hands on or under her for a minute or two in the hope that she thinks you're still holding her. You skillfully remove your hands with great stealth and sneak out of the room. Forgoing snacks, bathing, or even brushing your teeth, you quickly get into bed, hoping perhaps to have an intimate 15 seconds or so with your partner—or perhaps by yourself. Your fatigue, however, is palpable.

You forgo the pleasure and pull the covers up over your exhausted body and start to drift off to sleep. As you begin to lose consciousness, the baby monitor offers up a little sound. You're not sure what it is—a burglar, a fire? You couldn't care less. You ignore it and return to la-la land. A second later, the monitor beckons you with a peep or coo. Your eyes open, and you lie there, immobilized by exhaustion—the lower half of your body is still snoozing—depression and anger creeping up your limbs. The monitor starts to screech and whine. It's over:

> "At the end of a long day, all I want to do is get into bed and go to sleep. I'm too tired to read or have sex or watch TV. I've given up sports and friends to be here. We work so hard, sometimes hours, to get our baby to sleep. Then he starts to cry just as I'm twilighting. My wife and I both pretend we're asleep, even though the baby is starting to wail, each hoping that the other will get up. Sometimes I feel like pretending I'm dead just so I can sleep a bit longer."

Barring any major medical issues that are interfering with his comfort, your baby's sleeping habits will improve, but probably not anytime soon. Since he is not yet on a schedule, you'll need to deal with the depression and rage that often accompany nighttime follies. Your partner will be equally (if not more) exhausted, so it's important to help her at night.

Problems with Your Sleepless Baby

- **Your baby won't let you put her down:** Your baby may sleep comfortably when secure in your arms but will invariably wake up when put down in her crib. You may spend hours rocking your baby to sleep, only to have her sabotage your efforts. Some parents bring the baby into bed with them to avoid this unpleasant and maddening experience.

- **Your baby wakes up when bottle or breast is removed:** While all babies need to suck, some babies are far more sensitive to being fed than others. Having your chest sucked on all night, as your partner will attest to, is no treat. Parents may often try to substitute a pacifier for the breast or bottle, but most babies can readily tell the difference. Some babies nurse or drink so much, just to suck, that they develop stomachaches and gas that ultimately prevent sound sleep. With patience and time, your baby will learn how much to drink and how to sleep without assistance.

- **Your baby didn't burp:** Your baby may drink and drink and not burp. He becomes a milk-filled time bomb—fun perhaps in someone else's home, not yours. Since your baby can't burp himself, he needs your help. Often, when babies are put in their cribs without having burped, they puke or cry from a stomachache.

- **Your baby wakes up at the slightest noise:** While it's important for babies to learn to tolerate some noise at night, the use of a white-noise maker that covers other noises (it makes a soothing sound) can be a lifesaver for you. A bathroom fan or running water works too. Try taking a shower with the baby laying nearby. You will be relaxed, and the sound of the water will help relax your baby as well.

- **Your baby won't feed or nurse before bedtime:** Very often, the last bottle or breast of the day will be enough to get your baby to sleep. For any number of reasons, your baby may choose not to partake in this late-night snack. Since it's not appropriate to let your baby "cry it out" at this stage, you may need to rock him to sleep.

- **Your baby won't follow a routine or schedule:** Most two-month-old babies don't follow a routine, that is, go to bed or eat at the exact same times every day. More likely, you'll need to adapt to her fragmented, unpredictable schedule until she's a bit older.

- **Your baby absolutely refuses to go to sleep:** Sometimes, when I'm unable to get our baby to sleep, I give him to my wife, and he immediately falls asleep. The opposite is often true as well. Babies seem to be able to sense frustration and anger and do well when handed over to someone with a better attitude.

- **Your baby won't go back to sleep:** It's one thing to get up and give your baby a bottle in the middle of the night; it's another to be unable to get her back to sleep. My wife and I have spent many an early morning watching the sun come up over our exhausted, frustrated house. With time and practice, your baby will learn to go back to sleep. Try to alternate and take turns with the baby so one of you can rest while the other cares for the baby.

TIP

The middle of the night is not the time to stimulate your baby with smiles or play. Stick to the business of fulfilling his physical needs. Playing is for daytime.

- **Your rage and depression are getting out of hand:** It's not at all uncommon for you and your partner to feel like screaming at each other, into the pillow, or even at your baby. My wife and I have had some of our biggest disagreements in the middle of the night—

when we're run down, depressed, and tired—the worst possible time to resolve issues. Defer such disagreements until the morning, when you can think a bit more clearly about things.

Going Out with Baby

Sooner or later, you'll want to journey out with your baby (or be forced out by your partner). Whether it's to get a cup of coffee, go food shopping, or let your partner sleep late, taking your baby out alone can be an interesting and challenging experience. What's the big deal? . . . He's so small . . . how hard could it be? As any woman will tell you, taking a baby out is not as simple as it looks:

> "When my wife and I were arguing about responsibility, I told her that taking the baby out didn't seem like such a big deal. She challenged me to try it. I really didn't think it was that big a deal—I was wrong. It was a good experience, and now I know I can do it. It also gave me a new perspective on what my wife goes through nearly every day."

Taking your baby out on your own further tightens the bond between the two of you. Don't be fearful.

Going-Out-with-Dad Reminders

- **Reassure your partner:** Some women will be hesitant to permit their partners to take the baby out (while others will start the car and open the door for you). Try to understand this. Talk about it. Your partner will give you tips and will help you prepare for your outing. She'll also counsel you about your fears.

- **Change your baby before going out:** You may avoid a screaming scene during your adventure if your baby is comfortable.

DIAPER BAG CHECKLIST FOR TWO-MONTH-OLD BABIES

- ✔ Diapers (at least three)
- ✔ Cloth diaper for cleaning puke
- ✔ Diaper wipes (may be placed in plastic bag or plastic carrying case)
- ✔ Bottle (preheat prior to leaving home and secure top to prevent leaks)
- ✔ Pacifier, if used
- ✔ Change of clothing for baby
- ✔ Bib for feeding time
- ✔ Diaper ointment

- **Feed your baby before going out:** There's nothing worse than a hungry screaming baby strapped into a car seat en route to the bank or grocery store.

- **Pack the diaper bag:** The diaper bag is your lifeline. It contains all the items you'll need to care for your baby while on the road. Prepare it well. You'll be surprised how much stuff your partner has managed to mash into it. As your baby gets older, the contents will change, and you'll need to update it frequently. Don't leave home without it.

- **Properly dress your baby** for the weather conditions.

- **Wear an old shirt.**

- **Bring a baby harness or sling:** If you use these (they enable you to carry your baby while keeping your hands free), be sure you remember to pack it in the car.

- **Put your baby in the car seat:** It's be easier to bring the car seat in the house and place your baby in it rather than bringing her to the car seat while it remains in the car. Don't forget to buckle your baby in securely. The car seat must be positioned so your baby is facing the back of the car.

  - **Bring money:** In the midst of all the commotion of preparing the baby, I've often forgotten my wallet.

  - **Invest in a bottle warmer:** It plugs into the car's lighter.

TIP

Never put a rear-facing car seat in the front seat if your vehicle is equipped with a passenger-side air bag. You should avoid putting a car seat in the front seat even if there isn't an air bag.

Going out with your baby can be stressful. Depending on what you're doing and where you're going, you'll need to learn to juggle the baby, the groceries, and your wallet. Your baby may be content to remain in his car seat (which you'll have taken with you) and snooze. At other times, however, he may start to scream in the middle of the checkout line or while you're using the bathroom. Remember, if your baby does begin to scream, he will respond best to being removed from the car seat and held.

If your baby starts to cry while shopping, you'll need to do something. Remember

PSDB:
Pick baby up.
Sit down.
Check **D**iaper.
Give **B**ottle.

When you're out with your baby, never, ever leave her unattended. Never turn your back on your baby. At the grocery store, always keep your baby between you and the item you're purchasing. Never leave your baby in the car while you get money from the ATM machine. Even if you need to use the bathroom, never let anyone hold or watch your baby—take the car seat into the stall with you.

Taking your baby out opens up an entirely new set of opportunities. You'll also learn that each developmental stage has its own special set of challenges.

TIPS

• Transport your baby in the car seat rather than taking him out and carrying him. The car seat, with baby, can then be set into a shopping cart or on a table while you eat. Your baby may also fall asleep in it. Remember, don't ever wake a sleeping baby, especially if you're shopping.

• Politely shoo away doting grandmother types who approach your sleeping baby. They'll want to touch, pinch, poke, and ultimately awaken your slumbering baby. However, the biggest concern is the germs or illness they may be carrying. The same goes for small children who want to hold your baby's hand, touch him, or kiss him. Children are naturally curious about babies, and this curiosity along with a cold can equal a sick baby.

• To prevent fatigue and to avoid bumping into things, carry the car seat on your arm, not in your hand.

• Never carry your baby and a hot beverage simultaneously.

FOCUS: HOW TO BATHE YOUR BABY

As your baby grows and develops, she will be far more interested in being touched and caressed. Bathing your baby is one great way to fulfill your child's need for touching, smiling, and soothing. A nice bath before bed can be part of the bedtime ritual. While most babies find a warm bath soothing and relaxing, some are stimulated by it and prefer a sponge bath. A few babies react to a bath with the same enthusiasm as a cat. These babies will probably do best with sponge baths for a while. You could also try a bath sponge or some towels in the baby tub; some babies are scared by a hard plastic surface.

- **Run the bath:** If you're alone, put your baby in a safe place. Use a small plastic tub with a slanted bottom. This keeps the baby's head and body elevated. The water must be warm but not hot. Fill so that the water level comes halfway up the baby's chest. Because it gives greater control over your baby and so your back doesn't break, place the tub on a counter rather than in the bathtub or on the floor.

- **Get everything near the bath:** Be sure to position soap, shampoo, washcloths, and anything else you may need within easy reach of the bathtub.

- **Undress your baby:** Always a challenge. Wrap your baby in a light blanket or towel and carry her to the bath. Expect to be peed on—if not now, then later.

Help Your Exhausted Partner

Whether she's a "stay-at-home" mom or she's gone back to work, chances are that your partner will be absolutely exhausted by the end of the second month. She may still be sore from the delivery or c-section, may still be up all night, and may be trying to take care of the house and everyone in it. You need to help her cope.

- **Place your baby in the bath:** Put your baby in the bath slowly so as not to startle her.

- **Wash your baby:** Keep at least one hand on your baby at all times. When wet and soapy, they are very slippery and can get hurt. Talk to your baby and smile as you use a soft cloth to gently wash her. You don't need to scrub, nor do you need soap at this point. Start at her face and ears. Be sure to wash under your baby's neck. Support her head from behind and tilt it back slightly. This will enable you to wash the creases of the neck, where formula or milk has dripped. Wash the rest of her body. You can lift your baby up, flip her over, and support her with one hand under her stomach while you wash her back. Wash your baby's genitals and bottom last.

- **Remove your baby from the tub:** Babies are very slippery when wet. Grasp your baby under her arms and lift, then wrap immediately in a dry towel. Dry your baby gently, but completely, especially in genital area and under neck and arms. Powder or creams are generally not necessary.

- **To wash your baby's hair:** Wrap her in a towel and hold her over the sink like a football. Use a mild baby shampoo. When you rinse, use a small cup with warm water rather than a big cup or pitcher so as not to lose control over the flow of water. If your baby has cradle cap—dry, flaky scalp, sometimes yellowish in color—try washing his hair with a soft-bristled brush.

Some Ways to Help Mom

- **Take your baby** out for an hour.
- **Do the grocery shopping.**
- **Help to keep the house clean;** assign yourself some regular chores.
- **Pick up after yourself.** Although I frequently forget this myself, dirty underwear belongs in the hamper, not on the floor.

• **Cook a meal.** Even grilling something on a barbecue will be a great relief to your partner.

Bonding with Baby

By the second month, your baby will be more active and respond to play much better. This is also a good time to experiment with your little one and see what she likes and doesn't like. Begin bonding through play.

Laughing

Find out what makes your baby laugh. During the second month, babies will respond to facial gestures and laugh at silly faces. He may also laugh when you gently tickle him. The legs and shoulders seem to be the best places to try. Be careful not to tickle too hard, and be sure to stop if the baby does not laugh or begins to cry. You don't want to torture him. He can start to mimic you. If you laugh, he may laugh.

> "I would laugh a bit, and it would make my little boy laugh. However, his laughing would make me laugh harder, which in turn would make him laugh. I thought it would keep going until one of us exploded."

Dancing

Hold your baby up next to you like you would for burping and do a slow dance around the floor. You can either hum the music or dance to recorded music. Waltzes and other slow dances work best. No break dancing yet.

Baby Talk and Toys

Try mimicking your baby's sounds. It will consist mainly of gurgles. Most babies will really pay attention to you as you try to communicate in this gibberish. Also, use rattles or other toys to play with the baby. At this stage, you'll probably have to hold and shake the rattle. The baby will follow the sound of the rattle or the sight of toys as you move them around in their field of view. Whenever he does something good, like watch the rattle or talk back to you, praise him with a "Good Boy" or a "Yeah!" in a high-pitched but soft voice.

Growing Together

Having been a dad for two months, you've probably made some mistakes and had some terrible nights, but you've learned so much! Because you've remained involved, you're now an active, essential person in the life of your baby. If you're like most dads, you're probably wondering what happens next. The next stage will find you and your family growing in new ways—and at lightning speed. The house may become even more hectic, but your experiences will become richer as well. As your baby becomes more active and aware, you and he will grow even closer.

[A baby is] a loud noise at one end and
no sense of responsibility at the other.

—RONALD KNOX

4

The Third Month

You look in the mirror and see the blurry image of two dads—one is tired, withered, drained, and pale, while the other is vibrant, enthusiastic, proud, and eager to meet the next challenge. What a month it's been! Although you're not really that much older, like a piece of fine cheese, you may be feeling nicely aged. Fatherhood has been known to transform even the toughest and most resilient into a quivering mass. But why the dichotomy? The feelings of aging, exhaustion, and discouragement are matched by a new wisdom, a feeling of mastery, and a look into the future. You may be feeling more at ease with your fatherly duties and have probably mastered many tasks that just a month ago seemed foreign.

As your wisdom and sense of fatherhood develop, you're probably taking more notice of your baby's many new talents—she's starting to do some amazing things! Your little bundle isn't really a newborn anymore. In fact, you may actually be proudly referring to your baby as your "little boy" or "little girl":

"The first time I told someone about 'my daughter,' it seemed so unreal. After all, just a month or two ago, she didn't seem like a 'daughter'—she seemed like a newborn. But let's face it. She's not some tiny little newborn anymore, and I'm not as inexperienced as I was just a month ago."

The third month is an exciting time. It's really a transition month. While your baby isn't a newborn, he's not yet capable of the many physical feats that characterize development over the next few months. This month is a time when your little boy will be inching along in every way, practicing the skills that will soon develop into physical leaps and bounds:

"It's wonderful to think that in just a few short months, my baby will be crawling on his own. When I watch him, I can almost see him starting to go through the movements! I can't wait!"

Both you and your partner may be starting to emerge from the cloud of fatigue that's hung over your home and permeated your existence. You may even venture out and engage in social festivities. The third month is a nice time to sit back for a minute or two and reflect on the distance you've covered so far:

"I stayed up late one night after everyone had gone to bed. I went into my son's room and just looked at him. He was lying there on his back snoring—just like me! All the sudden, he didn't seem so little anymore. I felt a little older too. But I also felt proud that I had weathered the storm thus far."

What's New with Your Baby?

Everything about your baby will be in flux. Your baby's features will become more distinct, and her body will be changing. Your baby will be more engaged with the world and will want more of your time and attention. In addition to the many other skills and behaviors your baby previously engaged in, she will also be working on new ones.

Developmental Milestones

One of the many innate skills your child possesses is sociability, and she will use everything at her disposal—her motor, sensory, and psychological development—to draw you closer. Your baby will also employ these new and improved behaviors to propel her farther from helplessness and more toward independence:

"I always thought of my baby as so needy and dependent . . . and she is. But in the last few weeks, she's spent considerable time cooing to herself or just playing in her crib. She seems to be practicing independence."

Motor Strength: Having improved upon some older skills, your baby will do a number of new things. In an effort to become more interactive with the world, he may bat or swipe at objects and may even try to grab them, albeit clumsily. Your baby may be able to bring his hands together and might even be able to hold his head steady when sitting up. There's a chance that your baby will be able to bear a bit of weight on his legs when held up. Your baby's overall motor status and muscle tone will be enhanced, and some babies will turn over easily.

TIP

Prop your baby up in the corner of a couch and talk or play with her. Most babies love the new experience of being upright on their own.

Sensory Perception: Some three-month-old babies can follow an object across the room with their eyes. Your baby might turn his head in the direction of a voice, especially if it's yours or your partner's. By this time, your baby should be able to differentiate between you and your partner. Dad's voice is deeper, his hands are bigger and rougher, and his clothes feel different. He even smells different.

Psychological: Your baby's efforts to endear herself to you shouldn't go unnoticed. By responding with enthusiasm and smiles, you're teaching your baby positive interpersonal skills. Talk to your baby, allowing pauses for her to coo back. This will help introduce her to conversational skills. There's a chance that she will laugh out loud in response to being caressed or will spontaneously squeal with delight. Your baby will also be able to make new sounds and will start to engage in play.

It's important to remember that all babies develop and grow at a different pace. Don't be alarmed if your child doesn't precisely follow the standard developmental milestones. If you're concerned, however, don't hesitate to consult with your baby's pediatrician.

What Is Your Baby's Day Like?

Sleeping: Although your baby still requires massive amounts of sleep, it's a sure bet that he won't want to spend quite as much time snoozing. Three-month-old babies much prefer to interact with their surroundings. Although not always true, if your baby is still nursing, he may not yet be sleeping through the night. Even bottle-fed babies will often awaken several times. In general, however, your baby's sleep may not be quite as tenuous as in the previous few months. And your baby's increasing wakefulness can be an attractive attribute:

> "I used to like it when our baby slept—it meant she wasn't awake and screaming. But now, I'm really starting to like her better when she's awake."

Feeding: If your wife is nursing, she may or may not want to begin the weaning process. If she does wean your baby, prepare yourself for giving nighttime bottles.

Crying: Although there are always exceptions, by the end of the third month, you should start to see a decrease in the irritability and moodiness that originally formed the cornerstone of your new baby's personality. Your baby will more than likely spend less time crying and more time playing or observing the world around him. This may be due in part to your ability to anticipate your baby's needs. There are babies, of course, whose irritability will persist (see "The High-Maintenance Baby" later this chapter).

Curiosity: Your baby will be more interested than ever in all the new and exciting activities surrounding her:

> "I can't believe it, my baby watches TV with me! If I turn it off, or if I change positions so she can't see it, she gets crazy and starts to shake and cry!"

TIPS

• Use your nose to gently touch your baby's bare skin around the chest and under the arms. Many babies find this pleasingly ticklish and will respond with squeals and laughter.

• Studies show that fathers involved at this stage will help stimulate better social skills and problem-solving abilities in their children that will show up years later.

Reprinted with Special Permission of King Feature Syndicate

Your baby may grasp at objects or gaze at mobile or suspended toys. She'll also yearn to explore things—with you!

Playing: Although you may not have thought it possible, your three-month-old is clearly capable of playing! While I'd rule out a serious game of chess, your baby will soon develop the capacity to interact with you playfully. For

EAR INFECTIONS

Otherwise known as otitis media, an ear infection is an infection of the middle ear. Ear infections can occur at any age and for a variety of reasons. Since your baby isn't yet able to articulate her distress, and since she doesn't yet possess the ability to pull on her ear, detecting an ear infection can be a challenge. Typically, your baby will eventually develop a fever or may actually have a cold or the sniffles. Irritability, vomiting, and diarrhea are not uncommon. Your baby's already tenuous sleep or feeding schedule may be off. Your baby may want to be held all the time or may want to feed or nurse constantly.

Ear infections are diagnosed by use of an otoscope, an instrument routinely inserted into the ear canal that under the best of conditions is likely to bring screams to your child.

If your baby is diagnosed with an ear infection, she'll be treated with antibiotics. If caught soon enough, most typical ear infections have no long-lasting ill effects.

Sometimes, if your baby has had multiple episodes of ear infections over a given time period, your doctor may recommend a minor surgical procedure. The procedure—placing tiny tubes in the ear—is designed to rid repeated infections by relieving pressure in the ear and allowing any infectious material to drain. This procedure will provide pain relief and will usually stop the seemingly endless cycle of infection.

FOCUS: PLAYING WITH YOUR BABY

A little while ago, your baby could barely open his eyes; now, a few months later, he is ready for play!

"All those sleepless nights had me convinced that this 'baby thing' was really going nowhere. I was hostile to the idea of having more kids. To be truthful, I was even hostile to the idea of keeping this one. Then, all the sudden, my son started giggling and playing with me. It made all the difference!"

Up to this point, you may have treated your baby as a breakable object. His skin seemed paper thin, and his floppy limbs appeared to be easily breakable. Spending any time with a three-month-old baby, however, will convince you that they need more than just cautious handling. They crave attention and want fun human contact!

"I sometimes play with my baby for at least an hour. I love to sit with him and make faces or blow raspberries on his stomach. His skin seems so much tougher or thicker than it was when he was a newborn. He really seems to love the contact. He reacts to me and almost seems to beg me for more!"

Q: Why is play important?

A: Play is essential to babies. It brings you and your baby closer and teaches your baby what it means to be in a relationship. Play helps to form the foundation of interpersonal skills your baby will use forever—it helps with socialization and acclimates him to interacting with his surroundings. Play helps children develop motor and sensory skills as well. Serving as a signal that your child is happy and thriving, play also reassures those dads who were doubting their ability to go on living with a screaming child:

"When my daughter and I play, I forget about those sleepless nights . . . well . . . most of them. I feel like her responsiveness to me is almost her way of saying,

'Thank you for taking care of me.' It's a definite rush—better than any movie or baseball game!"

Q: Do all babies develop playing skills at the same age? My baby just doesn't seem interested.

A: Not every baby starts to play during the third month. This can be a source of disappointment for some:

"I try to stimulate my three-month-old, but he just seems to be a blob. He doesn't want to do anything. It's very disappointing."

Like anything else your baby does or will do, he will develop his own sense of "relatedness" to his surroundings in various ways and at different times. Be patient. Placid three-month-olds can turn into lively four-month-olds.

Rarely, as your baby grows older, a severe lack of awareness of his surroundings can sometimes signal a potentially serious problem. If you're concerned about this, contact your pediatrician.

Q: What should I worry about when I play with my baby?

A: Some dads have concerns about what they can or can't do with their babies:

"I was throwing my three-month-old up into the air when my mother told me that I was taking a big risk with the baby. Don't all dads toss their kids? I mean it wasn't like his head was going to get caught in the ceiling fan or anything."

A: There are a number of problems associated with being too rough with your baby. Here are some helpful guidelines:

- **Never toss your baby into the air:** Although she might seem to enjoy it, jolting your baby through tossing, shaking, or bouncing can cause substantial, irreversible damage to your baby's head, neck, and eyes.

- **Let your baby be the judge of what's fun and what's not:** Your baby will probably let you know if what you're doing is fun. If she looks

(cont.)

FOCUS: PLAYING WITH YOUR BABY

(continued)

uncomfortable or distressed or if she begins to cry or frown, stop and consider an alternative play activity.

- **Let your baby be the judge of how much is enough:** Some babies can tolerate more fun than others. Look for evidence of fatigue—if your baby is crying or beginning to show irritability or disinterest, stop playing.

- **Never hold your baby down against her will:** Pinning your baby down to tickle her may be perceived as an assault. Your baby shouldn't learn to tolerate this—from you or from anyone else.

Your baby will give you countless opportunities to engage her in play. Remember to go at a pace that will not overwhelm, frighten, or alarm your child. Be creative, have fun, and above all don't take chances with the physical well-being of your baby.

example, your baby may smile and giggle in response to being tickled. She may also start to play by herself.

What's New with Mom?

By this time, your partner may (or may not) have adapted to the tremendous increases in her workload and substantial decreases in her sleep. In addition to the variety of feelings she had in the months prior, it's a sure bet that she's trying hard to develop a schedule of sorts. That is, she wants to get back "into the swing of things."

Emotional—She May Be Trying to . . .

Get Back on a Regular Schedule: Your partner may be trying to organize her life. While it's likely the baby won't be terribly cooperative (I'll discuss baby's schedule in the next chapter), she may try to work around the unpredictability:

> "Even though our schedules are still crazy, my wife has started to plan for holiday events like birthdays and major holidays. She seems a bit more energized."

TIP

Capture your giggling baby on film.

She may become frustrated if her plans are met with a resistant baby:

> "My partner tried so hard to organize her life. She tried to pay all the bills and arrange for repairs to the house. When I got home at night, though, the bills were piled up on the dining room table, and she hadn't been able to talk to the repair people on the phone. The baby was so needy, she couldn't get a break."

PLAYING WITH YOUR THREE-MONTH-OLD

There are any number of creative ways you can engage your child in play. Here are a few:

- The best way to engage your child in play is to look at him and smile broadly.
- Babies prefer higher-pitched sounds and will respond to them by smiling and cooing. Look right into your baby's eyes and, with a high pitch, smile and say his name repeatedly.
- Babies enjoy the feel of your skin on theirs. Gently rub your nose on his nose.
- Lay your baby on a warm surface, like a bed, and clap his hands together.
- Provided your child has good head control (not all three-month-olds do), lay on your back with your knees bent toward your face. Lay your baby down on your legs, bring your head up toward his face, and smile or say his name.
- Sit your baby facing you on your lap and, while holding his shoulders, gently pull his left shoulder toward you and push the right shoulder away. Alternate slowly so the baby looks like he's doing the twist.
- Hold your baby out in front of you and bring him in toward your face while you say his name.
- Tickle your baby gently on his stomach or neck. Walk your fingers up his back. Be careful—too much tickling will lead to squirming and discomfort.

Work on Her Body: Your partner may try to work on returning to her pre-pregnant state by watching her diet or exercising. Again, sometimes the stress of caring for the baby can disrupt her efforts.

She May Feel . . .

Continuously Exhausted and "Burned Out": Even though she may be trying to get some control back, she's still probably exhausted, particularly if your baby is sleeping poorly at night or is a high-maintenance baby (see the following discussion).

Conflicted About Her Career: Some women who give up careers outside of the home in order to raise children may long for their old jobs back, while others couldn't be happier. On the other hand, women who return to work often wish they could be at home with their babies.

Excited That Baby Is Settling In: Some babies, by the end of the third month, are starting to "settle in." That is, they cry less, sleep more regularly, and are generally less irritable and more consistently pleasant to be with. This may be perceived by everyone, especially your partner, as very reassuring.

Confused About Weaning: By the end of the third month, some moms, if they haven't already, start to think about what life would be like without breast feeding. While many women continue to nurse for months, or even years, most women at one time or another weigh the benefits of continued nursing against the disadvantages. The thought of weaning the baby may be a source of relief for her but may also lead to feelings of sadness or loss.

TIPS

• Talk with your partner about each of you getting 20 minutes to yourself in the evening. This can really help both of you.

• Unless you want another child right away, always use contraception—no matter how soon after the delivery.

Happy and Satisfied with Your Baby's Growth: Most women seem to enjoy their baby's progress. A thriving baby can reenergize an exhausted parent.

Interested in Sex: Although there are no set time limits, the third month may signal the return of her libido. As I discussed in the previous chapter, be patient and take it slow. Also, unless you want another child immediately, be sure to use birth control, even if she's nursing (see the following discussion).

Physical—She May Have . . .

Less Milk Production: If your partner is not nursing very frequently, her milk supply may be drying up.

A Return of Fertility: Although this can return at any time postpartum, by the third month, particularly if she's not nursing, her periods may return to normal, and she'll probably be fertile. If she's been nursing, it may take a bit longer for regular periods to return (although some nursing mothers are back to their regular cycle as early as four weeks postpartum). Remember, however, that a nursing mother with irregular periods can still get pregnant.

What's New with Dad?

You may still be exhausted, but you also may be experiencing some new sensations, desires, and conflicts.

You May Feel . . .

A Renewed Sexual Interest in Your Partner: If you previously noticed a decrease in your sexual desires, the end of the third month with your baby may signal a resurgence of interest on your part.

Closeness to Your Baby: Many three-month-old babies are developing their own styles and ways of interacting with their surroundings. Your baby's new charm may engender feelings of love and admiration within you. You'll likely be drawn even closer to your baby.

Like a Parent: Since your baby is finally starting to settle in, you may actually start to put yourself in your father's shoes and see or redefine yourself as a parental figure:

> "I feel a bit guilty about this, but, before the third month, I guess I saw myself as a bit of a zookeeper. My baby was so uncooperative and awful to be with . . . like a wild animal or something. I felt like throwing her pieces of raw meat. Now, she's charming, and I feel like I'm really her dad!"

Overwhelmed with Responsibility: You may be finding it tough to successfully juggle your relationship with your partner, your life with your baby, and your work:

> "I'm spread so thin. I get so uptight when I think about all I have to do. I'm trying to be a good husband and dad and am trying to impress the boss with my work. It's all so hard. I'm exhausted. I don't seem to have any patience or stamina. Sometimes I feel like taking off. I just don't understand what my role is in all this!"

TIP

Try to find other fathers to talk to about the transition you're making in becoming a parent. Often, the men who were in your prenatal class will be willing to share their experiences with you. Just talking with other people in your same situation can be a good therapy for frustration or anxiety.

Like a Servant: As you help out more and more around the house, your partner may come to depend on you for certain tasks and may even seem to take you for granted. If this becomes a problem, be sure to take time to discuss it with her.

> "Whenever we went out with the baby, it was my wife, the baby, and the pack animal—me carrying everything."

In the next chapter, we'll look at some ways that working dads can find peace and happiness without leaving town. If you're feeling ready to pack your bags, feel free to skip ahead and read this.

An Urge to Organize Your Life: How nice it would be to get a grip on your life! Feeling in control of your life is crucial. With a more settled baby, it may now be possible to start organizing yourself. Try to catch up on some of the activities you had to temporarily abandon when your baby was born.

Being There for Your Baby

As your baby grows and develops, you'll probably feel the pull to spend more time with him. You'll find your baby to be far more engaging and pleasant, and he'll be able to do more things both with you and, for brief periods of time, on his own. With this pull to be increasingly involved with your child come questions and concerns.

Spending Loving Time with Your Family

You want to spend "quality time" with your family. You'd also like to be able to give and receive love. While you're learning how to juggle your personal and work life, you're faced with the burden of coping with unresolved questions and issues. As you'll invariably discover, being a loving partner and parent while pursuing a career takes a lot of practice! In time, though, you'll learn to master the concept of spending time with your family.

Many dads have a variety of issues and questions related to just exactly how to spend time with their families. Like virtually everything else related to loving, there's nothing specific you need to do!

How to Be Loving: It's common for some (certainly not all) dads to feel uncomfortable with the concept of love. After all, the generations that came before us were even less comfortable with it!

TIP

If it feels awkward to tell your baby that you love her, try whispering it to her in private. You may also want to depersonalize it a bit by saying "Daddy loves you" instead of "I love you." In time and with practice, you'll feel comfortable with the words.

Learning to give love comes with time and experience. Don't worry if it feels a bit awkward at first. Try to remember that there are many expressions of love. Some dads may feel comfortable telling the baby how much they love him or may do so by kissing the baby frequently, while other dads prefer to express their feelings through play or the day-to-day care of the baby.

FOCUS: HOW TO DRESS YOUR BABY

Dressing your baby can be a bit tricky, but you need to learn how if you're going to be spending time with her. Since infant clothing remains an enigma to even the most experienced dads, it helps if you're good with puzzles or play chess well—you never know how the clothing is going to respond to you. Dressing your baby gives you another skill, makes you an important person in the life of your baby, and also can be very helpful to your exhausted partner.

- **Diaper:** Remember, too loose they leak, too tight they shriek.

- **One-piece underwear snapping system:** The one-piece undergarment (with a long tail in the back) that snaps in the crotch is a bizarre-looking item. Bunch it up so as to form a ring through which the baby's head will go. With the baby lying down, place your left hand behind the baby's head and support her neck. Put the garment on the baby's head and, while lifting the baby's head and neck off the bed a bit, pull garment over her head.

  Lie the baby back down (older babies can be dressed sitting up). While the garment is still a ring around the baby's neck, gently bend her right arm up (as if the baby is taking an oath) and push her hand and arm through the sleeve. Take care not to bend the baby's fingers. Repeat for the other side. Pull the garment down over the baby's body and straighten it out. Make sure the material is not bunched up around the baby's shoulders. Pull the garment's "tail" down behind the baby's bottom, over the diaper, and up under the crotch and, making certain the snaps are aligned, snap the tail to the front section. Seventy-five percent of babies will be screaming and crying by this point. Sixty-five percent of dads may be doing the same.

- **Shirt:** Using the same technique as with the one-piece undergarment, put your baby's shirt on.

- **Pants:** Your wriggling baby won't like to wear pants and may try to kick them off. Start with one leg, then the other. Pull up gently and tuck the shirt in.

- **One-piece outfits:** One-piece outfits should be placed on a bed or floor with all their secret hatches, zippers, buttons, and snaps in the fully un-locked, open position. Place the baby directly on top. Legs should go in first, then arms. Buttoning the crotch is a challenge, and many dads will miss a snap. Don't fret if you do—minutes from the time you have your baby dressed, she'll wet or poop, and then you'll have the opportunity to practice your skills all over again.

- **Socks and shoes:** The trick here is not to hurt your baby's toes and avoid being driven even deeper into "dressing insanity." To avoid bending your baby's toes, try rolling the sock up first, then placing it on the toes and pulling up. If your baby is wearing booties or soft footwear, take care to avoid tying the booties on too tightly.

- **Snowsuits:** With snowsuits, make sure that the zipper doesn't bother your baby's neck. Also, he will roast if dressed in a snowsuit too soon before you go outside.

The best way to learn to dress a baby is to first undress the baby. This will give you a sense of what you're up against. Practice makes perfect! After you've taken the better part of the day getting the outfit on your baby, there's a 64.5 percent chance your baby will poop. Your baby may seem to enjoy your clothing struggles. Good luck, and may the deity of your choice be with you.

How to Respond to Signs of Affection: Some dads may feel confused about how to respond to smiles or squeals of delight from their babies. Often, squealing back or just smiling or giggling is the best way to start. In time, you two will develop your own ways of relating to each other.

The Importance of Spending Time with Your Family: Spending time with your family is essential. It *does* matter. You *are* needed. Even if it's on weekends or late in the evening, your consistent presence will be etched in your baby's mind. Your partner will also see you as available and supportive. Your "being there" will help your baby learn to think of home as a stable, safe, and loving place.

The High-Maintenance Baby

Okay, so maybe your baby isn't settling in. Perhaps she's rarely in the mood to play or be happy. Despite your best efforts, perhaps she doesn't care about the external world. Maybe your baby wants to be carried around all day or won't stop crying, or perhaps, just like your great-aunt, she just seems to have a sour disposition. Have no fear. You're not the first, nor are you the only, parent of a child who brings you a bit of embarrassment when you compare notes with other dads.

Your baby is high maintenance. As a result, your home is not relaxing. You and your wife are tense, yelling at the baby and at each other. You've had dis-

TIPS

• While dressing your baby, try to distract him. Use a running commentary, describing what you're doing. Animated speech works best. Make it fun for your baby by introducing the concept of "peek-a-boo" when putting clothing over your baby's head or using your nose to tickle your baby when putting his clothing on.

• When buttoning one-piece outfits, start with the snap nearest one of the feet and work your way up and over.

HIGH-MAINTENANCE-BABY CHECKLIST

✔ **Is your baby sick?:** If your baby was previously calm and is now inconsolable, this is an especially important question. Call your pediatrician to arrange for a checkup.

✔ **Feed, change, and burp:** Some babies, like me, are very sensitive to hunger, feeling wet, or gas.

✔ **Carry:** Many high-maintenance babies may insist upon being carried around all day. This can be very stressful, but a variety of carriers are available to make this task a bit easier. Harnesses, backpacks, and slings are just a few of the options.

✔ **Change temperature:** Don't automatically assume that every baby likes to be bundled up. Some prefer to feel slightly cool. Some like having access to their hands and can't tolerate being bundled.

✔ **Bath #1:** Give your grumpy baby a bath.

✔ **Bath #2:** Take a bath with your grumpy baby.

✔ **Bath #3:** Put your baby in a safe place and give your grumpy self a bath.

✔ **Distractions:** Try distracting your baby with toys, high-pitched noises, or mobiles.

✔ **Car:** A trip in the car, or an "almost" trip in the car, sometimes gets a baby to stop carrying on.

✔ **Change the routine:** Sometimes babies scream from boredom. If your baby is used to being held a certain way, try a different way. If he is used to a certain type of noise, try another. Try to change his environment.

✔ **Change partners:** After carrying your baby around for an hour, ask your partner to try. Your baby will sometimes appreciate the change and may quiet some.

✔ **Be patient:** Your baby will soon outgrow these behaviors.

✔ **Relax:** Your baby can sense your tension and will tense up herself.

turbing fantasies about what your baby would look like immersed in a bucket of ice water. From dusk to dawn, you don't get a break. What do you do?

Protect yourself with fail-safe options. Whether your screaming cherub has always been difficult or has just recently departed from his calm ways, you

and your partner need to protect yourselves and your baby from inevitable feelings of hostility. Talk to your partner about ways in which you
both can avoid shows of anger and hostility toward each other and your
baby. Your partner, for example, might decide to put the baby in a safe
place; call you at work for support and reassurance; ask a friend to come
over; take a three-minute shower; and take the baby out in the car for a
drive around the block. Most importantly, plan for stressful times and be
creative.

> "Sometimes, my child is a complete jerk. She screams all day, and I
> can't make her happy. Sometimes, if I put her in her snowsuit, for rea-
> sons I don't understand, she falls asleep. I keep her in the kitchen, on
> the counter, in a snowsuit, in her car seat. I don't even need to take her
> out. Ridiculous."

Make sure you have an appropriate outlet for your anger and dismay and
don't neglect your relationship with your partner. She's having a tough time as
well. Your baby will settle down in time. Some of my children were tough
babies, but eventually they settled in and are now charming and delightful.
Avoid making judgments about your child's future on the basis of a few tough
months.

TIPS

- Never, ever hit, slap, or shake your baby. A shaken baby will suffer severe, permanent brain damage that can even lead to death.

- If you start getting angry and feeling violent, even if you feel like yelling, put the
baby down in a safe place and get away for a moment. Step out of the room for
a bit until you regain your composure. Just a little time away from the baby can
make a big difference and can help prevent you from taking irrational and harmful actions. There is never a reason to yell at or hit a baby.

Bonding with Baby

With each passing month, your baby can do more and more things. During the third month, he can play much more than before. Here are some things to try.

Grabbing

Your baby should be able to grab things by now. When you are holding him, give him your finger to hold in his hand. This can be comforting to your baby and to you as well. It is continuing the bonding of touch; however, he is now taking the active role of holding you.

Place toys in front of your baby to see if he will reach out for them and grab them. You may have to put them in his hand and then move them away in order to get him to grab them. Babies will also want to touch your face or even hair. Move close enough so he can reach you.

> **DIAPER BAG CHECKLIST FOR THREE-MONTH-OLD BABIES**
>
> ---
>
> Add the following items to your three-month-old's diaper bag:
>
> ✔ Rattle
> ✔ Squeaky toy

Rolling

Your baby may start to roll from side to side at this point. As you see him start rolling, you can help teach him to roll completely over. Place your baby on his stomach. He will often have a difficult time trying to roll because babies often put their arms out like airplane wings. Instead, tuck them under his body so he is supporting himself on his elbows. Then slowly help him to roll onto his back. This will help him not only learn this skill but also build a relationship of trust between the two of you. He is learning you are there to help and to teach him. Later it will be easier to help him crawl and then walk.

Spend Time Together

Continue to spend as much time as possible with your baby. Take him out on walks. If you are doing something so you can't hold him, put him in a baby seat or even on a blanket on the floor next to you. Even though you may not be able to touch him, talk to him so he knows you are near. Just be careful he is not too close to your project so that he could be hurt by something falling or spilling. You can even take a nap with your baby. Just be careful he will not fall or that you will not roll over and smother him:

> "I enjoy taking a nap with my little son. He loves to lay on my chest and listen to my heartbeat as he falls asleep. I feel so close to him then."

Growing Together

Your three-month-old really seems like a little person. The next month signals both a new beginning for you and your baby and a continuation of the lives you already share together. You can look forward to even more enjoyable times as you and your baby continue to learn new skills together.

People who say they sleep like a baby
usually don't have one.

—LEO J. BURKE

The Fourth Month

Although months have passed, you, your baby, and your partner are still just getting used to one another. As the three of you experience new ways of interacting, the psychology of your family is bound to change virtually every day.

> "I can't put my finger on it, but somehow, we don't seem to look at one another in the same way anymore. We all seem to be orbiting closer together, becoming more intertwined."

You're probably enjoying most of this new family life, but you may also be facing major challenges—getting along at work with less sleep, dealing with a lack of free time, learning to relate to your baby, and trying to maintain a healthy relationship with your partner:

> "I can't keep track of everything. I feel like I need a guardian, or at least a calendar book that's as big as a car. I guess I'd need a big pencil to go along with that too."

The pleasures of raising a child and growing with your family are sometimes complicated by difficult or even painful times. While the third month served as an important transition time, the next few months find some dads thinking about the pleasures as well as the growing pains of being a dad:

"I love being with my family, but I often feel that too much is expected of me. On the other hand, maybe I'm not around enough. I do want to be with my daughter more. It's all very confusing. I think I need a guru. Maybe I just need a good massage."

The fourth month usually finds working dads wanting to spend more time with their babies. As we'll see, parents should also start thinking about their baby's financial future. Regardless of what issues emerge, one thing is certain— you and your family are continuing to grow and learn together.

What's New with Your Baby?

Although the changes are subtle, your four-month-old is learning and integrating new skills every day. Generally pleasant when awake, your baby will be more consistently happy, charming, and playful. She will have a far broader range of emotional responses to a given situation. Your baby may also be able to occupy herself on her own for greater periods of time.

Developmental Milestones

By the end of the fourth month, many babies are developing the capacity to move, or at least wriggle around a bit. Their perceptive abilities continue to improve, and they should be quite alert when awake. As their sense of "person-hood" continues to develop, they'll slowly become more independent and expressive.

Motor Strength: Your baby's repertoire is increasing exponentially! He may be able to hold his head steady while sitting on your lap and may even be able to lift his head to 90 degrees when lying on his belly. As your baby begins to experiment with his ability to shape and influence the world, he'll move his limbs frequently, spontaneously, and with purpose. Your baby's arms may lunge for hanging objects, and he will wriggle around, roll over, and may even be able to sit up by himself. Beware of the unrestrained four-month-old:

"How wildly maniacal this little peanut is. He's more active than I am! We try to get him ready to go out, but before we know it, he's wiggled out of his car seat before we can get him buckled. It's a two-person job."

Your baby's innate reflexive grip will slowly disappear but will be replaced by more purposeful grasping. Also, watch for his ability to pass an object from one hand to the other. Be sure that you do not let him get hold of small objects that could pose a danger of choking him. Remember, babies at this stage still experience their world with their mouth and will want to put everything in their mouth. General motor strength will be improved, and your little angel may be able to deliver a pretty swift kick to your abdomen or genitalia while being changed or played with:

"Oh my . . . I'm glad I don't use that part of my body much anymore."

Learn to dress your baby from his side rather than directly at his feet.

Vocalization: Your baby's ability to vocalize will be rudimentary but markedly improved.

Sensory Perception: Your baby's ability to perceive her world will be improved in virtually all spheres. She will have an improved ability to focus and hear—occasionally turning toward a familiar sound or voice.

Psychological: Your baby is quickly learning that there's more to life than just eating, sleeping, kicking, and screaming. Your baby is learning that he is a distinct, separate individual, capable of interacting with and affecting the world. Your baby will smile easily and laugh out loud to express delight or to please you. He will grab out of desire to obtain, express dismay or disgust, and turn his head toward you in curiosity. Look for a far broader range of emotional responses and expressions this month. These remarkable behaviors are steps your baby's taking to influence the world.

What Is Your Baby's Day Like?

Sleeping: As your baby gets older, she'll be spending less time sleeping during the day and, hopefully, more time sleeping at night. She may be starting to get on a schedule of sorts. (We'll look at the issue of "schedules" in detail later in this chapter.) The four-month-old baby may develop some standard routines, such as sleeping during the same time periods every day. Although many four-month-olds sleep through the night, your baby may have different plans:

"Is my baby the only one in the world who wants to get up and play at 3 A.M.?"

The best way to cope with your little night owl is through teamwork. Take turns trying to get your baby back to sleep. If your partner has been up all night, get up early and cover for her, allowing her to get some sleep, before you go to work. Your baby will eventually regulate his sleep cycle.

Feeding: By now, your baby is probably an expert at feeding and may attempt to grasp or hold the bottle. A four-month-old will tell you in no uncertain terms when he is finished with the bottle—usually by screaming, turning his head, or flailing and spitting the bottle out:

"My daughter is getting strong and really seems to know what she wants. I was feeding her one day, and she started to cry. She somehow grabbed the bottle and flung it out of my hands, onto the cat! She's going to make a great quarterback!"

TIP

Look for any opportunity to interact with your baby. Turn an unpleasant experience into a positive one. If she has a poop, talk to her while you change her diaper. Tickle her stomach, lift her legs up and down, or make faces.

Some four-month-olds may be ready for solid food. If your pediatrician has given the OK, take a closer look at this fabulous milestone on page 159.

Excreting: By this time, your little angel's poops may have begun to take on an unpleasant odor—particularly if solid foods have been introduced. You now may be able to detect a poop by sniffing your baby's butt, although you may feel like ignoring it in the hope that someone else will do the deed:

"I was holding my son on my lap when my wife asked me if he had pooped. It didn't help me to respond by saying that I couldn't tell. She snarled at me and said she could smell it from where she was sitting and that I couldn't ignore it anymore. I told her it was my butt she was smelling. She didn't buy it."

Independence: As your baby finds his own way in the world, you'll likely notice an increasingly strong sense of independence. To the extent that a preverbal, not-so-strong person can, your child will be making numerous efforts to gain a degree of autonomy. Drawing on experience and your guidance, your baby's behavior will become increasingly purposeful.

Playing: Growing even more sensitive to your input and attention, your baby is becoming stronger and more alert and engaged. Your four-month-old will thrive on your interest in her by brushing up on the play skills gained thus far.

TIP

Respond positively to your baby's early attempts at expression. Praise her verbally or respond by making positive expressions back.

Expressive Ability: Thanks in part to your baby's developing nervous system, his impressive ability to learn and integrate new information will be heightened. He will employ body language, facial expressions, and even vocalizations:

> "My daughter has gotten pretty good at letting us know how we're doing. Sometimes she almost seems to express disgust when we do something she doesn't like. When she gets going, she sounds like an excited chipmunk."

Health Issues: Fourth-Month Pediatric Visit

Barring any major medical problems requiring special attention, the fourth-month examination will consist of a history and a physical. Like the month two examination, it will also include another round of shots.

History: Your baby's pediatrician will probably ask you several questions: How is everybody getting along? Is your baby sleeping? Does he eat well? Have there been any concerns on your part regarding your baby's health? Can your baby engage in age-appropriate behaviors, such as grabbing at objects and smiling? Do you sense any deficits, such as hearing problems or visual impairment?

Physical Examination: Your pediatrician will examine your baby in much the same fashion as she has previously done. Head circumference as well as height and weight measurements will be taken so that the doctor will be able to assess whether your baby is developing normally. The doctor may also discuss vitamins and fluoride treatments with you.

Immunizations: Provided your baby is healthy, the doctor will likely order the DTP (diphtheria, tetanus, and pertussis), OPV (polio), and hemophilus influenza B immunizations. Remember, reactions to immunizations are typically not serious and may consist of fever, irritability, tenderness or swelling near the injection site, and vomiting. Rarely, certain shots can cause life-threatening problems characterized by very high fever, confusion, erratic behavior, seizures, and extreme fatigue or listlessness. Should any of these symptoms develop, your child might be developing an infection of the brain or nervous system called encephalitis. Call your doctor immediately.

What's New with You and Your Partner?

Both you and your partner have experienced a variety of feelings thus far—some familiar, some new, some shared, and some not. While it's important to recognize those unique and distinct feelings, in order to be healthy, effective parents, friends, and lovers, you and your partner need to function as a team. Examining your own feelings and emphasizing your own needs exclusively, without considering your partner's, can be destructive and disruptive:

> "My partner and I are having a lot of problems. She's been very tired, and when I get home from the self-esteem shredder I call "work," I'm in a terrible mood. Sometimes I feel like screaming and carrying on, especially when the baby won't sleep and my partner is tense. I feel like she's always complaining about this or that while I tend to keep all my feelings to myself. It makes me want to flee."

The fourth month of life with your baby is a great time to reflect together on where you've come from, where you are now, and where you're going. Since it's a time of great happiness and satisfaction as well as stress and fatigue, you'll want to share your pleasures as well as pains with each other.

Problems with Your Relationship

Competition: It's not unusual, particularly if you and your partner are both very involved in the day-to-day care of your baby, to develop feelings of com-

Reprinted with Special Permission of King Feature Syndicate

petition with each other. Often, you may differ on issues concerning the best way to soothe your baby or the easiest way to put him to sleep. When it comes to caring for your baby, both you and your partner may feel like authorities on what's best.

Jealousy or Resentment: While you may be jealous of your partner's special relationship with your baby and may also feel left out and neglected (or even replaced), your partner may be envious of your ability to leave a tense house and go to work. During the pregnancy, most couples grow very close to each other. However, fathers have a difficult time understanding why that closeness seems to disappear with the birth of a baby. It is not because your partner loves your baby more than you. Rather, she must give more attention to the newborn for its care and needs. As you raise your child together, your love for each other will grow.

Responsibility: Who gets up at night? Who heats up the bottle? Who changes a really disgusting poop? Who bathes your baby? Why should you get up in the middle of the night when you have to go to work in the morning? Why should she get up in the middle of the night when she too has to go to work (whether it's in an office or at home caring for your baby)?

Free Time: How do you and your partner decide who gets to relax and when? Some people get so caught up in trying to do it all—work, house, and baby— that they forget to have fun.

Fatigue: Exhaustion can skew even the most loving relationships, and you may find yourselves arguing about who works hardest.

Intimacy: While intimacy with your partner may have returned by now, many fathers still wonder when it will get back to the way it used to be. Fact is, it will never be exactly the same as it was before. Now that does not mean it will not be as good as it was before. Rather, it will be different and can be even more intimate and satisfying.

While your sexual attraction to your partner may still be strong, it may not be returned by your partner. She does not care for you any less. In fact, if your partner's sexual desire is decreased, it is probably normal.

Growing Closer to Your Partner

For some fathers, their experience with intimacy may be linked to their sexuality. Expanding the feelings of intimacy can be a challenge. This natural maturing of your relationship builds on mutual respect and appreciation for each other. Talk to your partner about sexuality in your relationship. While this may be difficult, it is important the two of you work together so your relationship can grow.

These are just a few of the many distressing but common issues that often arise in relationships. The conflicts clearly don't end here. Hopefully, you and your partner will notice your own unique set of problems. It's particularly important to recognize the insidious nature of stress and tension in your relationship—trouble doesn't start overnight. How can you deescalate the tension before it engulfs the three of you? Sometimes just raising the issues can be helpful. Some questions you may want to ask each other are:

Q: *Are we helping each other?*
A: Very often, couples develop their own schedules and go their own separate ways. Make certain you're not shortchanging yourself by shortchanging your partner.

Q: *Are we fulfilling each other's needs?*
A: Keep in mind all the reasons you chose to be with each other initially. Now is the time to renew your enthusiasm.

Q: *What is the emotional or symbolic significance of the baby in our lives?*
A: More than just a screaming poop geyser or a charming little angel, your baby's entrance into your lives signifies something very important. Whether

spiritual or otherwise, you and your partner need to wonder together what that something is.

Q: *What is the impact of the baby on our daily routines? How has it gotten better? How has our baby disrupted our lives?*
A: Caring for a child can be challenging since it tips the equilibrium that existed prior to the birth. Forget your guilt—don't hesitate to look at some of the ways your baby has messed things up for you. Be honest with each other. It's healthy to express mixed feelings.

Q: *How are we coping with our fatigue?*
A: Some cope by withdrawing or by getting depressed, while others become irritable and angry. Don't underestimate the role of exhaustion and its negative effects on your relationship.

Q: *Do we still talk with each other?*
A: If you find that you're not spending any significant time talking with each other, make a pledge to change your ways.

Q: *Are we listening to each other?*
A: Talking is one thing. Listening is another. Try to hear your partner out, without interrupting her. Then insist that your partner do the same for you.

Q: *Are there issues that remain unspoken?*
A: Harboring resentment or anger and not voicing it productively can lead to irritability, hostility, and resentment. Avoid accusations and criticism. Have a set time each week when you can both be together. Have dinner by candlelight or share some wine and review the week. Work on your differences by using your alliance with each other.

Q: *Are we taking each other seriously?*
A: While it's often difficult to empathize with your partner's exhaustion or difficult day, particularly since you may be feeling the same way, don't discount each other's complaints or issues.

Q: *Do we miss the old intimacy?*
A: Admittedly, it's often tough to find the time or energy to spend a romantic evening alone or to recapture the essence of what you each once found

so appealing about the other. Raise this issue if relevant. Arrange for a relative or trusted friend to stay with your baby while the two of you enjoy the privacy of a hotel or motel for an evening—or even an afternoon.

TIP

Regardless of your stress level, plan to meet once a week with your partner to talk about your baby's progress. Such discussions usually lead to a healthy exchange of ideas about your relationship.

Q: *How has our relationship improved?*

A: Like anything else, the substance of a relationship is usually not all negative. Couples should meet from time to time to discuss how their lives have changed for the better. Often, developing a consensus about your happiness is enough to propel your relationship forward.

Since children learn by observation and benefit from a stable, loving home, one of the most important factors in raising healthy kids is maintaining a healthy relationship with your partner. Unfortunately, when you're both exhausted and frustrated, your relationship can take a backseat to "just getting things done." Do your best to facilitate communication with your partner, try not to lose your collective sense of humor, and don't take yourselves too seriously—you're both still learning and growing together.

Being There for Your Baby

You're busy and sometimes feel as though you're running out of steam. You're juggling family and work as efficiently as you can. From time to time, however, you have very mixed feelings about both. Through it all though, you're continuing to brush up on all the skills you've learned so far. Finally, you realize that your reward—your baby's smile, attention, and love—is just what you need to keep going. Your blossoming relationship with your baby seems to propel you onward. How can you find new ways to foster your joyous relationship?

Since creative play is an important part of your four-month-old's life, this is a great time to develop new ways of engaging with your baby. Your increasingly strong relationship can also be used to help your baby in an indirect way. Since you've received your baby's social security number (if you haven't applied for this yet, do it now), this is also an excellent time to start learning how to painlessly save money for his education, his first home, or even his eventual retirement!

Entertaining Your Curious Baby

With a little creativity and innovation, you can keep yourself and your baby laughing and learning. You'll want to engage your baby in activities that are fun—fulfilling her need for play—and that are designed to hone her motor, sensory, and emotional skills. These activities don't need to be state-of-the-art. In fact, the ability to stimulate your curious baby requires only mild ingenuity and strong desire.

Activities for the Curious Baby

- **Dangling objects:** Dangling items of various shapes, sizes, and colors will stimulate your baby. Notice the improvement in her ability to track or follow an object. Make it "disappear" and see how your baby reacts.

- **Funny faces:** Some babies love it when grown-ups make ridiculous faces at them.

- **Tickle games:** Using your fingers, slowly walk up your baby's belly or back. Accelerate as you approach his neck. Let your baby "tickle" you and laugh.

- **Rattles:** Shake a rattle in front of your baby or let her grasp it and shake it herself.

- **Sing:** You can sing anything. Most babies love being sung to, particularly if the music is high pitched, and are appreciative even if you have the kind of voice that makes grown-ups cringe.

- **Bicycle kicking**: With your baby on his back, gently grasp his feet, bend his legs at the knees and hips, and bicycle his legs around and around. Many babies love this exercise.

- **Bouncing:** With your baby on a soft bed, on her back, very gently place your hands under her back and lift up and down, bouncing her ever so slightly.

- **Tours:** Your baby's perceptive skills are growing rapidly. Take a tour of the house and show him pictures, flowers, paintings, even the furniture. If weather permits, take your baby outside and show him trees and other outdoor items. Be sure to give a running commentary, explaining to your baby where you're going and naming things as you point at them.

Establishing a Schedule

The unpredictable nature of your baby's sleep-wake-feeding schedule can soon wear thin. With your help, a four-month-old baby can be somewhat capable of falling into a schedule. More often than not, your baby will start to toy with the notion rather than fully comply with the idea. Since it makes things more predictable, a schedule makes everyone's life easier.

There's no easy way to force a baby into a schedule. However, by four months, your baby should start to develop a partial pattern to her daily routines. That is, many babies will wake up in the morning at a certain time and may eat and/or nap in relatively predictable cycles during the day. You can capitalize on these patterns by, for example, trying to extend the amount of time that passes before you feed your baby again. Since your baby will need to be entertained or occupied during these times, you'll need patience and perseverance.

Likewise, at night, you can help establish a routine by putting your baby to sleep at a set time each night. Your baby can be bathed at the same time every day. By doing the same thing the same way every day, you're communicating to your baby that this schedule is the one you prefer.

Since your baby's biological "rhythms" are still maturing, you'll need to be patient and flexible. Gratifying your baby while trying to meet your own needs isn't easy. Remember, you want your baby to comply with your wishes, but you also want to exercise enough flexibility so as not to become overly rigid or controlling.

TIP

Mirrors are always fun with babies. They will often stare at the "baby in the mirror" and even take to her. Some babies may become concerned, though. She sees you holding the "other baby" and may begin to wonder who is holding her.

TOY SAFETY

As your baby begins to play with various objects, it is important to ensure safety. Toys are required to list an age rating. Never give your baby a toy unless it is for his age-group. However, even though the label says it's safe for your baby, it's important to still do your own check. Every year, toys are recalled because they caused the death of an infant, even though they were listed as safe for that age-group. Some things you should check are:

Small Pieces: Does the toy have small pieces that detach and can fit inside your baby's mouth, or is the toy itself too small? The best test to determine whether a toy presents a choking hazard is to use a toilet paper roll. If a toy will fit through the roll, then it will also fit in a baby's mouth and is too small. Most toys for this stage will not have pieces that detach by design. Rather, they may become detached through a defect in the product. Pull on anything that could come off with moderate force. You are not trying to break the toy but rather to ensure that the baby will not be able to pull it off. It is even important to check stuffed animals for this. Never give a baby a stuffed toy with eyes or other parts made of plastic or other material that is then attached to the toy by sewing. Instead, any features should be embroidered onto the toy and consist only of thread or fabric.

Suffocation: Can the toy or parts of the toy cover the mouth and nose at the same time and suffocate your baby? Watch out for rubber and plastic especially. Curved objects are particularly dangerous since they can cup over your baby's mouth and nose. Even though it may not look like it could suction on, keep it away. The baby may roll over and lie on top of the object, covering his mouth and nose.

Durability: Your little guy will be holding his toys and hitting them against things. Make sure the toys you give him are tough enough to withstand the impact. This can be a problem with older toys. Plastic can become brittle with age. Even though you beat the heck out of a rattle when you were his age, he may shatter it. You should also be concerned about small objects that can be sharp or cause choking or suffocation. As a general rule, use only newer toys.

No Strings or Cords: Some toys have cords or strings attached to them to pull the toy along the floor or make the toy talk or perform some type of action. Keep these away from your baby. They can strangle your child if they get wrapped around his neck.

Toys of Older Children: If you have older children around, you must be very careful they do not put their toys where your baby can get hold of them.

Supervision: Always keep an eye on your little one while he is playing with toys. Even after you have followed the previous rules, the unexpected can always happen. Therefore, don't put toys near the baby while he is sleeping or if you are going to be out of the room.

Finances—Saving Money for Your Baby

So far, much of what you've accomplished as a dad has been focused in the here and now. That is, you've learned to change your baby's diapers, play, go out, and so on. You've seen immediate results. There are some essential parental duties, however, that don't directly involve interacting with your baby. One of the wisest things you can do for your baby is to save money for him. Accumulating wealth for your child is a selfless act that will greatly aid him in the future.

Unfortunately, saving for the future, unlike the concreteness of changing a diaper, is an abstraction. Sometimes it's hard to put money away, especially when your budget is tight and your kid won't be attending college for another 18 years. Also, discussions about money, more than almost any other topic, seem to be "off limits" for many couples. Many parents would prefer to discuss their sex lives or other personal matters rather than talk "money." Saving money seems to conjure up fears and uncertainties. Anyone, no matter how rich or poor, can save. However, financial matters, and saving in particular, don't have to be taboo and surely don't have to be mysterious, scary, or dangerous, or even difficult.

Q: *I make next to nothing. How will I ever be able to save a substantial amount of money?*

A: If I offered you a penny today and then told you that for the next 30 days I'd double the previous day's money, would you rather accept a gift of $1,000 from me today or wait until the end of the month and then take the result of the penny-doubling offer?

Thanks to the magic of compound interest, by the end of the month, I'd have to give you $10,737,418 in pennies. Believe it. While it's unlikely that you'll be able to save that much money, you should be able to use compound interest to your advantage. Even just a few dollars a month can add up over the long run. Read on.

Q: *Why should I start to save now? I'm young. My kid is just a baby. Why can't I just start some other time?*

A: By employing denial, parents often ignore the realities of life in a financial world. By the time your little bundle pulls up to her first dorm room, four years at a public university could cost $150,000, while four years at a private college might cost at least $250,000—probably more. You'll need to either inherit a huge sum of money, embezzle, or extort from a troubled relative (not advisable)—or start saving, through careful investment, in order to secure sufficient funds for your child's education. The sooner you begin saving, the better. According to some complicated calculations, performed expertly and skillfully by my friend and personal accountant David Wasserman, CPA, there are incredible benefits to beginning your baby's nest egg now. Consider the following:

> If you waited five years after the birth of your baby and then started to save $200 per month at 10 percent, by the time your baby enters college, you'd have amassed $64,120—not bad.

> If, however, you started to save $200 per month at 10 percent the very year your baby was born, by the time she was ready to go to college, you'd have amassed $121,114!

Getting started now will give you the best chance of reaching your financial goals.

Q: *I'm not worried. I'm great with money. When my daughter is maybe twelve or so, I'll start to save. I can easily make it up in the stock market. What's wrong with that?*

A: Citing special powers or abilities to forecast the economic future (or perhaps forgetting that they may be blessed with more children), some parents, dads in particular, display unrealistic attitudes. In truth, the most effective way to save money is small investments made regularly over great periods of time. Unless you start to save soon, it's unlikely that you'll be able to amass the kind of money you'll need. Trying to outwit Wall Street when your child is only a few years away from entering college is an unwise move.

Q: *We barely have enough money to buy food and clothing. How can I save money I don't have?*

A: Many families, mistakenly feeling that saving requires huge stores of cash, cite a lack of financial resources as an excuse not to save. The good news is that you don't need massive amounts of money to be a successful saver. Even parents with little financial means can save for their child's future. A few dollars a day can mean the difference between college and no college. Consider the following facts:

FOCUS: HOW TO SAVE MONEY FOR YOUR BABY

- **Get motivated and start now:** Whatever savings vehicle you decide to invest in, do it now.

- **Discuss your saving's ideas with your partner:** Don't fall into the old male habit of making major decisions alone. Include your partner. Go over the numbers and your ideas.

- **Learn about investment vehicles:** In order to get where you want to go, choose the kind of investing that suits your needs and philosophy. While not a substitute for reading about money or discussing the issue with a trusted adviser or financial planner, here are some choices with recommendations:

Mutual funds: Mutual funds are nothing more than collections of stocks, bonds, or other similar securities that are managed by a professional money manager. Mutual funds allow you to buy small amounts of a multitude of securities without having to study each one and without having to plunk down large sums of money.

Stock mutual funds are probably the best way to buy stocks. For the purposes of long-term growth and savings for your baby, remember that, even taking into account market downturns, corrections, and crashes, stocks have produced the best overall returns over the decades.

Savings bonds: Savings bonds are basically IOUs that are issued to you, by the government, in return for lending it money. In exchange, the government promises to pay you back, with interest. The interest you receive upon redemption is not taxed on the state or local level. Also, for investors whose income is below a predetermined amount, you may redeem bonds completely tax free if you use them for your child's college education. Bonds are easy to purchase and are issued in many denominations. They are extremely safe. Their big disadvantage is that their payout is low.

Bank savings accounts and certificates of deposit: These are super-safe savings vehicles whose payout is usually very low. You don't want to save this way for your child. Consider the following calculations:

Fifty dollars invested each month for 18 years at bank rates of 5 percent will yield $17,533, while $50 invested each month for 18 years at 10 percent will yield $30,278.

Individual stocks: Buying individual stocks can be fun. If you have expendable income to toss away, feel free. Don't put your child's savings in jeopardy, however, by having fun. Unless you're very experienced or have a reputable broker, you're not likely to save much money for your child through the purchase of individual stocks.

Bonds: Bonds, or loans you make to an organization in return for a reward of interest, come in many different varieties—municipal, long-term, short-term, corporate, government, foreign, and junk. Some are safe, some are not. Unless you're an expert at buying and selling bonds, I'd avoid them at this point in your savings plan.

- **Pick an investment vehicle:** When all is said and done, my recommendation is that you begin to save for your child using a stock mutual fund. Don't be frightened. Remember, some time between today and the time your baby is ready for college, the stock market will fall. However, because you're investing for the long term, your mutual fund more than likely will recover. In fact, the market always recovers eventually. A market correction also gives you the opportunity to buy more of the stock mutual fund at a lower price.

  There are many different kinds of stock mutual funds—growth, aggressive, small company, global, and so on. If you feel a bit squeamish, then I'd recommend an index fund—one that keeps pace with or mirrors the overall performance of the stock market. For more aggressive investors, consider a fund that tries to beat the market, such as an aggressive growth fund.

  (cont.)

FOCUS: HOW TO SAVE MONEY FOR YOUR BABY

(continued)

- **Contact a mutual fund company:** Stick with one of the better-known companies—Janus, Twentieth Century, Vanguard, or Fidelity. Tell them that you'd like to open a custodial or uniform-gifts-to-minors fund. Ask them to recommend a fund that has either kept up with the market or has exceeded it. Ask them to send you literature on the funds.

  Custodial accounts have some tax advantages. Some possible disadvantages are that your child has a right to all the money when he turns a certain age; as a parent, you may not use this money on yourself; and there may be problems if your child applies for financial aid later on. Depending on your own financial situation, you may want to save in your name. Ask your accountant for advice.

- **Arrange for automatic transfer of funds:** When you fill out the application, check yes to the questions that ask if you would like a certain monthly amount deducted from your checking account automatically. This way, you'll never need to remember to send in money. Having the same amount of money debited from your checking account each month is called "dollar cost averaging," and it allows you to buy more shares of a stock when the price is lower and less of the stock when the price is high.

- **Forget about your investment:** Don't touch it or sell it. Don't worry about market swings or doomsday predictions. Call the mutual fund company once a year to determine if the fund is performing as well as other funds in its class. Five or six years before your child enters college, you'll want to protect your child's money from economic downturns by placing some of the funds in an investment less likely to fluctuate too wildly in the event of a market fall.

- **Consult an accountant:** If you're interested in learning about other forms of saving plans for your child, consult an accountant or attorney who specializes in estate planning.

$25 invested each month for 18 years at 10 percent would yield $15,139.

$50 invested each month for 18 years at 10 percent would yield $30,278.

$100 invested each month for 18 years at 10 percent would yield $60,557.

$200 invested each month for 18 years at 10 percent would yield $121,114.

$500 invested each month for 18 years at 10 percent would yield $302,784.

Even if you're not able to save enough to swing college expenses on your own, you still have many options. For example, if you own a home, you can take out a home equity loan or line of credit. However, if you've saved wisely, you'll need to borrow far less money from other sources.

Q: *I've never been able to make a buck in the stock market. Frankly, investing frightens me. Why should I get into something I don't understand?*

A: You shouldn't. Don't let a lack of confidence inhibit you from starting the saving process. Millions of inexperienced investors have successfully put together large nest eggs by investing small amounts, steadily, in mutual funds.

Q: *Investing seems far too risky. Why can't I just pay for my baby's education some other way?*

A: Any way you slice it, if you want steady financial gains, you'll need to invest or save through the stock market. You can reduce your risk by choosing to invest in mutual funds (see the following discussion). Stock market falls, corrections, and even crashes are to be expected. Remember, you're saving money over the long term and can afford to weather expected stock market downturns. In the long run, only the stock market will give you the returns you need to finance your baby's education.

Q: *How can I save when I have so little time for anything?*

A: With your job and family responsibilities, who has time to worry about saving money? Mutual fund companies, however, make it easy for savers with little or no time.

Q: *I'm not worried. Why can't I borrow the money later?*

A: Many parents dismiss savings because they think they can easily secure a loan. There's no telling whether loan eligibility will change or whether loans will even be readily available in 20 years. Also, why develop indebtedness when you don't have to?

Bonding with Baby

Your baby is able to do even more things by now. She should have mastered grabbing objects and holding onto them. This will allow her to play with some toys. Rattles are a good toy with which to start. I suggest using cloth-covered rattles with stuffing inside. The older plastic rattles can hurt if your baby hits herself on the head while shaking it. If she doesn't understand what to do with the rattle, show her by shaking it yourself. Then place it in her hand and shake her hand to make a sound. When she begins to do it on her own, praise her with smiles, laughs, or even clapping your hands. This will reinforce the process of learning by providing an incentive and a reward.

TIP

Dump every single monetary gift, no matter how small, into your child's account.

Babies like to look at lights. Several types of toys can be found with several lights that flash in patterns, some to music. These are not only entertaining to babies but also teach them to track motion with their eyes.

Your baby should be able to put your face together with the sound of your voice. When she hears your voice, she will be looking for your face—for daddy. This can make nursing difficult for your partner if you walk in and say something while she is breast-feeding and the baby turns to look for you.

When speaking to your baby, avoid using pronouns. Since the meaning of these words, such as "I" and "you," change depending on who is speaking them, babies have trouble understanding and following your meaning. Therefore, always use names in your conversation with her. Instead of saying "I love you," tell her "Daddy loves Jessica." Also, to help teach her names, when you say them, point to the person as you say your name. In the previous example, you would point to yourself when you say "Daddy" and then to her when you say "Jessica." During this time, you can also begin your speech therapy to teach your child to say "dada." As a father, your goal should be to have this word be the first out of your baby's mouth. So keep practicing.

Growing Together

By now, it has become increasingly apparent that there's more to your life than just you. You may have temporarily given up many of the things you cherished before your baby was born—time alone, sports, and going out. On the other hand, you've also seen the importance of maintaining your new family through communication and cooperation.

Your growing family will reward you. As your baby develops and your family matures, the time you spend with him will become irreplaceable. In the fifth month, your new family will continue to look to you for guidance, support, and nurturing. Your reward? Membership in an increasingly wonderful network of love, respect, and caring.

The most important thing a father can
do for his children is to love their mother.

—THEODORE HESBURGH

The Fifth Month

So far, you've managed to keep your head above water by practicing and employing child care skills, talking with your partner about important issues, and enjoying your baby. While the fifth month finds many dads pleased with their lives, some working dads may be feeling increasingly isolated from their families. In this chapter, I'll discuss some strategies to help working dads make the most out of the time they spend with their babies.

Now that your baby is closer to being mobile, it's a good time to learn about some common health hazards and how to prevent them. Finding a good babysitter is also important at this age because it gives you and your partner a chance to venture out and enjoy some time alone together.

What's New with Your Baby?

The five-month-old child is more personable—surprising you almost daily with new feats of charm, personality, and skill. Your baby will reveal a new ambition and increasingly strong displays of independence and autonomy. She may surprise you by wriggling off the bed just when your back is turned or by rolling around on the carpet until she reaches an electrical cord. Drawing on your nurturing and encouragement, your baby will have grown stronger and smarter, more curious and experienced.

Developmental Milestones

As your baby continues to prepare for life in the big universe, everything about him will be stronger and bolder. Don't be surprised if his grip on a pea and other dangerous objects is firm and unyielding. He will pay more attention to smaller details and will be better at interacting with his surroundings.

Motor Strength: As the fifth month rolls on, your baby will probably have better control of his head. When lying on his stomach, your little Hercules will be tempted to push himself up with his arms. More than likely, your baby will become pretty good at rolling over onto his stomach. Your baby's new ability to buck out of the baby carrier or an unsecured car seat may drive you crazy. He may manage to get stuck in strange positions on your bed or in the crib. Your baby may possibly be able to partially stand with assistance and might be able to sit unattended for brief periods of time.

Vocalization: Your baby will be experimenting with sound—babbling, cooing, and even starting to run sounds together! Your baby will love it when you mimic the sounds he has produced.

Sensory Perception: Attention to detail is the name of the game. Your baby should respond to you and other familiar voices and likely will watch you walk around the room. It wouldn't be unusual for your baby to show interest in a very small object, like a toy or coin, when waved slowly around in front of her.

Psychological: By this time, most babies are readily smiling and responding to your facial expressions. Many babies will laugh out loud or squeal with delight. Expression, verbalization, and curiosity—all behaviors that bring your baby closer to the world—will become far more evident as the months go by:

> "When I stop to consider how much my son has accomplished in such a short time, I'm astounded. When I watch him babbling or rolling around or see the determination in his eyes when he's just trying to reach an object, I can see the bits and pieces of a walking, talking, thinking human being."

What Is Your Baby's Day Like?

Exploring: As your baby learns that the universe is far more than the breast or bottle, she will reach out in an attempt to make contact:

> "If I put my baby on the bed, it's amazing. She'll roll around and actually look at the objects around her, like a blanket or a toy. She wants to touch them."

Curious: Although your baby's motor skills are still not as refined as they will be, he will, with perseverance, try to examine items of interest:

> "My son is grabbing at everything. He's so inquisitive. He even poked himself in the eye."

Playing: Your baby will enjoy being lifted into the air, rocked on your knee, and held in an upright position on the bed or floor. She may be able to stand with help:

> "My daughter loves it when I lie against some pillows on my back, with my knees bent like I'm about to do tough sit-ups. I put her on top of my knees, and rock her backwards and forwards. She goes bananas—laughing and giggling. I can't get over the fact that she was so fragile and incapable of doing anything just a few months ago!"

Interactive: Your baby will use all of his newly discovered skills—play, curiosity, verbalization, and enhanced motor strength—in an attempt to interact more easily (and sometimes insistently) with the environment. By this time, your baby will probably enjoy playing "peek-a-boo" with you. While in the past you may have been the one to cover your eyes to play, she can now cover her own eyes. She may need help from you at first. Say "peek-a-boo" when she uncovers her eyes, and eventually she will make some type of verbal sound trying to mimic you.

> "Getting my daughter's diaper on has become a two-person job. It's very clear that she doesn't like it. She cries and tries to roll away from us. When we stop and let her go naked, she smiles."

Health Issues

Provided that your baby is healthy, your pediatrician will likely not need to see her during the fifth month. That's not to say your baby won't be developing some common ailments (most of which can be safely treated at home). I'll discuss these illnesses in appendix A, "Common Childhood Ailments." There are, however, some important health issues unrelated to common medical illnesses.

Up to this point, your baby has probably spent most of his time either in someone's arms or in a crib. As your baby begins to explore the world, however, he is at far greater risk of encountering hazards that we as adults rarely deem to be safety concerns. Remember, as your baby grows, his helplessness will diminish, but his judgment about what's safe and what isn't will lag far behind his mobility. Thus, at every stage of your baby's development, it's *your* responsibility to make certain the environment in which your baby grows is safe.

What's New with Dad?

Much of what you'll be feeling during the fifth month is in response to your baby's increasing independence, physical and emotional abilities, and sharpened interpersonal skills. If you're fortunate enough to be able to spend a lot of time at home, you'll see your baby change before your very eyes. If you're like many working dads, however, and gone much of the day, you may resent spending time away from your little pride and joy:

> "I feel like I'm getting ripped off. It's true, when my baby was smaller, I couldn't wait to get out of the house. I freely admit it. But now, I feel like I want to be a part of everything he does. I'm missing stuff. I don't get home until late, and I'm up early. It's not fair. My wife doesn't want to work, and I don't really want her to. How can I possibly spend as much time with my son as I'd like?"

> "I resent the fact that I have to work outside the home. I'm petrified that one day, I'm going to wake up and be 75 years old—having missed the formative years of my daughter's life . . . and for what? Just to please some arrogant boss?"

If you're feeling like these dads, remember, you always have options. Listed here are just a few of the many different ways you can interact with your baby when time is short. Above all, be creative and flexible.

Hints for Working Dads

- **Flexible work hours:** Ask your employer if it's possible to work longer one day, in exchange for leaving early, or coming in later on another day. Can you work weekends occasionally?

- **TV time:** If you must watch TV, do it with your baby. Place him on your knees and gently bounce him up and down, give him a bottle, or sit him next to you. If necessary, stand up and walk with your baby. Just be together.

- **Exercise:** Many men enjoy spending time on a treadmill, stationary bicycle, or cross-country ski machine and ask their partners to watch the baby while they're exercising. If you have an exercise machine in the house, don't waste time alone. Place your baby in a baby carrier or on a blanket on the floor near you. She will probably be mesmerized by the sound and rhythmic motion, and you can make faces or talk to her as you work out. Or, as an alternative, get outside with your baby, using a jogging stroller or a bicycle trailer designed for infants and small children. The two of you can get some fresh air together.

- **Bathing:** Giving your baby a nighttime bath is a nice way to be together. However, as your baby grows older, it's also fun to bathe with him. Make sure you have your towel and robe ready as well as a towel for your baby. When your baby gets a little older, you can shower together.

- **Nighttime bottle:** A genuinely nice way to feel close to your baby is to give the last bottle of the day. Take this time to talk to your baby about your day and mention how glad you are that she is an important and special member of the family.

- **Dressing baby:** Dressing or undressing your baby before bed is a nice form of interaction. Make a game of it—perhaps peek-a-boo or a tickle game. Your baby will appreciate your attention and will grow more accustomed to being touched by you.

FOCUS: PREVENTING HEALTH HAZARDS

All of the following hazards are preventable, and many of them are applicable to both older and younger babies. As a protective, concerned dad, you should have your finger on the pulse of household hazards. While I'll be discussing safety-proofing your home in chapter nine, the guidelines here form the basis for home safety. Don't leave these important matters up to your partner—it's too much responsibility for one person.

Feeding Hazards

Avoid Using the Microwave for Bottles: While microwaves can be a quick and convenient way to warm up a bottle, it can also lead to burning your baby. Since microwaves heat unevenly, the bottle may feel just right. However, the liquid in the center may be much too hot for your baby. Instead, place the bottle under hot running water or in a sink with hot water. Take it out to shake and check occasionally until it is the correct temperature. At times it may be necessary to use a microwave. In those cases, be sure to heed the following tips.

Hot Rubber Nipple: Use caution when heating a bottle. On occasion, particularly if the nipple is old or worn, it will cook and become boiling hot. If you must use the microwave, always unscrew the top of the bottle first and microwave only the bottle and formula.

Worn Rubber Nipples: As a general rule, throw out any nipple that appears the slightest bit worn, cracked, melted, or sticky. They can be a choking hazard. The same is true of pacifiers. When in doubt, throw it out!

Hot Formula: Always test the temperature of the formula, particularly if using a microwave oven. The oven heats fluids nonuniformly, causing certain areas within the fluid to be hotter than others. Shake the bottle first, then test by squirting a small stream onto the back of your hand. The liquid should be body temperature. If it feels hot, run the bottle under cold water to cool it off or let it sit for a few minutes.

Foods: I'll discuss solid foods in the next chapter. Never give an infant honey or corn syrup during the first year. These substances contain botulism spores that can make your baby seriously ill. You should also never give an infant eggs, in particular the whites of the egg. Babies under a year old can develop an allergy to eggs if introduced to them early.

Sleeping Hazards

Suffocation: By this time, your baby probably has good head control. However, if not, don't allow him to sleep on his stomach. Don't put stuffed animals, pillows, or heavy comforters in the crib with your baby. Make certain all screws and bolts are periodically tightened in your baby's crib. Side rails can collapse, trapping your baby in the sides of the mattress.

Strangulation: Since a wriggling baby can accidentally strangle herself easily, never put a child to sleep wearing a bib. Never allow a child to sleep unattended in her carrier or unrestrained car seat while wearing a bib. Remove drawstrings from coats or other outfits (this is true for any age). Also, keep them away from the cords of blinds or curtains by watching where you place cribs, bassinets, and even baby seats. Since your child is now grabbing things, she may reach out a bit and grab a cord and get it wrapped around her neck.

Falls: Never allow your child to sleep (or play) in a baby swing unattended.

Environmental Hazards

Weather: Your baby's skin can burn very easily. Make certain to use a strong sunblock and a hat when venturing out in the spring or summer. Don't forget about exposure in the winter, as sunlight can burn tender skin even on cloudy days.

Smoking: Little lungs don't do well with smoke. If you must smoke, do it outside, away from your baby. Secondhand smoke is dangerous, and falling ashes or burns can be devastating to the skin of your little beauty.

Traveling Hazards

Car Seat: Make certain the car seat is installed properly (no easy task) and that, for infants, it faces the rear of the car. Make sure your baby is properly restrained. Also, if your car has a front passenger air bag, you mustn't place your infant seat in the front seat. If the air bag inflates, your baby would be forced against the back of the passenger seat and could suffocate or be injured by the force of the air bag.

(cont.)

FOCUS: PREVENTING HEALTH HAZARDS

(continued)

Lonely Baby: Never, ever leave your baby in a car, under any circumstances—not even for a minute. Never leave your baby in a running car, particularly in the garage.

Hot Baby: Never leave your child in a hot car. A car left in the sun for a few minutes can heat up like an oven. Babies die every year from hyperthermia. On an 80-degree day, it only takes 10 minutes to heat the inside of a car above 100 degrees.

People and Other Living Things

Siblings and Other Children: Young siblings, cousins, or other little children should never be left alone with your baby. Even the most gentle, reasonable child might resent the baby or fail to recognize his own strength.

Pets: Like siblings, pets, even golden retrievers and other ordinarily kindly creatures, must never be left alone with your baby.

Abduction: Most abductions are perpetrated by persons known to the abductee or her family. Nonetheless, never trust your child with anyone you aren't completely familiar or comfortable with. Never leave your baby unattended. Never discuss your home life with a stranger or give out your address. Don't allow babysitters to have friends over in your absence. Keep your doors locked when traveling in your car. Have the outside of your home well lit at night and have secure door locks installed.

Parental Rage: Some parents suffer from feelings of anger and rage, often, but not always, associated with lack of sleep, pressure on the job, marital difficulties, or psychological turmoil precipitated by having a child. Since they'll invariably reemerge, such complex issues need to be discussed and not buried. If you're feeling the urge to hit your partner or child, get help now. Violence in the home—whether verbal, emotional, sexual, or physical—toward one's partner or children is simply unacceptable. Call your local emergency room or medical doctor for help. I'll discuss more issues relevant to sexual and physical abuse and anger in chapters eleven and twelve.

Accidents

Fires: Don't use extension cords. Electrical cords shouldn't be warm or hot to the touch anywhere along their path. Space heaters located in your baby's room should be state-of-the-art with automatic tilt shutoffs and should be kept away from sources of water, curtains, toys, and stuffed animals. Your house, especially the area where your baby sleeps, must be equipped with smoke detectors. Consider a carbon monoxide detector as well and have a fire extinguisher in easy reach on every floor. Clean air conditioner filters from time to time. Clothing or other items should not be stacked too near a closet lightbulb. Remove stuffed animals from near baseboard heaters. Figure out a route to safely evacuate your baby if needed.

Falls: Never leave your baby unattended on a changing table or counter. Walkers should never be used. Even though these items are still available for sale, child safety experts warn against their use. Instead, use a stationary walker, which allows the child to bounce and turn but does not have the danger of moving around or tipping over. Never leave your baby unattended in a stationary walker, a jumper, or a baby swing. Take your time walking up and down stairs when holding your baby.

Bath: Pay attention to water temperature and don't assume that water from the spout will maintain the same temperature. Always test the water. Every year you read about it—never, ever leave your baby alone in the tub for even a second. Let the phone ring—they'll call back. It's also important to adjust the temperature of your water heater to decrease the maximum temperature to prevent accidental burns.

Hot Beverages: Have your hot cup of coffee, tea, or soup later, when you're not holding your baby. Beware of cooking on the front burners, especially if you have a baby in a walker. Beware of waitresses carrying hot meals over your baby's head.

Medical Hazards

I'll discuss life-threatening illnesses and other medical emergencies in appendix A. Remember to always keep medications out of baby's reach. If you spill a pill, search the floor until you find it so that your baby doesn't find it instead.

- **Holding baby:** When time is short, use whatever means necessary to familiarize yourself with your baby. I've held each of my squirming kids on my lap while eating—not that easy but, with practice, not that hard.

- **Play:** Play can be accomplished anytime and anywhere. Games can be played while dressing or undressing your baby, giving him a bottle, or holding or carrying him.

- **Baby's routine:** Even when you're not with your baby, you can be involved in the process of caring for her. Become an expert in your baby's normal routine and rituals. Help your partner make bottles for the next day or get the crib ready for baby's bedtime. Be involved with the bedtime rituals. Get the washcloth ready for the bath and lay out the towel. All of this brings you closer, spiritually and otherwise, to your baby.

- **Take baby out:** Don't forget that your baby is now an official explorer and will want to tag along. Take him out on short excursions to the post office or bank.

Reflect on Your Role as a Father

By this time, you have gained a lot of experience in fathering. It's a good idea to take some time and compare what you expected from fatherhood prior to your baby's birth with what fatherhood is actually like. All fathers start with an idea of the type of father they expect to be. Now, after five months, take some time to reflect and compare how you expected to be and how you actually are. Do you spend as much time with your baby as you wanted to? Are you as emotional and warm as you expected? With some experience under your belt, talk to your father or another older father-type in your life about the ups and downs of being a dad. Ask other fathers with newborns about their experiences. If you're far from your target of the father you wanted to be, is it because you were not realistic or because you need to make some modifications? No matter what the case, you must be comfortable in your role as a father. Trying to live up to someone else's expectations if they are not in line with your own will usually cause unhappiness or other problems.

Reprinted with Special Permission of King Feature Syndicate

Being There for Your Baby

Will ignoring your relationship with your partner upset the dynamic balance of your family and have a negative impact on your relationship with your baby? Yes. Can you stay involved with the day-to-day activities of your baby while relaxing a bit and enjoying some time with your partner? Yes. Are you a bad dad if you feel the urge to get away once in a while? No.

By this stage, some parents feel guilty about going out together without their child. However, spending quality time alone with your partner is possibly as important to your child's mental health as it is to yours. A child with parents who actually like each other and have grown-up fun together will grow up feeling secure and loved. In order to go to the movies, however, you'll need to find a babysitter. Carefully choosing the people you'll entrust with your precious child is an important responsibility. As a dad, you must be involved in this process.

 TIP

To help you decide on a sitter, put yourself in your baby's shoes. Ask yourself this question at the end of each interview: If I were immobilized, mute, weak, and completely dependent, would I want this person caring for me?

Take Your Partner Out on a Date

By this time, you and your partner have hopefully started to settle in a bit. You're more experienced and your home should be more relaxed and content. Although you may have ventured out with your partner, without your baby, you're probably interested in making it a more common occurrence. If you haven't gone out alone with your partner since your baby arrived, now is the

FOCUS: HOW TO PICK A BABYSITTER

Q: *Where can I find a decent babysitter?*

A: Usually, the best way is word of mouth. You may need to be mildly intrusive and inquisitive, as many people guard the true identities of trusted babysitters. Also, try high schools or places of worship. Relatives can come in handy as well. Agencies are a good but expensive source.

Q: *What's the appropriate age for a sitter?*

A: Many dads feel funny about leaving their baby home alone with a very young person. As long as the sitter is responsible and capable of learning, age shouldn't matter too much. Of course, you'll want someone who has attained a certain degree of maturity. Check to see about the local law regarding age limits. Some states have set a legal age for babysitters. If you hire one below this legal age, you could be charged with child neglect, especially if something goes wrong.

Q: *Male or female sitters? Does it matter?*

A: The bias of some, perhaps considered by others to be an irrational one, is to use female sitters. These parents have a harder time trusting a boy or man with their children, as I do. I will not allow a man or boy to sit for my children. You need to use your best judgment. While many, including myself, fear males' inexperience with children or that they may respond violently when angered, the same can be said of female sitters. Most sitters you'll find available are female. However, there are also some very good male sitters, and as your son grows up, he may be more comfortable with male sitters.

Q: *How much experience should the sitter have?*

A: While it would be ideal to find a sitter with a great deal of infant experience, it's not always possible. There's nothing wrong with training a younger person to care for your baby as long as she meets the criteria listed here and is willing to learn. It's sometimes possible to find an inexperienced sitter who's willing to "grow" with you and your family over a long period of time. Many communities offer babysitting courses, often through the Red Cross. Also, find out if your sitter is trained in infant and child CPR.

"We had initially searched for someone with a ton of child care experience. Finally, we found a young woman, and we trained her. She's great, and she's made a commitment to be our regular sitter for the next year!"

Q: *Should I ask for references? What if she doesn't have any?*

A: References are a must. If you're not provided with references, insist on it. If none are given, reject the applicant. (Even a sitter with little or no experience should be able to provide a list of neighbors or clergy familiar with her personality.) Ask the reference if the person is capable, reasonable, reliable, kind, and teachable. You'll want to know if there are any negatives and whether the reference would hire her again.

Interviewing prospective candidates is essential, and you need to be there. Don't make this your partner's sole responsibility. The interview can help screen out candidates who don't seem to be safe choices, who have obvious signs or symptoms of impairments such as drug or alcohol abuse, major mental illnesses, or unpleasant or even dangerous personalities:

"My partner is perfectly capable of deciding on who's safe. If the girl walks into my house carrying a howitzer, my wife will know that she's not the right one."

Unfortunately, the warning signs are likely to be far more subtle. You should have a say in these most important matters and should be there to help with the selection process. Don't take someone else's word that they have a great kid for you. The interview also gives the sitter a chance to meet you and to determine if it's the right job for her:

"This one girl came to our house. She sounded great on the phone, and the people who gave us her name loved her. No howitzer or small handguns, but when she got to the house, she seemed really freaked out by the baby, who was crying. She said she didn't think it was the right job for her."

General Appearance: You'll want to note the person's general appearance. Does she take care of herself? Is she well groomed and clean? You'd be

(cont.)

FOCUS: HOW TO PICK A BABYSITTER

(continued)

surprised at what may walk into your house. Does she appear to be healthy, awake, alert, and focused? Does she look at you when you speak, or does she seem to be preoccupied? If the latter, she's not the one for you.

Personality: It takes time for some people to open up and feel comfortable. Don't be put off by someone who seems quiet or reserved. On the other hand, someone who appears excessively withdrawn or has difficulty relating to you or answering questions may not be the right one for you. Refusing to answer reasonable questions and/or a guarded or suspicious appearance are warning signs that she's not quite right.

Her speech should be clear and her statements to the point. Beware of someone who seems to ramble on without purpose or who fails to end one thought before moving on to another. It's important that she be emotionally engaged with you. Beware of excessive sarcasm and a tendency to be controlling. Beware of sitters who go on about the importance of discipline—there's no need to discipline a five-month-old infant.

In general, you want someone who's attentive and open and who displays enthusiasm for her work. You want someone who is excited about caring for your baby, who is warm, loving, and willing to learn.

"We interviewed a woman once. My one-year-old crawled over to her and tried to open her purse. The woman snapped at him and told him to 'please leave the purse alone.' Her reaction to a normal one-year-old's behavior really annoyed me. She didn't get the job. We sent her away to the land of consolation prizes."

Capabilities: Remember, little or no experience shouldn't necessarily exclude the candidate, but you want a sitter who is teachable. Let her hold the baby. If she has little experience, teach her how to hold the baby. Is she confident but also receptive to being taught? Observe her reactions. Does she talk to the baby? Is she stimulating to the child? Does she smile?

Would she be willing to take an infant and child CPR course? Has she ever cared for children before? Has she ever helped in an emergency or crisis? What would she do if a medical emergency arose? Don't be afraid to ask reasonable questions.

Fee: The fee should be commensurate with experience. Beware of an older sitter who charges a very low fee.

Training Your Sitter

In-House Training: Once we've chosen a sitter, my wife and I like to see how she does on the job. It also gives us an opportunity to teach her about our baby's needs. Invite the sitter to come over one afternoon to show her around. Make sure she carries the baby and gets used to feeding him.

Ground Rules: Establish rules regarding safety issues and hazards and let your sitter know how you want her to care for your baby. For example, my wife and I don't allow any visitors while we're away. That means no pets, boyfriends, relatives, or even girlfriends. We want the sitter to be exclusively focused on our children. We insist that the sitter stimulate our baby by playing with or holding him.

We review the way we like our baby to be fed, burped, and changed. We also go over the bedtime routine and what to do and who to call in case of medical emergencies. You'll need to be clear about whether you want your baby bathed (we tend not to allow it until we feel very comfortable with the sitter).

Some families prefer live-in help—a nanny or au pair, for example. When choosing live-in help, you should employ the previous tips. The wrinkle is whether you can all live together. It's important to arrange a trial period, after which either party can bow out without losing too much face. In your search for live-in help, you'll need to use a reputable organization, perhaps one that a friend has used in the past. Make sure you and your live-in sitter negotiate all conceivable problems up front before they happen—privacy issues, salary, form of payment, whether she can have friends in the house from time to time, boyfriend/girlfriend issues, what time to start, responsibilities, vacation, quitting time, weekend coverage, whether you or your partner will be around during the day, and so on.

TIP

Churches, health clubs, and other locations where they hire child care workers are often good sources for babysitters. Some of the workers may be interested in making a little extra money. If your child goes to these child care facilities, they may already know the sitter and feel comfortable with her. Don't be afraid to ask the supervisor about a sitter if you are unsure.

time to start. While going out is fun, it can also be nerve racking and with good reason: You should have some real concerns about who'll be looking out for your baby's interests while you and your partner are out.

A good babysitter can vastly improve the quality of your family life. Even if you decide not to go out, having an extra pair of hands in the house can make a world of difference. You'll need to work through your ambivalence about leaving your baby or even being in the house and not being together. Since being with a babysitter allows your baby to grow accustomed to being with someone else for a change, having a sitter can also help your baby become even more socialized. Choosing the proper person for the job can be difficult, but as discussed in the preceding Focus, it's possible.

While I won't be discussing issues related to choosing a day care facility, you'll want the "character" of the facility to be comparable to a loving, caring, gentle, stimulating babysitter. Make sure the facility is clean and licensed and has experienced, sta-

HELPING YOUR BABYSITTER

- Call your new sitter once or twice while you're out. Ask her if she feels comfortable in the house. Reassure her that you'll be home at the previously agreed upon time.

- Carry your car phone or beeper with you in case the sitter needs to contact you. Often, just knowing that you are reachable can help diminish anxiety (yours as well as the sitter's). You should also give your sitter an itinerary of where you will be along with the appropriate phone numbers. Also, list another adult, such as a neighbor or nearby friend, the sitter can contact in case of an emergency when you cannot be reached.

ble employees. You'll want to be certain that they're in it for the kids and not the money.

Inappropriate Behavior with the Nanny or Babysitter

As a therapist, I have worked with numerous nannies and dads who have had sexual relationships with one another. If you are considering having a fling with the sitter or nanny, don't do it. That is not why she is there, and it will ruin your family. If you are tempted to do such a thing, you need to ask yourself what is going on in your relationship with your partner. Don't act on your impulses. Talk it over with a counselor or other mental health professional.

Bonding with Baby

Your baby just keeps growing and maturing. Now it is time to try something new. Explore the great outdoors. This may not be an option, depending on where you live and the time of the year. I don't recommend taking your newborn out to build snowmen. However, if the weather is moderate, take him outside to play.

Some ideas for activities include going for a walk or even a hike using a stroller or carrier you can wear. Be sure to face your baby out away from you so he can look around. It's always a good idea to apply some sunscreen to the exposed parts of his body. Make sure to use only baby sunscreen. The skin of most babies is very sensitive to ultraviolet light and will sunburn easily, even on cloudy days. Also, be sure you have him dressed in clothing appropriate for the

---

DIAPER BAG CHECKLIST FOR FIVE-MONTH-OLD BABIES

Add the following to your five-month-old's diaper bag:

✔ One ball (large enough not to be ingested) to roll on a table: Your baby will love to follow it and bat at it.

✔ Suction-cup toys that stick on the table are handy for entertaining babies in restaurants.

temperature. You don't want him to get cold, but at the same time you don't want to roast him either.

As a part of your walk or anytime, really, lay out a blanket on the grass and set your child down on it. From the blanket, he can look at the grass or other nearby plants. If you let him hold flowers and such, be sure to watch carefully so he doesn't put them in his mouth and start eating them.

Take along some type of toy or activity. This is a good time to introduce your child to the wonders of soap bubbles. As you blow the bubbles, watch his reaction as he tracks them with his eyes or even tries to grab them. If you're planning to be out for a while, be sure to bring a diaper change and possibly even a bottle for feeding. The outdoors provides a new experience and a change from the everyday inside life of most babies.

Growing Together

Some of the toughest times are now behind you. Hopefully, your baby's sleeping habits have improved, you've established some regularity to her schedule, and you and your partner are getting out a bit. The next stage of your baby's life will bring some pretty incredible new behaviors that are bound to please you. Your baby will soon become even more independent. Get ready for some excitement as your baby develops an increasing sense of who she is.

I was the same kind of father as I was
a harpist—I played by ear.

—HARPO MARX

7

The Sixth Month

H ow can it be? It probably seems amazing that your baby is halfway to being a one-year-old:

> "It all seems like a blur. I sometimes have to fight very hard to remember what he was like even one month or one week ago. Every time I turn around, he's doing something new. I feel like I should just keep the video camera on him all the time. I don't want to miss anything. It all makes me wonder whether I've been around enough."

Likewise, you've got nearly six months of on-the-job training under your belt. So much more a child than an infant, your previously completely helpless babe may start to give you a run for the money!

> "She laughs, she rolls around, she sits up! My partner and I aren't noticing as much tearfulness either. Our baby's still tons of work but *so* much more enjoyable."

This month is a nice time to do an emotional reality check. How are you feeling about being a father? Is it everything you had expected? Are things going the way they should for you? We'll take a much closer look at these and other personal issues later in this chapter. I'll also cover other important issues, such as the drama of solid foods and what to do about your baby's sleep problems other than bang your head against the wall.

What's New with Your Baby?

The developmental gifts your baby will bring you during this month are fabulous. You'll be astounded by her ability to interact with you. Your baby will figure out new and different ways to charm you.

Developmental Milestones

Your baby's strength is growing exponentially. He will be bulkier and heavier. You'll probably start to notice hints of the next new wave of independence as well as your baby's attempts to move freely on his own.

Motor Strength: Everything your baby could do before she'll do better—sitting on her own, pushing with her feet, and driving you crazy during changing time by rocking and rolling around. Don't be surprised if superbaby starts to stand on her own with a bit of support from a willing dad:

> "I stand my daughter on my stomach while I'm lying down and hold her hands. She bounces up and down on her feet, no problem!"

Your baby will likely have better head control as well. When you place him on the ground, your baby may try to move or wiggle around. He may even push up to his knees and hands! Your baby's dexterity will also be improved, but beware: Don't be too surprised if your child reaches for a tiny object, successfully grabs it, and throws it into his mouth.

Your baby's increased ability to get around will place her at new risk. Whenever babies obtain new abilities or improve upon old ones, you must be prepared to shift your focus as well and make your environment safe. I'll discuss such safety issues in detail in chapters nine and ten.

Vocalization: While your baby is adapting to and influencing his surroundings, his language skills will also be notably improved. Your baby is now far better at raising or lowering his voice—particularly when your attention is required. He will likely be fascinated by his new language skills. Babbling and making sounds of all kinds is fun!

Sensory Perception: By this time, your baby's eyesight is probably very well developed. She will watch you enter the room and will track you wherever you go. Your baby's ability to discriminate voices is improved as well. Caution: Babies sample the world by placing just about anything they can grab in their mouths.

Psychological: Your baby's ability to reach out emotionally is heightened. There's a good chance that your baby will respond to his name and will draw you near by laughing, smiling, or otherwise indicating his desire to play. A broad variety of emotional states will be present. Your baby will probably become angered or frustrated when unable to reach an object and may howl in protest when an object is removed from his grasp.

While certainly not yet firmly established, your baby is developing a style or personality all his own. Your baby may exude warmth, happiness, and enthusiasm; may be full of energy; or may be more reserved, shy, or less mobile.

What Is Your Baby's Day Like?

Purposeful, reactive, and responsive, your baby is quickly growing accustomed to life in the big world. I like to think of the sixth month as a juncture—a time when your baby is developing and growing into a person while maintaining all the qualities that endeared her to you for the past months. When I consider all the fantastic traits that six-month-old babies continuously refine, update, and improve, I think of the "10 Es":

Exploring: Propelled by an intense curiosity, your baby's relentless pursuit of all things new and different will astound you. You've probably noticed that if left alone in her crib, your baby will toss and turn, grasping anything that looks new and interesting.

Engaged: Your baby is far more likely to fix his gaze upon you. He will smile spontaneously and will try to engage you in spirited play.

Emotional: Did your baby drop a favorite toy? She will probably let you know by screaming or crying. And when your baby feels happy, look for a big, broad smile and giggle.

Energetic: While still needing lots of sleep, your baby may insist on staying up later or may be a bit more resistant to naps. Employing energy reserves based on her desire to be with you or to just be independent, your baby may seem battery driven at times.

Expressive: New expressions—shows of disgust, pleasure, anger, or sadness—will illuminate your baby's face and body. His verbalizations will be louder and more forceful as well.

Expanded Repertoire: Your baby will be able to do everything better. She will have more knowledge of the world and will be stronger and more capable of new and exciting feats. She'll be more familiar with the contents of her crib and playpen and may even seek out a particular object. She'll make you feel noticed and loved. One nice characteristic of the six-month-old is her sense of relatedness, that is, her ability to engage with you emotionally. You may see the beginnings of more formal personality development.

Extremely Playful and Silly: Given the proper circumstances, your baby will probably be a ball of goofy, happy energy. Since your baby has more energy, is smarter, and is more familiar with his surroundings, play seems to come easier. Your baby will be quite the comedian—for example, spending copious amounts of time chewing on his feet while smiling and laughing.

Entertaining: Using her newly found sense of playfulness, your baby will entertain not only you but herself as well. Watch for improved eye contact—almost as if she's trying to draw you into her world. Your baby will gaze in fascination at her fingers and toes and may sometimes be content to coo to herself and play alone in her crib.

Endearing: There's no getting around it. Your baby is now the most social, loving, and fun he's ever been. If you haven't fallen in love with your baby yet, you probably will this month.

> "Before the sixth month, I loved my son, don't get me wrong. There's something about this stage, though, that brings me closer to him. I can't believe how he and I can relate to each other, even at his age. If I didn't know better, I would swear he is learning to feel the kinds of emotions I thought only adults feel. He responds to me, and there seems to be a kind of reciprocity between the two of us."

Eager to Please: Believe it or not, your baby will sense your satisfaction during playtimes and will attempt to do things she thinks make you happy. Laughing when you laugh, smiling when you smile, and staring at you, she'll do her utmost to keep you riveted.

Health Issues: Sixth-Month Pediatric Visit

Barring any major medical problems, the sixth-month examination will consist of a history and physical. Like the fourth-month examination, it will also include another round of immunizations.

History: Your pediatrician will probably ask you several questions: How is everybody getting along? Is your baby sleeping? Have your started your baby on solid food? If so, does she eat well? Have there been any concerns on your part regarding your baby's health? Can your baby engage in age-appropriate behaviors, such as attempts at mobility, vocalizations, or showing interest in her surroundings? Do you sense any deficits, such as hearing problems or visual impairment?

Physical Examination: Your pediatrician will examine your baby in much the same fashion as he has before. Head circumference as well as height and weight measurements will be taken. Your doctor may also discuss vitamins and fluoride treatments. He may test your baby's complete blood count to check for anemia by way of a pinprick.

Immunizations: Provided your baby is healthy, your doctor will likely order another round of the DTP (diphtheria, tetanus, and pertussis), the hemophilus influenza B, and possibly the OPV (polio) immunizations. If your baby received the first two hepatitis vaccines, he will receive the last in the series which is good news for your baby!

Of course, you may again have noticed some changes in your baby, and you may have questions for your baby's pediatrician. Remember, the only bad question is the one not asked. As well, there are a few normal conditions you may be curious about that may arise during or around the sixth month:

Q: *Why is my daughter always drooling? It's so disgusting. She reminds me of an Irish setter.*

A: Try to look lovingly upon your spitting, slobbering, drooling youngster. See it as a milestone. It's very likely that your baby is starting to teethe. Teething can begin anytime—some babies don't get teeth until they're a year old, while others may have teeth as early as two months. You may notice a small swelling or white spot on the top of your baby's gums. Typically, the front teeth come in first.

Along with your joy at knowing that your baby will soon have a mouth full of pointy little chomping razor blades (which she will invariably test out on your shoulder), you may find that teething can be a painful experience for everyone. While not all babies suffer from painful gums, many do. Teething can interfere with the ordinarily tranquil child and may impair her appetite and sleep cycle. Your baby may become irritable and may be biting and chewing anything in sight, including you.

Some experts dispute the notion that a teething child can develop a brief fever or an episode of vomiting or diarrhea, but many moms and dads attest to these symptoms.

TIPS

- Let your teething baby chew on a cold, clean, wet washcloth.

- Don't give any medications that contain aspirin to your baby. Aspirin can cause Reye's syndrome, which can be fatal.

Q: *How can I help my teething baby? He seems really bothered by his new teeth. I know I'm bothered by them.*

A: Judicious use of an anti-inflammatory drug like Ibuprofen or an analgesic like acetaminophen, with the doctor's approval, can help your baby get through a tough night. Additionally, mild topical anesthetics can be applied to your baby's gums. Cold fluids, frozen teething rings, or pressure applied to the area can also bring relief. Never apply alcohol to your baby's gums, no matter what grandma says. In addition to helping relieve the pain, just holding your baby close to you can help soothe her quite a bit. She is hurting and uncomfortable. Just knowing you care by holding and making physical contact can go a long way.

Q: *Now that my baby's first tooth is here, how do I keep it clean?*
A: A moist, clean washcloth or gauze pad gently rubbed against the tooth is all that's necessary. Avoid fluoride toothpastes for now—too much fluoride is not healthy for baby.

Q: *I never minded changing my daughter's diaper before. Now her poop smells like . . . well . . . mine. Why? Is there something wrong with her? Is she part water buffalo? Is there some way I can evade my paternal responsibilities and have my wife change all the diapers?*

A: Unfortunately, all neutral-smelling things must come to an end. Assuming that your baby has recently started solid foods (we'll discuss this milestone shortly), her bowel movements will start to act and smell just like yours. There's nothing wrong with this. Keep changing them.

What's New with Dad?

By the sixth month, you may be feeling more secure in your abilities to father. In fact, if you've remained active in your baby's life, you're probably able to confidently anticipate his needs and attend to them as they arise. Perhaps you're working well with your partner and have even developed a predictable routine.

Watch out—the "middle-month-routine" syndrome can often get the best of you. In fact, moms and dads can fall into such a rigid pattern or routine that they actually miss out on special opportunities. Sometimes, a seamless, seemingly "perfect" system can squelch creativity and can actually be inhibitory:

> "My wife and I were into the 'routine' so much so that we were like machines—automatons. She did this, I did that. I did the requisite things with my son, and so did she. After a while, it became obvious that she and I were on parallel tracks—never intersecting, hardly talking with each other. I was starting to forget to do basic things like being polite and loving to her. I just wanted to get my part of the 'job' done. I was also a bit grumpy with our baby as well. I guess I was just bored or something."

It takes willpower to watch oneself from a distance—but that's what you need to do this month because sometimes as you slide into a routine, it's easy to lose sight of what's actually happening. Take a look at how you're interacting

TIPS

• At diaper-changing time, when all else fails, breathe through your mouth.

• Dump as much of the poop down the toilet as you can. Despite your best efforts, poop wrapped tightly within a disposable diaper will still stink and constitutes a health and environmental hazard besides.

• When changing your baby while out, don't forget to remove the offending diaper from your car. If you don't, the next morning the inside of your car will smell worse than yak breath.

with your baby and partner. Check in on yourself and make some changes if necessary. If you're feeling too much a part of the cement that is the "routine," as an involved dad, you should be asking yourself a variety of questions:

Dad's Sixth-Month Checkup

- **How do you feel about being a dad?** Believe it or not, many dads rarely stop to consider this monumental issue! Feeling content with fatherhood is a slowly learned process. Try to be honest with yourself. Do you like it? Do you like some of it? None of it? The sixth month is a great time to ponder these questions. If your answers indicate that you're really unhappy, try to understand to what extent your feelings or behaviors are affecting your life with your baby and partner.

- **What are your responsibilities?** Are you satisfied with your part of the care of your baby? Do your responsibilities seem like onerous chores, or do you feel satisfied?

- **Are you bored?** Boredom can lead to irritability, miscommunication, and disinterest—traits that don't work well for three people trying to live and love together.

- **Is it time to make a change?** Sure, you're great at changing diapers, but can you put your baby to sleep? Spice it up. Be wild. Put your baby to bed once or twice. Changing responsibilities with your partner can lead to innovative or novel ways of caring for your baby. If you do most of the diapering on weekends and your partner puts the baby down for a nap, try switching. The best way to beat boredom is through change.

- **How is your career?** Freud said that work and love are required for happiness. For some, it's hard to imagine one without the other. For others, it's hard to imagine having both together. Careers can sometimes interfere with effective fathering. Many dads find themselves in jobs they disdain and bring their irritability home with them—making work and love all the more difficult. Remember, your family is probably pretty good at picking up on your unhappiness.

  If you decide to leave your present job, do so with a plan. Avoid impulsive decisions. Research the job market, seek advice from job banks, and send out your resume. There's nothing more stressful than no job and conflict at home. If you feel that you're unable to leave your job—it may only be a temporary inability—continue to look for alternatives. While you're doing so, avoid sinking into the abyss that can occur with job unhappiness. See chapter eleven for some tips on how to stay healthy in stressful times.

- **Are you treating yourself well?** As we'll see later (in chapter eleven), being a dad is a bit easier if you're good to yourself. Treating yourself well—eating right and exercising, for example—can make a huge difference.

- **Is there tension between you and your partner?** Your child will learn the most from you by witnessing the integrity of your relationship with your partner. Is your relationship mutual, loving, and supportive? As we've seen, it doesn't take much to tip the balance between harmony and discord. Always try to keep an eye on your relationship.

- **Can you express both your joy and your unhappiness?** Men have traditionally flunked the "are-you-in-touch-with-your-feelings" test. Don't worry—you don't need to sob buckets to be aware of your emotional states. But remember that your moods and emotions have a direct impact on the members of your family, whether or not you choose to express them. For some men, the take-home message is to learn to talk rather than yell, slam doors, or behave rudely. For others, the message is that good and bad feelings can coexist.

- **What scares, depresses, or angers you?** Is fatherhood what you expected so far? Have you been able to identify and remedy, hopefully with your partner, important, unresolved issues? If you're a typically angry person, have you been able to constructively express these feelings? If anger, resentment, or envy seem to be bubbling up inside you, can you allow yourself to appropriately express these feelings? Do you know what it is about fathering that frightens you?

- **Are you involved?** Watch for the signs of an uninvolved father: inordinate amounts of free time, tension with your partner over responsibilities, feeling isolated from your family, and feeling unfamiliar with your baby and her routine.

    Ask yourself these questions: Do you know the names of your baby's peers or your partner's friends? Do you know the name of your baby's pediatrician? Have you been involved in feeding your baby or putting her to sleep? Do you talk to your baby? Are you comfortable holding your baby? Do you feel awkward in play? Does your baby seem like someone else's? Are you able to provide the basics of care, and can you soothe your child? If you've not been involved, for one reason or another, it's not too late.

If these areas are problematic, ask yourself why. Discuss them with your partner and ask for her help in resolving them. Don't wait for these problematic areas to magically resolve on their own. Remember, your baby is growing at an astounding rate. Don't miss out.

Your Relationship with Your Partner

Now that the two of you have been at it for six months, it's time to see how you're doing not only as parents but also as partners. Are you spending enough time alone together? Are you communicating?

Often there will be tension between you and your partner. It can be based on a number of things. However, one of the most common is scheduling. This boils down to what needs to be done, when, and by whom. Between work, taking care of a home, and the responsibilities of a baby, there's not a lot of time for yourself. Therefore, you have to try to schedule when you do each thing. Unfortunately, your partner is doing the same thing, and it will rarely square up exactly with your schedule. The best way to solve this possible problem is to sit down together and work out a common schedule that works for both of you.

Another source of tension can be your individuality. Both you and your partner will be required to do the same jobs. However, often you will go about it in different ways. This can range from doing dishes to changing diapers to just about anything. What works for your wife may not work for you. Compounded with other trials, such as lack of sleep, these little differences can easily become blown out of proportion. Your partner may get upset at you because you're not changing the baby like she does, and therefore you are doing it wrong in her view. In most cases, there's no right or wrong, just preferences. If this gets to be a problem, discuss it with your partner. She may be doing things you think are wrong as well.

Being There for Your Baby

Your responsibilities at home never seem to diminish. In fact, as you and your baby grow older, you'll likely realize that there's more to raising a child than just changing a stinky diaper (although you still have to do that, too). In this section, we'll take a closer look at a variety of important issues relating to the care of your baby.

Sleep Problems

One way you can "be there" for your family is to help your baby learn to sleep through the night. While many babies are sleeping soundly during the night (six to eight hours straight) by this time, some haven't yet mastered the skill. For parents of sleepless babies, irritability, anger, and even clinical depression can occur, causing disruptions and stress in the house:

> "Even at 12 months, my son still woke up three times each night. It was literally torture. I couldn't function—as a father, husband, or employee. I was always sick, tired, and depressed. One night, I was so frustrated, I punched a hole in the door. I'm usually pretty even tempered, and that's when I knew we had to do something."

Getting your baby to sleep soundly is better for everyone. Your child will probably benefit from a full night's sleep as well. In the following Focus, we'll look at ways to help your little night owl learn to sleep through the night.

Up to this point, you've had to tolerate your child's unwillingness to sleep through the night. Your six-month-old baby should be able, however, to put herself back to sleep upon awakening and to remain asleep for much of the night. There are many valid exceptions for a baby's inability or unwillingness to sleep through the night—teething pains, ear infections, stomachaches, and other illnesses. If your baby has generally slept soundly and is only now waking up shrieking, a trip to the pediatrician is in order.

Barring unresolved medical issues, however, perhaps the most common cause of persistent awakenings is simply a learned response to environmental stimuli. Babies learn to become dependent upon bottles, binkies, breasts—all kinds of attention—for soothing. Some parents blame sleep problems on

FOCUS: WORKING AT HOME

With the advent of telecommuting and other wonders of modern communication, many fathers are finding it easier to work at home. While this is not possible for all men, those who are able to do so are finding it rewarding and at the same time challenging. Some occupations can be accomplished completely at home. Others may allow for a day or two to be spent at home and the rest of the time at the office.

The amount of flexibility one has while working at home can vary. While some must be on from 9 to 5, others need only get in their eight hours sometime during the day. If your employment allows you to work at home, even for only a portion of your workweek, I recommend at least trying it out. While not for everyone, it can be very rewarding once you get used to it and overcome the obstacles inherent in working at home with the family.

Rewards

There are a number of bonuses that fathers who work at home are able to enjoy. For starters, they are there as their child is growing up. If your hours are flexible, you can take time during the day to play with your child or to help out your partner in the day-to-day jobs of raising a child. If your partner has to go out, you can watch the baby for a while so she can get a break and go by herself. The list goes on and on, but the most important aspect is that you're there at home.

Challenges

Working at home is not all rose petals. It also can have its thorns. The main challenge is the same as the reward—you're at home. Home is filled with distractions: your partner, your child, the phone, the TV, and so on. Your partner can be the hardest one with which to cope. She may think that since you're home, she can come in and talk to you, ask you to hold or change the baby, and numerous other things. In addition, the sounds of the daily routine of running a home may be a distraction, such as vacuuming, a crying baby, and so on. Nothing is worse than talking to a co-worker or client on the phone with a crying baby in the background.

While these are external distractions, it can also be difficult for some fathers to concentrate on their work at home. They may want to keep taking breaks to go to the refrigerator, to watch TV, or a number of other activities that are so close at hand. If you have little self-control or need a structured schedule, this may not be for you.

Helpful Ideas for Working at Home

Here are some tips to help make your job at home more productive. While it might not be possible to follow all of these, each tip will make working at home much easier.

Designate One Room as Your Office. It should have a door and, if possible, be separated from where most of the daily action takes place in your home. Keep everything you need for your job in your office so you don't have to leave it regularly. Some fathers even keep a coffeemaker in their office!

Discuss the Challenges with Your Partner. She must realize when she can interrupt your work and when not to. Let her know your schedule for the day. The two of you must be able to work out any problems. Some partners find it difficult to have the father home during the day. She may feel you are invading her space and time!

Try to Make Your Schedule as Flexible as Possible. This allows you to go to doctor's appointments and such with your partner and take a more active role in your child's growth and development.

Focus on Your Job. It may take practice to tune out the sounds at home. You may also need to clear your office of non–work-related items that may distract you from your tasks.

(cont.)

FOCUS: WORKING AT HOME

(continued)

Realize Your Limitations. If you're having trouble working at home, don't push it to the point of losing your job or your sanity. It's not for everyone, and each father's circumstances are different. Some people just work better in an office or other structured environment.

"I have really learned to enjoy working at home. My wife and I have come to an understanding about interruptions. I have made my schedule flexible. It allows us to take our child shopping, to the zoo, or on other activities during the week instead of on weekends so we can avoid the crowds. I get to spend part of the day with my daughter, then can do some of my work at night when she is asleep."

hunger. The truth is that most healthy six-month-old children should be able to go six to eight hours without a feeding at night and soothe themselves back to sleep.

Some parents choose to deal with the issue by tolerating sleeplessness, while others ignore it and let their children scream. Some give the baby a bottle whenever he wakes up, and other parents bring the baby into their own bed. Some parents will go to any length, satisfying or gratifying the baby in all sorts of ways, to peacefully get the child back to sleep:

"She gets up at 2:30 A.M. We play with her. I flunked my 'Intro to Business' final, but I can roll a ball and stagger around in a sleep-deprived daze like no one else I know."

Parents are often at odds with each other about such sleep issues:

"I just want to let her scream all night long but my wife goes in every two seconds and picks her up. I don't think our baby will ever learn to sleep on her own."

Introducing Solid Food

While there's no specific time line for starting solid foods, your baby's pediatrician will probably have given the go-ahead by six months. Watching your baby taste solid food for the first time can be very satisfying and is usually accompanied by some dramatics:

> "The first time we fed our son rice cereal, he made the most impressive look of disgust I've ever seen. It was almost like his face curled up into a ball. I caught it on film. It was hysterical. He had some of his food in his mouth, I had some of his food in my mouth. Most of what he took in was immediately spit out. I don't think he swallowed any of it. He seemed insulted. It was almost as if he had to take some time to learn to swallow."

Solid food can, in some cases, be given as early as the fourth month. Your pediatrician will help you choose the appropriate kinds of foods and advise you on when to start them. There are, however, certain foods that shouldn't be fed to your little eating machine, and you should be aware of these. Make sure to get a comprehensive list from your pediatrician. Here are some:

Forbidden Foods

- **Raw eggs** should never be fed to anyone.
- **Cooked egg whites** can introduce an allergy to eggs in children under a year old.
- **Corn syrup or honey** can be started only with an older child (12 months or older).
- **Strawberries** can precipitate an allergic reaction.
- **Raspberries** have seeds that are difficult to swallow.
- **Milk and other dairy products** can be started slowly only after consulting with your pediatrician.
- **Raw fish or meat** should never be fed to your baby.
- **Avoid nitrite- or nitrate-containing foods,** such as smoked fish or bacon.
- **Acidic fruit juices,** such as pineapple or grapefruit, can give your baby diarrhea or a rash.

FOCUS: HOW TO TEACH YOUR BABY TO SLEEP THROUGH THE NIGHT

Since teaching your baby to sleep through the night can in itself be a sleepless proposition, it's best to work together with your partner. Make sure you and your partner are on the same wavelength and are committed to the project.

There are several different techniques. The simplest is to allow your baby to "cry it out." I don't care for this model because of its impersonal and unnecessarily harsh methodology—babies still need to know that you exist and are looking after them. A better alternative is to teach your baby to put herself to sleep, gradually.

Your goal is to acclimate your baby to falling asleep without the various aids previously afforded her—bottle, breast, rocking, pacifier, and so on. It'll undoubtedly take some practice for everybody (plan on at least three or four rough nights).

- **Caffeine-containing foods,** such as chocolate, coffee, and tea, are not good for your baby.
- **Avoid feeding your baby foods he can choke on,** such as nuts, hard candy, pretzels, hot dogs, and grapes.
- **Never feed your baby anything containing alcohol.**

Above all, go slowly and be sure to check with your baby's pediatrician before you introduce new foods. At my house, feeding our babies for the first time was a ritual of sorts. We'd all gather around the table and marvel at the baby's first attempt. It's truly a rite of passage. Don't forget that she can swallow the new substances about as easily as you can swallow baby food. Wear a poncho, cover the furniture, protect your eyes . . . YOU'RE OFF! . . . Have fun!

After the nighttime feeding, place your baby in her crib while awake and leave the room. If your baby cries, return in a minute or two and soothe her with a pat or two on the back and some loving words of encouragement. Don't pick her up.

As the evening progresses, allow your baby to cry for longer periods of time between your visits but always return periodically to let her know you haven't forgotten her. You can pat your baby and talk briefly, but resist the temptation to pick her up. Your baby will likely scream or cry loudly. It may take an hour or more before your baby goes to sleep, but as the days go by, her crying will diminish.

You'll need to do the same thing when your baby wakes during the night. Resist the temptation to pick your baby up unless she needs to be changed or is in some medical distress. If your baby is on solid food, has eaten dinner, and has had a bottle or been breast-fed sometime in the evening, it won't be necessary to feed her again in the middle of the night. Within a few days, your baby will likely be sleeping well. Good luck. May the sandman bestow an entire bag of sand upon your baby.

Play Update

Your baby's increased motor strength and improved neck tone allow for slightly more vigorous play. Her enhanced psychological sensory skills will enable more intense interaction. Try the following:

- **Talk with your baby** continuously. Engage her in dialogue.

- **Play peek-a-boo.**

- **Play hide-the-ball.** Show your baby a ball, then hide it behind your back. See if he can realize it hasn't disappeared. Some babies will try to look for the hidden object.

- **Sing to her** and encourage use of expression and language by responding with glee to baby's utterances.

FOCUS: HOW TO FEED YOUR BABY SOLID FOOD

- **Setup:** Your baby will need to be secured in either a high chair or a baby carrier. Cleanup is easier if you place a plastic mat or newspaper underneath. There'll be lots of squirming and maneuvering. Prepare the baby food by dumping some of it out of the jar and into a dish or bowl. Heat it slightly and stir well. Use a small spoon. Have plenty of rags or dish towels ready in anticipation of the mess. Put a bib on your baby. Put a bib on yourself. Get the video camera ready. Seat yourself comfortably.

  TIP: *Use a plastic, not glass or ceramic, dish to feed your baby, in anticipation of him batting it out of your hands.*

  TIP: *For health reasons, don't feed your baby directly out of the baby food jar unless you're planning to throw the entire jar out. A jar of baby food that has saliva from baby's mouth in it is a breeding ground for germs and bacteria and should not be used again.*

- **Load the spoon:** Since most of the food will fall out of the little slob's mouth, place just a small portion of food on the spoon.

- **While singing or reciting a rhyme, bounce your baby on your knees or legs.** Say one particular word more loudly than the others and give her an extra-high bounce.

- **Play standing games** by gently pulling your baby up by her arms to a standing position on your thighs or stomach.

- **Pull your baby up to a crawling position.** Support your baby's belly if necessary.

- **Put your baby on your shoulders and dance** in front of the mirror like a lunatic.

- **Put your baby in a jumper toy** suspended from the top of a doorway. Never leave your baby while she is in the jumper.

- **Distract your baby:** One of the keys to successfully introducing your baby to solid food is to get her interested in the process . . . or something completely unrelated. Your baby will probably be looking at the camera instead of the food. To get her attention, make high-pitched noises, open your mouth wide, and play games with the spoon.

- **Feed your baby:** After testing the temperature of the food (yuck . . . by tasting or touching it), put the spoon up to your baby's lips. Let her taste the food before you try to shove it in. Look at your baby and open your mouth. Put the food in gently, tip the handle of the spoon up, and pull out. Chances are that your baby will dribble most if not all of the food out onto herself. Sometimes your baby will sneeze. *That's* fun.

   TIP: *Avoid gagging and choking your baby by not pushing food too far back into your baby's mouth.*

- **Patience, perseverance, and praise:** You'll need to practice all these things. Smile at your baby, congratulate him, and encourage him to try again. Eventually, your baby will catch on.

- **Invest in a stationary walker.** This will enable your baby to experiment with her standing and bouncing abilities without exposing her to the serious dangers of a mobile walker.

Hazards Review

While I'll be discussing safety-proofing in detail later in the book (chapters eleven and twelve), beware of your baby's improved mobility. He is now capable of grabbing small objects and eating them. Also, since his rolling skills are improved, his falling and tangling "skills" are also heightened. Be sure to review the hazards discussed in the previous chapter and the safety tips on pages 130–133. Never leave your baby unattended on a bed or counter or near clothing or toys with cords, the telephone, or an open door leading to a stairwell. Be sure to remove drawstrings from all his clothing.

Bonding with Baby

Wow, you have made it to six months! You probably feel like celebrating the halfway mark to your baby's one-year birthday. So go ahead and do so. It doesn't have to be anything major. Just you, your partner, and your baby. If you know some other couples with a baby born about the same time, invite them to join you. The purpose of the party is to have fun. Don't structure it out. The key is to acknowledge your achievement. Try watching a movie, especially a comedy about parenting. Even if you have seen it before, it will be even funnier now that you have experienced some of the same things the characters in the film are doing.

This is also a good time to view video or pictures from your baby's birth. See how much the little guy has grown and changed in the last six months. You may even be surprised by how much you have changed!

Play Ball!

Your child should be able to play ball with you now. No, he will not go out for a pass or be able to hold a bat to hit a home run. However, you have to start

---

DIAPER BAG CHECKLIST FOR SIX-MONTH-OLD BABIES

Add the following to your six-month-old's diaper bag:

✔ Baby food

✔ Cheerios (if OK'd by your pediatrician)

✔ Baby spoon

✔ Toys capable of being chewed on

✔ Extra wipes

✔ Bib

somewhere. Try rolling a ball to him and then getting him to roll it back to you—or just hitting it somewhere. Remember, it will take some practice. At the start, he may just grab hold of the ball and try to chew on it. The key to this activity is to set up a game or even just an interactive exercise the two of you can do together.

Growing Together

Remaining an active participant in the life of your baby can sometimes be a challenge. You've probably done more than you think! You've fed your baby and have the carrot stains on your shirt to prove it. If you're like most involved dads, you're being rewarded daily by your baby's smile and attention.

Can it get better? Although hard to believe, your relationship with your baby can and will get better. You've already seen vast improvements in your baby's ability to influence her surroundings. As your baby gets older, her mobility and personality will develop more fully, and you'll have newer, even more meaningful experiences. In the next chapter, I'll discuss ways in which you can continue to protect your baby, have fun with her, and benefit from her improved social skills.

WORKING DADS UPDATE

Dads who work away from home may want to do the following with their babies:

- Take copious amounts of photographs to show at work.
- Bathe in the tub with your baby.
- Take a shower with your baby.
- Feed your baby solid food at dinner.
- During lunch break, meet your partner and baby for a picnic.

There are times when parenthood
seems nothing but feeding the mouth
that bites you.

—PETER DE VRIES

8

The Seventh Month

The seventh month is a great time to admire your baby's accomplishments and marvel at her improved strength and mobility. It won't be long before your kid is crawling around and getting into all sorts of new predicaments—adorably ruining expensive antiques, gleefully pulling glasses full of juice onto the new carpet, and painstakingly chewing up the newspaper. It'll be entertaining:

> "My son is like some kind of snake. He woke up one day and decided that he wanted to see a bit more of the world. I can't hold him anymore. All he wants to do is wiggle and squirm his way out of my arms and onto the floor. He grabs at anything. Once in a while, just to impress me with his enhanced fine motor skills, he jams his fingers up my nose. Sometimes he just lies on his back and flops around, like an overturned turtle."

While we won't be looking at ways you can protect the inside of your nose, we will examine wills and life insurance and how to protect your little turtle's future. We'll also focus on how to use medical basics to detect illness in your child.

What's New with Your Baby?

One of the hallmarks of the seven-month-old baby is his burning desire to get around and see the world. Since your baby won't always cooperate with *your* desires, this drive to explore can be a bit of a pain. Try, however, to put yourself in your child's tiny shoes for a minute. Consider how awesome and exciting the world must appear! Remember, for the longest time, your baby's world consisted of not much more than mom's breast or dad's bottle, so the vast vistas opening up—under beds, inside cupboards—are endlessly fascinating.

Developmental Milestones

Your baby's intense curiosity, coupled with her improved ability to squirm around and grasp smaller objects, forms the majority of new behaviors and milestones this month. Be on the lookout for your baby getting into a variety of things she shouldn't have access to.

Motor Strength: Your baby will be better able to swivel or turn his body in response to a voice or in an attempt to grab an object. While a few babies are crawling by seven months, most end up rolling toward a destination or will wiggle around until reaching their goal.

Your baby's ability to push her body up is greatly enhanced, and you'll frequently find her up on her arms, looking around. When pulled up on all fours, your baby may be able to remain that way for a while before falling onto her belly. Your baby will also probably bounce up and down on your lap. Her grip will be firm and strong—whether it's the hair in your armpit or your paycheck, her clenched fingers will fiercely resist any attempt to remove an object.

Fine motor skills will be put into practice. Using the gift of opposable digits, he will start to pick items up by coarsely grasping them between his thumb and another finger. Your baby will vigorously shake things, like rattles, toys, or your nose. He may insist on holding the bottle. He will also be more adept at bearing weight on his legs when standing with assistance and will be better at sitting.

Sensory Perception: Your baby will be constantly testing her skills by feeling and touching just about anything. Touching small objects will hold especially great interest. Seven-month-old babies love to watch things move or fall.

Psychological: As your baby gets to see more of the world, the world will, as it does with each of us, give her reasons to be displeased. Purposeful vocalizations of glee and delight will appropriately be replaced by anger, anxiety, or disgust. To your baby, the entire world is opening up. In response to the challenges of the world, you may witness the beginnings of familiar adult emotional states—discomfort with strangers, for example. Rather than shows of enthusiasm, those people not well known to your baby might be greeted with expressions of distrust, suspicion, fear, or stony-faced indifference. Your baby may also become easily frightened or overwhelmed.

What Is Your Baby's Day Like?

You've undoubtedly noticed that as time passes, your baby's world expands—she realizes that there's more to life than simply being fed. Maybe your baby understands that her ability to smile conditions an emotional response from others. Being carried around in mom's or dad's arms further increased her zone of familiarity. Now, newly mobile, your baby's "10 Es" will be more exciting and fun for everyone!

Exploring: At seven months, your baby is faced with the overwhelming prospect that with a bit of perseverance and propelled by wriggling legs and arms, she can reach new worlds! Whether left alone (with you secretly watching) or while being held, your baby's desire to explore will be impressive. Tossing and turning, moving, and perhaps even crawling, your baby will reach and touch just about anything:

> "All of a sudden, my daughter developed a deep love affair with the remote control, which also happens to be my favorite household item. It's like a religious icon for her. She and I actually compete for it. I have to wrench it out of her hands. It's always coated with saliva and generic baby slime of unknown origin, so I usually cave and give it right back to her."

Engaged: Once your baby latches onto something new, it's likely that she will be determined to possess it, until, of course, something better or newer comes along. Despite this fact, your baby will still be completely fascinated with you—your nose, eyes, and ears—and will squeeze, poke, pull, push, rip, and tear her way into your heart. A healthy sense of humor will get you through the painful playtimes:

"My baby loves to play with me but rips my chest hairs out. I'm trying to enjoy it. She's come so very far—it seems like just yesterday that she was vomiting on me."

Emotional: Since he now suspects that getting around on his own is a distinct possibility, your baby's emotionality may be somewhat heightened:

"Sometimes I just want to hold him, but he refuses to stay in my arms. It's maddening! He tries to reach stuff on the couch when I'm trying to watch TV. I can't stand it. If I try to stop him or hold him closer or tighter, he gets insane, screaming and carrying on—almost like he's having a tantrum!"

Energetic: Seemingly coming from nowhere, your baby's energy level will be enhanced by her desire to explore the world. Even when tired and cranky, your baby will give you a run for the money:

"The energy thing was definitely an adjustment for me. My wife typically cares for my daughter all day, and when I get home, the baby's usually near sleep. But lately, she has so much energy that I can't even hold her anymore. All she wants to do is play and fidget around. My wife is used to it, but sometimes, since I'm beat when I get home, it's a little annoying for me. On the other hand, it's fabulous watching her grow. I can't stand to be without her!"

Expressive: Your baby will continue to experiment with both sound and his ability to express a variety of moods by facial expression:

"My son seems to be mimicking or trying to copy some of the things I say. We play a sort of game. I babble foolishly, then he repeats it."

Expanded Repertoire: Your baby will be more expressive and better able to maneuver. Play will be expanded, and she will demand extra attention. Your baby's strength and size will be increasing, enabling her to accomplish things unimaginable just one month ago. Watch for the subtly increasing art of manipulation. Even at the young age of seven months, your baby is quickly learning how to influence her surroundings:

"My daughter definitely knows when I'm about to put her down. She pouts and starts to curl up her lips. Sobbing comes next. It stops, of course, when I pick her back up."

Extremely Playful and Silly: Bubbling with happiness and life, your seven-month-old will still be a comedian—a more mobile one. Your baby will clown around, chewing on your feet, your fingers, or your good furniture.

Entertaining: Your baby will expend an unprecedented amount of energy trying to move around. He'll be fun to watch:

"My baby squeals with laughter when I put him on the floor. He wriggles around in circles like one of the Three Stooges. If he could make that 'woo-woo-woo' noise, it would be truly hysterical!"

Continuing to use his sense of playfulness, your baby may be better at entertaining himself than in previous months.

Endearing: Watch for your baby to become increasingly genuine in his love for you:

"Sometimes my son will sit with me and just softly play with my nose or lips. I smile, then he smiles. I've always loved my baby but now I'm in love with him!"

Eager to Please: Your baby will get better at making you happy:

"If I laugh when my daughter pinches my arm, she keeps doing it. From time to time, she even sits still on my lap because she senses that it makes me happy."

What's New with Mom and Dad?

You're now on the downhill slide to the one-year mark as a father. However, that doesn't mean things will be getting easier. Instead, because of all the pressure and changes you've been through the last several months, you may even feel like you're ready to blow. Your patience is just about to run out between the household duties, keeping track of finances, and keeping up at work. In fact, you may be to the point of "fight or flee." Before you really lose your temper or decide to run away from it all, reflect on what you have become.

While growing up, most boys are taught to be self-sufficient as well as the importance of competition and winning. Looking at other model males in our world, we see that a man is judged by the work he does. For example, when you first meet a person, one of the first questions that comes up is, "What do you do for a living?" or something similar. Our job defines us. Rarely do you ask another man how many children he has or if he is a father.

The importance men often place on their careers neglects the profound influence they have on future generations by being a father. How do you want your child to remember you? By your job or by what you did with him? So before you start to think fatherhood is not all it is cracked up to be, just remember how important you are to the little one drooling in your arms. You've made it this far, and you're still alive. Just keep on going. When the pressure begins to build, take some time for yourself. Schedule a regular activity, whether it be a nightly walk or even a hobby of some type. While your baby and partner need you, if you get too worn down and stressed, you won't be of much help.

> "Each night after the baby is asleep and before I go to bed, I take some time to read a book. It helps me unwind and clear my mind by letting me concentrate on something outside of the home, family, and job. I read until I'm just about to fall asleep and then turn in. I find I rest better because I'm not laying in bed thinking about the day with my mind working instead of resting."

> "I find a daily workout really helps alleviate the stress that builds up as a result of the many roles I now play as a father, a husband, and an employee. It burns off the tension in my body and allows me to relax when it's over."

Being Prepared for Any Eventuality

In a prior chapter, we discussed steps you can take to save money for your baby. What would happen to your baby, though, if you weren't around or if you and your partner were severely injured? What would happen if you became disabled and couldn't provide for your family? If you and your partner died in an accident, who would guarantee your baby's financial future or attend to his emotional and physical well-being?

While many parents prefer not to think of such things, death, like spit and drool, happens. Disabling illnesses that take away your livelihood, vitality, and productivity can occur as well. Although you may be young, healthy, and strong, there's always a chance that you might die or become impaired long before your time. It's up to you to foresee these possibilities and take steps to protect your child.

Q: *I don't want to think about wills and things yet. My wife and I are young and healthy. I don't feel like we're going to die anytime soon. If we do, and I think it very unlikely, someone in my family will take over and care for my daughter.*

A: What young person *does* feel like he's going to die? The realities are that young people do become disabled or die. And if you die without a will, the state will decide where your assets go (it will take some) and who will care for your children.

Q: *I know that ensuring my baby's future, after I'm gone, means that a lot of people will know all my personal business. That really bothers me.*

A: Don't count on the *New York Times* to publish details relevant to your net worth. Careful selection of trustworthy people is all it takes to maintain your privacy.

Q: *It seems very expensive to me. All those lawyers and accountants and policies, in addition to those pesky insurance salesmen! How am I going to pay for it all?*

A: Try to look at the expense of proper legal or financial advice as an investment. When you stop to consider the lifelong implications, the expense is minimal. Your employer may offer some of these services as part of your benefit package. Ask. Also, unions and professional organizations may offer insurance at a discount.

Q: *I know it needs to be done. I just don't have the time to get out and meet with people.*

A: The time it takes to create important documents is minimal. Some of the recommendations in the Focus on page 176 can even be accomplished at home, on your computer.

Q: *I know we should write a will, but it seems too complicated, and it intimidates me. We keep putting it off.*

A: It'll be far more complicated for everyone—including your surviving family and child—if you fail to take advantage of your good health now and make clear to the world what you want done should you die.

Being There for Your Baby

There was a time, not so long ago, when dads relegated complete care of their small children to their wives. Fortunately, times have changed. Up to this point, we've discussed many of the things you can do to be and feel close to your baby. There's another important area of care, however, that modern dads need to be familiar with.

Since we're with our children more than ever, every dad should be familiar with the basics of baby health care. In this section, we'll spend some time looking at simple techniques you can employ to evaluate the health of your baby.

Health Issues

There's nothing worse than feeling alone with a sick child—having to make important decisions is no easy task. The job can be made simpler, however, when you and your partner work together. Unfortunately, this isn't always possible, and since dads are now spending more time alone with their babies, they need to be familiar with their baby's health history and some medical basics.

While nobody would want you to diagnose and treat your baby by yourself, the observation that "something is wrong" can be of enormous help to your baby's pediatrician. If you've been paying attention, you're probably aware of the typical behaviors your child displays when feeling well. In other words, you know her "baseline" health status. Deviations from this typical set of behaviors or a marked change in appearance should be looked upon with some concern.

Do yourself and your baby a favor this month and read appendix A, "Common Childhood Ailments." This appendix will familiarize you with medical terms, typical courses of treatment, and the basic medical supplies you should keep on hand. The Focus on page 180 will help you learn to read your child for symptoms. Remember, you're not expected to be a doctor, just to be alert and observant.

Health-Education Assignment

As soon as you're finished with this chapter, read appendix A, "Common Childhood Ailments." The appendix not only defines common illnesses but also explains how to take care of your sick baby and what signs and symptoms indicate a medical emergency.

High-Tension Diaper Change: An Update

Did you ever think you'd have a child whose shorts smelled like the inside of a hamster cage? Consider the following scenario: Your increasingly strong, kick-boxing, noncompliant baby has a huge, wet, stinky poop in his shorts. Your partner doesn't feel like you've been very helpful today and gives you the honor of changing the child. You're upset and impatient because the game has started and you've already missed the best part. The only thing more foul than the odor coming from his diaper is his attitude. He's in a horrible mood—hissing and screaming like an angry cat. You pull off the diaper and take a look. It's much worse than you thought. He immediately pees on you. Poop is flying everywhere. What do you do? . . .

 **TIP**

To prevent the spread of infectious disease, always wash your hands before touching your sick baby and again when you're done.

- **Quality control:** Quickly place a cloth diaper or other expendable absorbent cloth under your baby's butt and back.

- **Yell for help:** I'm not proud. Lest you stand frozen like a deer caught in the headlights of an oncoming car, remember that some poops are a two-person job.

- **Do it yourself:** If no one is available to help you, or if your partner is purposely ignoring you, you'll need to distract your baby by trying to make a game of it. Gently but firmly grasping both feet, pick her legs up

FOCUS: HOW TO PROTECT YOUR CHILD'S FUTURE

- **Start now!:** Don't delay. Your child's future depends on you.

- **Do it together:** Enlist the help of your partner. Since you'll be making monumental and long-lasting decisions, it's important that the responsibility be shared.

- **Create a list of assets:** If you and your partner die, your family, lawyer, and/or accountant will need to track your assets to help settle your estate. No estate is too small. Make a list of account numbers, insurance policies, and all other assets and property. Give copies to trusted family members, friends, and your attorney or accountant.

- **Buy life insurance:** Life insurance should do one thing only—it should pay when you die. Its purpose is to provide your surviving family with enough money to pay for the necessities of life and to educate your child. Purchasing high-quality term life insurance is a great way to protect your baby and family should something happen to you.

  Term insurance is inexpensive—depending on how much you purchase, usually a few hundred dollars each year or less. The concept is straightforward. If you die, the insurance company pays your benefactors. Plain and simple. This is pure insurance with no bells or whistles. You should purchase enough renewable term insurance to provide your loved ones with the lifestyle to which they are accustomed. This amount generally equals at least six times your current yearly income. Choose a conservative, highly rated, major insurance company.

  Some people purchase more expensive forms of life insurance as savings vehicles. Since there are better ways to save, I would avoid it. Should your partner buy life insurance? Even if she doesn't work, it's a good idea. Should she die, insurance can help pay for babysitting expenses and household help and perhaps give you the financial margin to take time off work to emotionally support yourself and your family. Should you buy life insurance for your child? Does your child work? Are you dependent on your child for income? Of course not. Don't bother.

- **Buy disability insurance:** What would happen in the unlikely event you're severely injured in an accident or need surgery that will prevent you from working for a long time? How will your family survive? Disability insurance is designed to replace a percentage of your income. Your policy should include the following characteristics: noncancelable coverage until you're 65, long waiting period to avoid high cost, and waiver of premium should you become disabled. For more information, you may want to read about disability insurance at your library.

- **Purchase health insurance:** Should you or a family member become seriously ill, spending your hard-earned savings on health care can be devastating to your family. If health care is not available through your or your partner's employer, join a health maintenance organization on your own.

- **Make a will:** This is an essential component of any long-term plan to ensure the security of your baby. You and your partner must have wills. Without wills, should you and/or your partner die, the courts will decide who gets what and, more important, what happens to your baby. There are other negative consequences of dying intestate (without a will) as well—custody, taxes, and property being but a few. Many families have been torn apart—feuding and fighting with one another—because of a poorly written or nonexistent will.

  Wills can be made at home by your own hand or on a computer with special software. Because of the legal complexities, however, my advice is to use an attorney. Drafting simple, uncomplicated wills (both you and your partner should have one) is not expensive. You'll also want to name an executor for your estate. The executor will help the lawyer settle the estate fairly, efficiently, and honestly. An executor should be a family member, trusted friend, or attorney.

(cont.)

FOCUS: HOW TO PROTECT YOUR CHILD'S FUTURE

(continued)

- **Name a guardian:** If both you and your partner die, who will raise your children? A will specifies who will care for your children. Without a will, a court will appoint the guardian. Choose a guardian who shares your values and who is suited, physically and otherwise, to raise a child. A guardian can be a family member or trusted friend. Be sure to discuss these issues with your choices before naming them in your will.

- **Create a durable power of attorney:** This document, which can be easily created by an attorney, names someone you trust to make legal, financial, and business decisions for you should you become disabled and unable to competently make choices.

- **Consider creating a living will:** This nonbinding but important health care document lets those around you—family, friends, and physicians—know what you would have wanted for yourself if you were presently capable of deciding. A living will, created while you're healthy, specifies your wishes should you become incompetent to make medical treatment decisions. Valid in the majority of states, this document will make clear, for example, your wish to be kept alive on life support or to be removed from it.

fairly high (while you wipe) and make a ridiculously high-pitched noise to capture her attention. Repeat as often as needed.

- **Distract, distract, distract:** Use your imagination. Cough, sneeze, dangle saliva from your mouth, or chant like a lunatic.

- **Work quickly:** Once your baby is distracted, you'll have a narrow window of opportunity in which to complete your vital mission.

- **Hold baby down:** If your baby is truly thrashing, hold his chest down gently but with authority to prevent twisting. Wipe as best as you can with the other hand.

- **Distract, distract, distract.**
- **Undress baby:** Sometimes, particularly if your baby has made a mess everywhere, the best way to get the little thrasher to hold still is to get her naked. If she's truly a mess, fill the sink with warm water and dunk her butt.

Bonding with Baby

Your baby is getting stronger and more able to play games with you. However, in addition to working on her motor skills, begin to stimulate her socially and perceptually. One thing you can try is to teach your child to expect new things. Bounce her on your lap as you sing a song or recite a nursery rhyme. Follow the beat of the song or rhyme with your bouncing. Stop every so often, both the voicing and bouncing, then, while holding her body firmly, lower her between your separated knees. Babies like the unexpected surprise. After a while, when you stop singing, she will anticipate the change. Therefore, alternate the pattern and lower every other time you stop.

You can begin to teach your baby to clap her hands by sitting her in front of you and clapping your own hands together. When she begins to follow you and claps her hands, smile and praise her. Together you can begin to play patty-cake kinds of games. For a real test of her dexterity, introduce toys into bath time. It requires much more hand-eye coordination to grab a toy bouncing up and down in a bathtub than one just sitting stationary on the floor.

During all types of activities, whether playing or changing a diaper, talk to your child. Tell her what you're doing. Explain why you're doing it. Tell her about your day. Anything. The key is talking. Babies learn speech from listening.

DIAPER BAG CHECKLIST FOR SEVEN-MONTH-OLD BABIES

Add the following to your seven-month-old's diaper bag:

✔ Newer foods approved of by your pediatrician

✔ Toys that baby can grab, chew, watch, or roll

FOCUS: HOW TO USE MEDICAL BASICS TO DETECT ILLNESS

Most parents can sense when their children don't feel well. Mostly it's a matter of paying attention to your child's normal routine and becoming particularly alert if the routine changes in any way. Listed next are a few simple screening techniques you can use to quickly assess whether your child is sick. If you have any doubt, call your pediatrician.

> **TIP:** *Remember, your job is not to diagnose illness, it's only to determine if your baby seems different in some way.*

- **Behavioral:** While each child will respond to sickness in a different way, behavioral changes often accompany a variety of illnesses. Is your baby responsive and alert? Is he eating and drinking? Look for changes in energy level, tearfulness, or irritability, for example. Some sick babies will insist on being carried constantly. Watch for changes in your baby's routine:

"Whenever my baby starts to get sick, he clings to me and sobs. When he was younger, he would actually sleep later in the morning when getting sick. In fact, whenever he slept past 6 A.M., without even going in to see him, I knew he was coming down with something."

Older babies may be able to point to areas of discomfort, while younger children are more difficult to diagnose.

- **Vital signs:** Your child's vital signs can be an important gauge of how he's doing. Vital signs consist of pulse, blood pressure, respiratory rate, and temperature. Abnormal vital signs can signal the body's response to some form of insult, such as an infection. While not always abnormal during illness, the presence of a markedly abnormal vital sign should alert you to the possibility that something is amiss.

Most parents are intimately familiar with an elevated temperature. A fever may, for example, accompany a variety of medical illnesses, ranging from the common cold to more serious conditions. Some parents can detect a fever by touching their babies, while others need to use a thermometer.

TIP: *Electronic ear thermometers are expensive but well worth the investment when you have a screaming, wriggling baby to check.*

A baby's pulse, normally quicker than an adult's, is really a measure of the heart rate. It can be taken by placing a few fingers (not thumb) over the heart. A resting pulse of 100 to 130—150 while awake and active and under 200 when upset—is normal. Any deviation from these figures, above or below, should be reported to the doctor. A very rapid pulse can signal a variety of conditions, including dehydration. A low pulse can also be cause for concern. An accidental ingestion of medicine—blood pressure pills, for example—might drive the pulse down dramatically.

Your baby's rate of respiration can be an important measure of how well air is moving in and out of her lungs. In a newborn, the respiration rate can be greater than 40 per minute, while an older baby's rate can drop to 25 to 35 per minute. Elevated during periods of excitement or anxiety, an increased rate can also signal fever, respiratory illnesses, and distress.

- **Color:** Your baby's color can provide valuable clues to his clinical condition. Pallor (pale skin) can indicate dehydration or other conditions, such as anemia. A bluish color, usually a serious sign, can signal a lack of oxygen, such as can occur in breathing disorders, choking, or allergic reactions. Reddish skin, lesions, or a rash can indicate infectious disease or fever. Yellowing of the skin or whites of the eyes can signal a serious problem as well. A tender, red, swollen area of the skin could indicate a local infection caused by injury—for example, a splinter.

- **Face:** Look for sunken eyes, which can occur in dehydration. Glassy eyes or a vacant stare can indicate a variety of illnesses. Drainage from the eyes or eyes that appear bloodshot can signal an infection. Many parents have learned to detect illness in their children just by looking at one particular area of the face:

(cont.)

FOCUS: HOW TO USE MEDICAL BASICS TO DETECT ILLNESS

(continued)

"Whenever my son gets a fever, his lips become bright red."

Another useful way to assess your baby is to gently pull down her lower eyelid. The inside of the lid should be nice and red. The inside of her mouth and tongue should also be red and moist. Dry, cracked lips and a dry tongue could indicate dehydration. Your baby's breath might become *ketotic* (a fruity or chemical smell) during an episode of dehydration. Look for drainage from the nose and observe its color. Watch to see if your baby is touching her ears.

- Excretory system: Is your baby's diaper wet? A persistently dry diaper could indicate a variety of problems, including dehydration. Very dark, concentrated, malodorous urine may also be a sign of dehydration. Diarrhea that persists for more than a day or two should be phoned in to the pediatrician, as should a persistent lack of stools or constipation.

- Appetite: Some children naturally eat more or less as they grow older. Any rapid change in your baby's desire to eat could be due to as simple a prob-

You should also be careful what you say around your child. If you don't want her repeating a word, don't say it in front of her. Nothing embarrasses a parent like a child repeating a vulgar expletive in front of everyone at a family gathering.

Growing Together

For some, it's unfathomable to think that just a few brief months ago, their baby was a helpless infant, incapable of significant movement, completely dependent on the breast or bottle, and unable to interact with the vigor they're

lem as teething but might also be more significant. Vomiting (not just spitting up) should be phoned in to the doctor.

- **Respiration:** A honking cough or the production of green, yellow, or blood-tinged sputum should be phoned in to the doctor. Watch your baby's chest. Is your baby laboring to breathe in or out? Is her chest rising and falling normally? Is your baby wheezing or honking during inhalation or when she breathes out? Is your baby choking on a foreign body?

    TIP: *Sign up for a CPR (cardiopulmonary resuscitation) class today.*

- **Abdomen:** A touch or gentle poke to the belly that elicits pain or crying should be investigated further. Call your pediatrician if you see or feel any obvious lumps or bumps.

- **Swollen glands:** Small tender balls, located around various parts of the body, can become evident during infectious or other disease states. These lumps can become noticeable to the touch on the back and sides of your baby's neck, the sides of his groin, or under his arms or chin.

- **Skeletal system:** A bone protruding from the skin or a lump under the skin over a bone is an obvious sign of fracture. A persistent swelling over an injured limb could signal a fracture as well.

now witnessing. Soon, your baby will become even more independent. Are you ready? What'll it be like for you? These are really only the first baby steps on the road to a more fully developed independence. In the next few chapters, we'll review some common feelings about your growing, thriving baby. We'll also look at other ways you can help protect your baby from harm.

A baby changes your dinner party
conversation from politics to poops.
—MAURICE JOHNSTONE

The Eighth Month

By the eighth month, you and your baby may be yukking it up together pretty regularly. By this time, many babies have a fairly well developed sense of humor, and it doesn't take much to get them chuckling. What is it about babies that drives dads to do crazy things? You're very likely acting in ways you never thought you would:

> "I feel like we're a comedy team—he's Chuckles the clown and I'm the dancing lunatic. We respond with such glee to each other's antics that I'm left in stitches."

Not all babies are clowns, however:

> "My daughter doesn't really ham it up like some other kids. She seems more reserved. On the other hand, I've noticed that she can do things that other kids her age aren't doing yet."

Because of her always improving sense of desire, curiosity, and strength, your baby will be far more tempted to take new risks—and challenge your patience by getting into even more "interesting" predicaments:

> "She seems like a little roving computer, downloading everything she sees onto her hard drive. Rather than the randomness that characterized her behavior just a couple of months ago, her scanning, seeking,

and attacking seems planned and methodical. My wife and I watch with pleasure as she stalks, tracks, and tries to eat the family dog."

Because of your baby's raw enthusiasm, however, you'll need to pay special attention to safety issues. In this chapter, we'll look again at health and safety issues.

What's New with Your Baby?

While not *every* eight-month-old baby has the desire or ability to crawl, most do. No longer content to sit on the floor like a bag of pineapples, your baby will be squirmy and inquisitive. Your baby's new activities and mobility, while usually greeted with howls of approval, may also be met with a general lack of enthusiasm from a tired dad:

"I realize it's important, even essential, for my daughter to one day walk. But for the life of me, I can't take it anymore. She never sits still anymore! When I pick her up to get her away from the garbage can or some other similar hazard, she flops forward, almost falling out of my arms."

Nor can you turn your back even for a second:

"I put my son on the ground and went to answer the door. I was gone for maybe 15 seconds. When I came back, he had already rolled himself into the fireplace. No fire, fortunately, but a very sooty baby. I brushed him off with the fireplace brush—very handy. I had always wondered what that thing was for."

Every now and then it's valuable to stop and satisfy your curiosity about the growth process. The following questions are designed to address common concerns about eight-month-old babies.

Q: *I've noticed that my baby isn't that great at crawling. By this time, isn't she supposed to be motoring around—you know, driving me crazy?*

A: It's important to understand that your baby will grow and develop at her own pace, one that depends on a number of important factors—the interplay of your baby's nature, genetics, biology, emotional maturity, and the environment in which she is raised. Every human being grows differently, and your baby has a right to grow at her own pace.

Your baby's motor skills—crawling in this case—will continue to improve as she grows older. Some babies are great crawlers at six or seven months, while others crawl much later, and some never crawl at all, choosing instead to focus on standing and walking. In most cases, an eight-month-old who cares little for the crawling journey will likely develop perfectly normally. If you're concerned about your baby's disinterest in crawling, however, feel free to call your pediatrician.

Q: *Is it normal for my baby to try to pick up every little thing he sees on the floor? I mean, sometimes he tries to pick up pieces of lint or even tiny little marks that are actually part of the floor. Once, he even tried to put the cat in his mouth. Is there something wrong here? I feel bad for the cat.*

A: It's much to your baby's credit that he can use his various senses to notice minute changes in his surroundings. One of the hallmarks of babies this age is intense wonder and curiosity. When coupled with the vision and touch necessary to put curiosity to use, watch out! Combined with his improved fine motor skills and ability to use his thumb and fingers to grasp, you'll need to watch your baby carefully.

Babies are particularly interested in change—that is, any perceived alteration in their environment. Your baby sees a floor and is then attracted to something in or on the floor that looks different or interesting. He doesn't yet possess the capacity to realize that some things can't be picked up, and he doesn't yet fully grasp the issues of dimensionality—height, length, width, and depth.

Your baby's ongoing love affair with putting objects in his mouth is normal. Your child may gross you out by trying to eat the cat, a dust bunny, or dirt and not be much worse for wear. The real danger is he will pick up something that seems innocuous to you but that is actually very dangerous, such as a deflated balloon (or a broken piece of one), which can easily suffocate a small child.

Q: *My daughter is very possessive of toys and other stuff she finds around the playroom. If another kid tries to take something away from her, she goes nuts—screaming and howling. Is this normal? Should we do something to try to make her share more? Is she going to grow up friendless? Does she need a therapist already?*

A: In the Wild West of babyhood, possession is ten-tenths of the law. Most babies who are old enough to grab, pick up, and possess an object will, with great vigor and force, protest wildly when that object is removed. This is completely normal. In terms of sharing, an infant doesn't yet have the capacity to understand the interpersonal skills that the concept of sharing is built upon. Don't bother trying to teach your baby this concept yet. Let her enjoy owning something. After all, she climbed over the cat to get it.

Q: *I've noticed that my son has a real interest in trying to stand. Whenever he's on my lap, he almost begs me to pull him to the standing position. Is it okay for me to allow him to stand and bounce around?*

A: It's not unusual for an eight-month-old to want to stand. As a matter of fact, some babies this age may actually start to walk around while holding onto a couch or table. Your baby will probably limit such standing if he doesn't feel ready.

Q: *What kinds of perceptive skills can I expect from my eight-month-old daughter?*

A: Your baby will continue to be flooded and sometimes even overwhelmed by sensory input. You may have already noticed that she's better able to respond to you by turning around when you call her name—even from a distance. Not only will she turn toward your voice, but she'll actively search for the origin of the noise, scanning the area until she finally focuses in on you.

Your baby will also very likely pay far more attention to the features and expressions of your face. Your voice, and the sounds you can make with it, will fascinate her. She'll study you intently, looking at your forehead, lips, eyes, and ears, and may even try to imitate your vocal patterns or expressions.

Q: *I could have sworn my eight-month-old son said, "Get me a cheese pizza," the other day. I told my wife. She told me to get some rest and stop reading conspiracy novels. What's going on here? Do I have a little genius?*

A: Don't count on your baby to order calamari for you next time you're out. Your baby's language skills are developing quickly—but not that quickly. You've probably noticed that he will often try to imitate some of the vocalizations he's been hearing. As he experiments with sound, he'll be fascinated by his own babbling. Often, random words and sounds that have meaning for us, but very likely none to the baby, will emerge. There's a possibility that he can understand a few words, such as his name or a command such as "No."

Q: *Can you help me understand how my daughter is developing interpersonally? At times she seems so grown up and at others like a sullen, miserable, cranky little pest.*

A: Still only eight months old, your baby is making great strides toward purposeful and meaningful interaction with the world. You may have noticed your baby reaching out to touch you or stroking your arm, feeling your face, or patting your leg while you hold her.

At the same time, your baby is also a bit overwhelmed by just how big the world can be. Since her power to discriminate friend and family from nonfamily is heightened, she may be gripped by fear and anxiety and respond with screams or tears when left alone or introduced to strangers.

Bolder in expressing her pleasures, desires, dislikes, and anxiety, your baby will often appear to be temperamental. Remember that a quick hug and a broad smile are often enough to send your unhappy baby into a fit of glee.

What Is Your Baby's Day Like?

Seeing the world and attacking it with enthusiasm will be one of your baby's favorite activities. Get on your hands and knees and explore it with him.

Exploring: Attentive to details, your baby will carefully examine items in his grasp and will make haste to reach distant items as well. Look for your baby to be easily distractible—exploring the bookshelf one minute and switching direction and looking intently at the TV the next. Your baby will travel great distances (by baby standards) to achieve a desired goal:

> "With vigor and enthusiasm, my daughter scoots, rolls, and crawls across the floor, striving and straining to reach her objective, to engage in her favorite activity—chewing on the dog's ear."

Engaged: You'll enjoy your baby's sense of relatedness. That is, by now you and your baby will probably be able to "talk" to each other in a variety of different "languages"—verbally, through play, by way of facial expressions, and through the use of emotionality:

> "When I can finally get the little guy to sit still for two seconds, we can actually talk to each other. I know he doesn't understand most of what

I'm saying, and I clearly haven't a clue as to what he's gleefully shrieking about, but my sense is that in many ways, we're speaking the same language."

Emotional: By this time, many babies have lost their "baby" cry (waa-waa). They now possess the capacity to howl and scream with unparalleled vigor. It'll no doubt annoy you when this occurs in the middle of the night. At the same time, even if you're not a very good comedian yourself, your baby's belly laughs will be more spectacular, and he will giggle and howl with delight more readily:

TIP

Videotape your dialogues with your baby and capture her reactions. As you watch it, you'll see two people speaking the language of love. In many ways, it's the culmination of all your hard work to date. Enjoy it!

"I've never considered myself to be very funny, but it doesn't take much to get my son to laugh. Hey, maybe I am funny. Maybe I'll quit my job and write a book."

Don't quit your day job—you're not that funny. The truth is that you don't need to be very funny. Your baby will appreciate you for just being you. Babies can very definitely feel your good intentions.

Energetic: Where does it come from? By this month, your baby is eating more, playing harder, and enjoying life to the fullest. With all this vitality, you'd almost think she was filming a Duracell commercial:

"Before I know it, my baby is out the door, motoring around the dining room. I bring her back; she leaves again. I bring her back, put the gate up, and find her trying to crawl into the garbage pail. I pick her up, she's still crawling—in midair! If her hands were sticky, I bet she could crawl up the side of the wall."

Expressive Ability: Your baby's experimentation with sound and vocalization continues. He will probably surprise you with babbling that sometimes sounds like words or phrases.

Expanded Repertoire: Your baby will be more "grown up" in her ability to express ideas, emotions, and discomforts. Since your baby's growing rapidly and is more sturdy, new games and play will be easier and safer.

Extremely Playful, Silly, and Entertaining: Look for your baby to smile and laugh spontaneously when playing alone:

> "Sometimes we just watch our daughter sitting in the middle of the room while she 'eats' one of her shoes. She screams with delight and babbles incessantly. Who knows what she's thinking."

Endearing: Many dads prefer this age to all others. Your baby is old enough so as not to need constant attention, is fun to be with and watch, and is still cuddly:

> "I'm so much more in love with my son now that we don't have to carry him around all the time while he screams bloody murder, pukes, pees, and poops. At the same time, he still has this little smooshy baby face that drives me nuts!"

Eager to Please: More so now than ever, babies in their eighth month will sense your satisfaction during playtimes and will continue to do things they think make you happy:

> "My son's crawling. He comes bouncing up to me, smiling his head off. It cracks me up, and I laugh hysterically. He crawls right up on my lap and nibbles my nose."

What's New with Dad?

For some dads, the birth of their baby, while experienced as wonderful and joyous, may also unexpectedly feel like a loss. How? Since raising a baby is like nothing you've ever experienced before, as well as time consuming and intense, many dads worry about losing their friends. Will you be able to maintain your friendships? How will your single friends respond to your new life? As a new dad, the structure of many of your relationships may change dramatically:

> "After I had my daughter, I seemed to lose touch with my friends. My college buddies, people that are really important to me, stopped coming over, and I felt a bit isolated from the outside world as I had known it. I really want to share this with them . . . you know, my pride and everything. But I guess losing friends is the price you pay for having a baby."

Or is it . . .

> "My single friends just don't get it. I don't want to see them much any-more, but they keep calling and coming over as if nothing has hap-pened in my life. It's getting to be a pain in the neck. How do I let them know I can't see them anymore?"

These changes can be disheartening, but there's good news. Nowhere is it written that you have to abandon, or be abandoned by, your peers in order to be a great dad. While it's not uncommon for new dads to experience marked changes in the nature of their relationships with others, change for the worse is not inevitable. In fact, it may be possible to take your relationships with your friends to new heights. Let's take a look at this important topic in greater detail.

Dad's Changing Relationships with Friends

Sure, your world has changed—for the better in most cases. But what does that mean for you and those who came before your baby? Friends may feel the following:

Envy: Because of what you now have—a beautiful baby and a nice relation-ship with your partner—friends can experience feelings of envy or even com-petition. These feelings can put a strain on your relationship:

> "I don't get it. Ever since my son was born, my best friend has been doing strange things. He went out and bought a high-powered sports car, and when we play catch, he throws the ball so hard, it hurts me."

Inexperienced: Single friends and those without children will marvel at your ability to pick up or change your baby. They may feel distanced, though, be-cause such skills are not in their repertoire.

Awkward: Not knowing how to behave around you, your partner, or your baby, your friends may feel strange or awkward in your home:

> "My best friend came over. We were all just sitting around watching the baby. He got up and sort of wandered around the house aimlessly, not knowing what to do with himself. It was really uncomfortable."

Or . . .

"For me, having a baby seemed to signal the beginning of a great new world for me and the end of another. My friends shied away from my baby. They didn't know what to do when they came over and saw me playing with him. They felt uncomfortable. Soon, they stopped calling."

Abandoned or Left Out: Not uncommonly, friends can resent your new relationship with your family and react against it:

"Although I'm not with him much, I've noticed that when I'm with my buddy, he seems strangely irritated with me."

In Denial: Sometimes, losing you and your attention is too much to bear:

"My best friend never called to congratulate me. When we talk, he never mentions the baby. It's weird. It's not like him at all."

Happy and Proud: Of course, many friends go on to be just that—good friends. Thrilled with your accomplishments and pleased with your success, many of your peers will be excited with you as you go along your journey.

Being There for Your Baby

As your baby grows older and becomes more independent, her risks of injury or accident increase. You've probably noticed your little daredevil crawling around the house with little regard for her own personal safety.

While bumps and bruises are normal, your job is to make sure the world your child lives in doesn't do her in. In essence, your home is a hazardous-waste site. Since your baby doesn't yet possess the capacity to discern right from wrong or safe from dangerous, she must depend on your experience and love to ensure her safe passage from one place to the next.

In this section, we'll look at some of the ways you can make your home a safer place for your baby. In the next chapter, we'll take a look at outdoor safety issues. Remember, though, there's no substitute for careful observation of your child at all times.

FOCUS: HOW TO REPAIR AND MAINTAIN YOUR RELATIONSHIPS WITH FRIENDS

While juggling friends and family can be tough, try to remember that friendships are an essential part of your life and are important for your own mental health. Your relationships will undoubtedly change, but they can change for the better.

- Don't write your friends off. Allow them instead to do what you've done—grow accustomed to your new life slowly and gradually.

- Like you do with your partner, go through the turbulence of novelty together.

- Help them get acquainted with your new life by involving them in it.

- Teach them how to hold your baby.

- Engage your friends in a play session with your baby.

- Haven't had a good talk with your best friend lately? Invite him out on a walk with you and your baby.

- While not a substitute for face-to-face meetings, use the telephone or e-mail more.

- With your partner's help, create a schedule and carve out time for your friends. Ask your partner to do the same for hers.

Making Your Home Safe for Baby

Safety-proofing your home is a full-time, ongoing job—you should update the process constantly. You've hopefully already done some safety-proofing—putting the crib together properly, installing the car seat, not allowing your baby to sleep in his bib, removing drawstrings from his clothing, and so on. Now that your baby is capable of some mobility, however, safety-proofing takes on a whole new meaning. While safety-proofing has a beginning, the end never seems to come. Since babies develop new skills daily, parents always need to be one or two steps ahead of their child's development. Because a safe home helps your child learn to trust his world and can save his life, safety-proofing, while time consuming and laborious, serves a very useful purpose. You can start by following these four tips:

Don't Put It Off: The squirming baby of today will soon become the crawling, walking, and running baby of tomorrow. Your baby's increased fine motor skills, strength, and curiosity will lead her into all kinds of adventures. Make sure the adventures are safe.

Think Like a Baby: Grow accustomed to understanding what your baby's capable of doing. Familiarize yourself with your baby's current abilities and try to anticipate what's next. Try to stay one step ahead.

Plan: Go from room to room—crawl around the floors—to anticipate what your baby would want to do, touch, pull, push, and insert in this particular room. Look up, down, around, and on the walls. Look for objects that could fall or tip over. Your goal is to try and obtain some control over the environment through which your baby journeys.

Pace Yourself: Rome wasn't built in a day (but your baby could probably tear it down over a long weekend). Although there's a lot to be done, start with the absolute necessary measures.

General Tips

Make a room-to-room sweep of the inside of your house, removing all tiny objects that can be picked up off the floor, beds, counters, ledges, and shelves and eaten (money, batteries, food, bits of plastic, garbage, papers, screws, nuts, balloons, and so on). Remove dangerous plants (all should be considered poisonous unless you know for sure they're not). Lock up weapons, including mace, pepper spray, guns, rifles, and knives. Place plastic rings on the doorknobs to prevent them from being opened by little hands.

Have a small, multipurpose fire extinguisher easily accessible in the kitchen and on every floor of your home. Plan a fire-escape route with your family and install working smoke and carbon monoxide detectors in the proper places throughout your house.

FOCUS: SAFETY-PROOFING—ROOM BY ROOM

Kitchen

- To prevent poisoning, cuts, and bruises, secure cabinets and drawers with spring-loaded safety clasps or even magnetic locks that use a magnetic key to open. These are preferable to the all-plastic clasps because they're easier to operate and break less often. As a general rule, toxic substances, like cleaning agents, should be placed high up in another cabinet or area of the house.

  > TIP: *Drilling tiny starter holes into the cabinets will help guide the miserably tiny screws that accompany the latches.*

- Plug up electrical outlets with outlet covers or plug-in plastic covers.

- Buy a stove shield. This is a plastic or metal shield that attaches to the front of the stove. The shield prevents curious hands from touching the hot surfaces of the stove and pots and pans from being pulled over.

- Place plastic rings, easily purchased at a specialty store, around the stove's burner knobs. These disks fit over the burner controls and prevent little hands from turning on the oven. This will help prevent a fire or a burn, and if you have gas burners the baby could fill the home with natural gas and asphyxiate everybody or even cause a major explosion.

- Be sure that anti-tip brackets have been installed on your oven to attach it to the wall. While this may not be a concern yet, once your baby can stand, he could pull the oven over on top of him, resulting in serious injury or even death.

- Obtain Velcro latches for your refrigerator and oven. You won't need them yet, but your baby will soon try to seek shelter in these enticingly cavernous appliances.

- Cook on the back burners and turn pot and pan handles inward toward the back of the stove. This prevents pots and pans from being knocked over onto your crawling, soon-to-be-walking baby.

- Tighten the knobs on the cabinets. Loose knobs can fall or be pulled off, leaving tempting screws available for eating.

- Consider putting a small playpen or portable crib in the kitchen so your baby can be safe while you or your partner cook.

- If your baby sits at the dinner table in a clip-on seat, make sure the area on the table in front of her is free of utensils and hot beverages. Place a chair under the clip-on seat to prevent falls in case the latch on the seat loosens.

- When using a high chair, strap your baby in so he can't slip under the tray and fall out.

- *Never* carry hot items over a crawling baby.

- Avoid drinking hot beverages when holding your baby.

- Smart use of gates can make life in the kitchen easier. Buy several. Use them to block access to dangerous areas and also to corral your baby and keep him in sight. Make sure they are securely fastened and that the baby cannot pull them down. Later you may have to make adjustments to this strategy as your child learns to use boxes or other objects to climb over them.

- Raw pieces of pasta and other difficult-to-swallow foods can choke your curious baby. Beware of small items of food dropped on the floor.

- Keep the garbage can in a cabinet or closet or secure the top with a bungee cord.

- Don't set knives or other utensils on the edges of the counters. Push everything in toward the walls. Some babies can scale cabinets even before they learn to walk.

- Coffeemakers must be pushed back on counters.

- Hanging telephone cords should be wound around a hook. Consider purchasing a retractable cord holder that takes up the slack.

- To prevent injury from falling items, the door to your pantry and other closets should be secured with a clasp. If your baby has access, he will try to climb up these shelves and will be beaned.

(cont.)

FOCUS: SAFETY-PROOFING—ROOM BY ROOM

(continued)

- Resist the urge to tip back in your chair. Little fingers and feet may be near the legs of your chair.

- Lazy Susans (rotating corner cabinets) are notorious for injuring the fingers of inquisitive babies. Make sure to latch it safely closed.

- As aesthetically pleasing as they may be, lobby to get rid of all unnecessary items on eventually reachable ledges and counters.

- Beware of the mystical power of electrical cords attached to appliances such as coffeemakers, blenders, and mixers. These snakelike objects, the pied pipers of the kitchen, will inevitably entice your child.

- Place a box of baking soda or a small, handheld fire extinguisher, approved for grease fires, near the oven.

Family Room/Study/Living Room

Use your common sense to duplicate the relevant measures taken in the kitchen—install outlet covers, remove dangerous and breakable items from ledges and shelves, use gates, and don't leave food and beverages that could injure your baby within reach. Use a playpen or portable crib for containment.

- If your television set is on a stand, make sure it isn't wobbly or capable of being pulled off. Consider Velcro or rubber feet if slippery. If the TV seems like it could easily fall over with the stand, ask a carpenter to secure the stand to the floor with bolts. If your VCR sits high atop the TV, secure it with Velcro.

- Power cords to lamps and TVs should be hidden or rolled up in a special power cord container that can be purchased at a baby specialty or hardware store.

- Hanging articles, like pictures, pose a risk because they can be pulled down by your baby. Remove them or rid the room of climbable objects.

- Fireplaces should have glass doors or other protective covers installed. Use an elongated U-shaped plastic bar (this can be purchased at a baby specialty or hardware store and is usually used to secure kitchen or bathroom cabinets) to keep the two glass doors closed. Even so, when a fire is blazing, you'll need to keep your baby away from the fireplace; the glass doors can get hot enough to burn your baby too. Remove fireplace hardware.

  Purchase protective padding for the corners and edges of the hearth. If the hearth sticks up above the level of the floor, it can be an obstacle for your baby to trip over, and the corners and edges can cause serious injury if fallen upon.

- Coins that fall out of your pockets and end up in the couch cushions are a choking risk and should routinely be collected and spent.

- Freestanding book cabinets, a popular climbing temptation, should be fastened to the wall.

- Be careful of rocking chairs. They have a way of squashing little fingers and toes.

- Your coffee table hates your baby. Sharp edges or corners should be protected with large rubber bumpers, which are easily purchased at a baby specialty store.

- Your baby likes to eat the walls and furniture. Make sure that none of your walls or furniture is coated with lead paint. Even if lead paint has been overcoated with latex, it can sometimes shed as dust as the newer paint peels or cracks.

- Blinds or curtains that have long cords are a strangulation hazard. Small plastic hooks, used to hang the cords around, should be installed next to each window.

(cont.)

FOCUS: SAFETY-PROOFING—ROOM BY ROOM

(continued)

Bathroom

- The only time your baby should be in this room is when you're using the facilities or if you're bathing him. When not in use, the door to the bathroom should be closed.

- Cabinets and drawers should be secured with plastic latches.

- Fingernail polish and remover, hair compounds, and many other toiletries and beauty products are very poisonous. Lock them up.

- The toilet lid must be down and secured with a child-proof latch. (These are often adult-proof—my four-year-old has to open the toilet for me.)

- Never leave standing water in the sink or bathtub. The shower door must be closed. Buckets must be emptied of water or cleaning solution as soon as you've completed the job.

- Medicines should be stored securely in a locked closet. You can lock any closet by purchasing a sliding lock-bolt at the hardware store. Designate one closet for dangerous items, such as medications.

- Turn the heat down on your hot water heater so that even when the shower or tub is on full hot, scalding is impossible. Alternatively, purchase scald protectors that can be installed into the water spigots. Buy an inflatable spout guard to prevent your baby from bumping or cutting her head in the tub. Place a rubber bath mat or nonslip decals in the bottom of the tub or shower.

- Babies like to lean against the tub while waiting to get in. Make sure your bath mat has rubber on the bottom to prevent it from sliding out from under your baby.

Laundry Room

Laundry rooms typically contain power cords, large machines, water, and buckets full of dangerous chemicals—not exactly a vacation spot for your baby. Gate it off or keep the door closed at all times.

Dining Room

Since the dining room often contains expensive china and other treasured items, your baby really shouldn't be in there. Like a bull in a china shop, your baby will have his way with all your family's nice things, and there may be little left but the broken bits and pieces of previously beautiful antiquities. Gate the room off.

Stairs

For obvious reasons, stairs are notoriously treacherous for your baby. Serious injury can result should your baby fall down them.

- Access to stairs must be denied by way of careful supervision and closed doors and gates.

- Your crawling baby may have access to a landing that leads to a staircase and can easily fit through spaces in the railings. Buy a stiff plastic sheet or netting (obtainable through baby specialty shops) that fits over the railings supporting the banisters.

Basement

The only reason for your baby to be in the basement is if it's part of your living space. If so, follow the same rules as for the family room. Make sure the doors to the furnace room or workshop are secured. If the basement is not finished, your baby has no business being there.

(cont.)

FOCUS: SAFETY-PROOFING—ROOM BY ROOM

(continued)

Hallways

Babies love to race down hallways. Make sure electrical outlets are plugged and access to stairs is denied.

Bedrooms (Including Baby's Room)

Use the same safety precautions common to other rooms we've reviewed. Take care to safeguard the windows (open them from the top, install window guards, or remove the cranks from casement windows) and curtain cords. Gate off closets or other potentially dangerous areas. Remove power cords, floor lamps, and dangerous or breakable items from the dressers and ledges. Plug electrical outlets.

- Dressers can severely injure or kill a child who pulls one over onto himself. Keep the drawers closed. While you're in your baby's dressers and closets, inspect his clothing and remove or cut off any drawstrings. These can *easily* strangle your baby.

- Make sure any dresser knobs or handles are securely fastened because loose screws will tempt your child.

Bonding with Baby

After securing the home, you may feel more like a warden than a father. However, you still need to play with your little prisoner and teach her at the same time. Remember, babies learn from play, and so you are teaching her something whether you know it or not. Your child will be starting to try and

- Pillows and fluffy, heavy comforters can smother an infant. Don't use them. Dress your baby as warmly as necessary for comfortable sleep so that you won't need to rely on dangerous blankets and covers.

- Make sure your baby's crib isn't under or near any objects that can tip over, hanging pictures, power cords, heaters, heavy items, fire hazards, or windows.

- To prevent your baby from falling out (or climbing out) of her crib, lower the mattress when you notice your baby can easily reach the top rail.

- Change the filter in your baby's air conditioner several times each summer.

- If you are using a humidifier, fill it with cool to warm water—never hot. If the baby does manage to knock it over, hot water will burn him.

- Periodically tighten all the bolts and screws on your baby's crib.

- Windows should be screened to protect your baby from insects.

- Make sure that stuffed animals are not leaking and that the noses and ears of her teddy bears are fastened securely.

- Inspect rattles and other loud, shaking toys for damage.

Finally, only through continuous inspection can you safeguard your baby's environment. Periodically review your work and fix broken clasps and locks. You must also watch to see how effective some of your safety modifications are as the baby matures. Some babies look at locks as challenging puzzles to solve. Always stay on your toes.

talk, and even if she is not quite there yet, it is a good time to begin teaching her names of different things.

The parts of the body are an easy lesson to teach. You don't have to teach her enough to pass an anatomy midterm, but the basics are always good. Start with the parts of the face. Point to each part as you say the name. Use both your face as well as the baby's. She can't see her own, but she can see what a nose looks like on you. Then you can show her where her nose is located. Continue with hands, feet, and the rest of the body. Ask her, "Where is Jessica's nose?" "Where is daddy's hair?" Be sure to smile and acknowledge her right answers with praise. If she is wrong, give her encouragement.

From the parts of the body, you can move on to clothing as you get her dressed. Or you can teach her the parts of a car or airplane using toys. As she begins to speak, you can then ask questions like "What is this?" as you point to something to elicit a verbal response rather than a pointing finger.

Your name game can continue around the house. Crawl around with your little one, identifying things as you go—door, rug, cat, and so on. This game teaches the child the names of items and also builds a relationship of learning. She knows she can turn to you for answers to things she does not know or understand.

MEDICATIONS AND ALCOHOL

Without thinking, many of us expose our kids to dangers. Common, everyday items can pose a serious threat to the health and welfare of your baby. Here are a few:

• There are many different kinds of alcohol. Not only does alcohol come in the form of adult beverages, it's also found in many items around the house—cosmetics, rubbing alcohol, various elixirs, and mouthwash. To your baby, alcohol—any type—is a poisonous drug that can cause convulsions, coma, and death. Don't give your baby alcoholic beverages, and don't allow him any access to them whatsoever.

• Most antidepressant medications can be extremely hazardous to your baby. In overdose, they can cause cardiac arrhythmias, coma, convulsions, hallucinations, and death by cardiac arrest.

• Acetaminophen, a commonly used analgesic, is a particularly toxic drug when taken in high doses. Liver failure may result.

• Aspirin, another common analgesic, is very dangerous when misused. In overdose, aspirin can cause rapid breathing, sweating, fever, vomiting, disorientation, kidney damage, convulsions, and coma.

Growing Together

Wow! In this chapter, we covered some fairly scary but necessary topics—how to prevent your baby from being poisoned, burned, clunked, squashed, and so on. Who said being a dad was easy? Growing together also means facing the harsh realities of life. The good news is that prevention is clearly the key—particularly since accidents claim so many lives. In the next chapter, we'll look at ways in which you can help your baby stay safe outdoors, and we'll explore what's going on in your relationship with your partner.

WINDOWS

Every summer, the media report multiple fatalities and horrific, lifelong injuries due to falls from windows. It's your responsibility to prevent this tragedy from occurring. Children are naturally drawn to open windows. Often recommended are bars that fit over windows to prevent falls. This can be an expensive and difficult solution. One way to prevent falls is to open the tops of the windows rather than the bottoms. Make sure to keep climbable furniture away from windows. As your baby grows older and stronger, remove the hand cranks from casement windows, storing them in a place easily accessible to you.

Children make your life important.

—ERMA BOMBECK

CHAPTER

10

The Ninth Month

What a "workday" your baby has! Busy all the time, she will be better at getting around and will employ new skills—or old but updated behaviors—to better reach out to the world. Your child's bigger, better, and faster status may find you saying, "Who can keep up with this kid?"

Since your baby will be more adept at concentrating and focusing on a given task, the ninth month is a great time to explore new forms of play and games. It's also a good time to review your own sense of well-being:

> "I'd been spending so much time with my baby that I was neglecting some very important areas of my life—bathing, eating, going to work. In all seriousness, though, I finally realized it's also important to keep up with myself, so to speak."

Sometimes it's easy to lose sight of your own needs as you get caught up in the joys and pains of raising a child. In this chapter, we'll focus on, among other things, updating your ability to interact smoothly with your family.

What's New with Your Baby?

This is a very exciting time for your baby. He should be moving around the house with a new confidence. Your baby will be moderately graceful in attempting to manipulate his body. Standing, creeping along while holding the couch, sitting down—all these behaviors, combined with his new intensity of focus and concentration, will delight you. Your baby's ability to learn from his mistakes is incredible:

> "With all the grace of an intoxicated gazelle, my son staggers up to grab the couch, spins around and falls flat on his butt. To top it off, he howls with laughter. It's fun to watch him learn how to control his body, and I must say, he's getting better and better at it."

Keeping an eye on your baby becomes hard work:

> "Before I knew it, she had crawled out of the room and was heading up the stairs! I felt like saying, 'Hey, as long as you're heading up, could you take the laundry with you?' She just laughs at me. I'm sure if she could talk, she'd probably say, 'Hey, c'mon fat boy, just try to catch me.' After spending a day with her, I'm winded. I need to eat better. No more hot dogs and milk shakes for me!"

Developmental Milestones

While crawling is probably still your baby's main form of transportation, look for terrific advances in her ability to stand and attempts to ambulate. A few determined babies are even walking by nine months. Coordination, language, and emotional reactions will also be more polished.

Motor Strength: Crawling quickly and with greater skill, your mischievous baby will be scurrying in every direction. In addition to his improved ability to navigate, your baby will also be able to coordinate behaviors that one month ago were impossible. Don't be too surprised if your baby crawls while holding a toy in one hand. And learn to keep a close watch on your baby, or you may find him starting up a flight of stairs! Your baby will also have far better control over his limbs and digits. Fine motor skills will be enhanced as well, and he will likely be able to do two things at once—play with a toy with one hand, for example, while destroying a piece of fine china with the other.

With a little help from a chair, couch, or table, your baby may become an expert at standing up. He may be able to inch along a bit, stepping cautiously to the left or right while holding on to the furniture. In order to secure a desired object on the floor, he may also be able to bend down while standing and have less difficulty going from a standing position to sitting.

Vocalization: Your baby's language skills will surprise you. Look for the production of two-syllable sounds as well as the ability to alter the volume, intensity, rate, and pitch of sounds.

Sensory Perception: Not surprisingly, your baby will want to touch everything—being involved with everything around her is a priority. Your baby's hand-eye coordination will be markedly improved. Look for your baby to spend great amounts of time experimenting with the movement, shape, and size of things.

Psychological: The ninth month brings with it several new and important phenomena related to emotional development. Your baby's sense of autonomy and separateness becomes more evident, which may manifest as fear of strangers. Since she is developing a sense of individuality, look for your baby to begin protesting things she doesn't like very much—eating, dressing, bathing, wearing a diaper, or being limited in her ability to crawl into a dangerous place.

A longer attention span will help your baby concentrate and focus on current tasks in a way not previously possible. She will be able to sit for longer periods of time, play games with you, and perhaps search for a desired but hidden object.

What Is Your Baby's Day Like?

Spending time with your baby may exhaust you. Let's take a look at some common but rarely voiced questions:

Q: *Why does my baby chew up and eat my* Sports Illustrated?
A: While your baby is likely not yet a sports aficionado, he still enjoys putting things into his mouth. Also, there's nothing like the sound of ripping, crinkling paper to drive your baby wild with pleasure. As your baby's sense of curiosity and adventure grows, so will his appetite for newer experiences. Unfortunately, eating paper is a choking hazard, and it should be discouraged. You should keep your magazines in the bathroom, on top of the toilet, where they belong.

Q: *How can I get my baby to stop crawling into the fireplace?*

A: You haven't read the previous chapter! (Do this now.) Your baby will crawl into any place that needs exploring. Babies love to get themselves into tight spots. The fireplace is very attractive because of its interesting appearance. Your baby may also happen upon it while trying to look at herself in the protective glass doors that you should have had installed already. Make sure the brickwork in front of the fireplace is covered with a soft cover to prevent your baby from injuring herself.

Q: *Will my child always have the attention span of a fruit fly?*

A: As your child grows older, the distractibility so commonly found during the first seven or eight months should start to disappear. In time, your baby should be better able to focus and attend to things for increasingly greater amounts of time. Playing peek-a-boo games or hand clapping should hold his attention.

Q: *My baby's standing great. When will she walk?*

A: Your baby will grow more stable on her feet, more adept at moving around, and better coordinated. While some babies, especially strong crawlers, take their time before walking, others may start at a very young age. Look for your baby to learn to hold a couch or table and start inching along.

Q: *What's the deal with my daughter's coordination—or should I say lack thereof? How will she ever learn to throw the javelin?*

A: Fear not. Look for a steady increase in her ability to move and grasp with improved coordination. This repertoire of more coordinated movements may soon propel your baby to new heights of havoc, destruction, and exploration of the far reaches of the inside of your VCR.

Q: *My son seems to have an affinity for putting his tongue on the electrical outlets. Thank goodness they're covered. I tell him not to, but he ignores me. Why is he doing this?*

A: Even at this age, babies understand some of the subtle differences between "Yes, by all means, go ahead and put your tongue in the outlet" and "Heavens no, don't put your tongue in the outlet!" and will rebel against your rules. Your baby's intense curiosity, improved ability to manipulate his environment, and adventuresome spirit will all work together to create a person who rarely exercises good judgment. Thank goodness he has you.

Q: *I've noticed that my daughter can remember things a bit better recently. Good for her. Unfortunately for us, she remembers not liking to take baths and eating. What's this all about?*

A: The days of you and your partner being completely in control of your helpless little baby will soon grind to a distressing—but fascinating—halt. The older your baby gets, the more she'll remember liking something a lot and wanting more and disliking something and wanting nothing to do with it.

Health Issues: Ninth-Month Pediatric Visit

The ninth-month visit will be much like the others. Your pediatrician may choose to spend more time assessing your baby's developmental milestones but will also perform a complete examination. If you have any concerns, be sure to ask questions.

Measuring Height, Weight, and Head Circumference: As is typical for these visits, the doctor or nurse will attempt to check your baby's height, weight, and head circumference. Your little propeller-driven road cruiser will likely resist. Regardless, the doctor will assign a percentile to the figures, comparing the measurements to other same-age babies. All children develop and grow at different rates. Feel free, however, to ask your doctor what the measurements are and whether she has any concerns.

History: After the measurements, you'll be asked how things have been going and whether there have been any noticeable problems with your baby. Your pediatrician will also want to know how your baby is feeding, sleeping, and acting. Feel free to join your partner in describing how home life has been. Since two people living together may have different views of how things are going, it's important for your pediatrician to obtain your perspective as well.

Physical Examination: As usual, you can expect your pediatrician to perform a thorough examination. He will check your baby's heart for abnormal sounds or murmurs, lungs for breathing sounds, mouth and throat for any abnormalities, eyes for reactivity and clarity, ears for infection, and nose for blockages. He will also assess your baby's general well-being, neurological status, musculoskeletal system for tone and strength, abdomen for hernias, extremities, and genital and excretory systems.

In order to assess your baby's development, your pediatrician may also spend some time playing with her—testing responsiveness, coordination, hearing, speech, and strength. Again, feel free to ask questions if you have any concerns. At the end of the meeting, you may be given the OK to begin new foods and instructed to give your baby vitamins or fluoride drops. The doctor may test your baby's blood count by way of a pinprick.

What's New with Mom and Dad?

Even in families where both parents work, mom may still be the primary caregiver. Odds are that she has her finger on the pulse of what's going with your baby on an hour-by-hour, even minute-by-minute, basis. By this time, she's no doubt accustomed to the routine of caring for your baby and you as well. But is she enjoying it?

Reprinted with Special Permission of King Feature Syndicate

Now is a good time to take stock of your relationship with your partner. How's your partner coping with motherhood? Is she happy? Does she feel overwhelmed? Does she feel like you're involved and pulling your own weight? Is she getting your support and thanks for all her hard work? Let's take a look.

While many of the stresses that characterized the first few months of your baby's life at home are gone, or are at least markedly improved, the fact that your baby has "settled in" can in itself have a negative impact on your relationship with your partner. In fact, as is often the case, once moms and dads have no common "enemy"—baby screaming all night, spitting up constantly, colic, and so on—they may be far less likely to rally together.

The reality is, however, that you two need to be on the same wavelength now more than ever. The challenges of raising an emotionally healthy, well-adjusted person are great. Your baby's growth and development depend heavily on the health and integrity of your relationship with your partner. Both you and your partner should be working together to solve a problem, yet emotionally you two may have gone your separate ways—you may even be working against each other!

While it's important to recognize individuality and autonomy, too often moms and dads during the latter parts of the first year can drift a bit apart. For example, dad focuses on work, while a stay-at-home mom raises the baby, cares for the home, and looks after dad. The routine becomes firm and unyielding, and partners may take each other for granted or worse:

> "It's not just she and I together anymore—there's my son. It's not fair to him that we're always fighting. He's not learning how to be in a good relationship by looking at us."

If the two of you are leading so-called parallel lives, consider questioning your routine with each other. Since early parenthood can be a time of great happiness and satisfaction as well as mundane and boring routine, you'll want to share your pleasures as well as your pains. Take the time to review some of the problems in your relationship—they'll affect all of you.

Being There for Your Baby

In this section, we'll continue our discussion of safety-proofing. As you've probably guessed, the outdoors is an entirely new world for your baby—one whose size (even if it's just your driveway) can be enough to overwhelm and confuse your baby. Nonetheless, as your baby's locomotive skills improve, he'll be far more likely and willing to engage in risky behaviors. It therefore falls upon you to make outside as safe as possible.

FOCUS: WORKING ON YOUR RELATIONSHIP

Many couples experience the same problems. Below are some examples, as well as ways to discuss important issues:

- **Selfishness, rigidity, and entrenchment:** Some couples become so firmly fixed in their day-to-day lives that they end up living in a world in which only *they* "fit" or belong.

- **Boredom:** It's not uncommon for moms and dads to become understimulated in their roles as parents.

- **Responsibility:** Whose responsibility is it to care for the house, care for the baby, and make money? Hopefully, both of you will be sharing some of these responsibilities.

- **Leading separate lives:** Sometimes, before you and your partner are even slightly aware, you and she have emotionally or symbolically moved into different rooms of the house.

- **Neglecting each other's emotional states:** Commonly, moms and dads fail to attend to the important issues of emotionality and conflict in each other's lives. This can happen through "benign neglect" or forgetting to listen to each other. Remember to keep the lines of communication open.

- **Taking the other person for granted:** It's easy to assume that you're all that matters and that everything will be in its place when you get home. If your partner is home with the baby, you may fail to appreciate the stress in her life. Conversely, you may be feeling underappreciated for all the backbreaking work you do on the job.

- **Lack of empathy:** When you and your partner cease feeling for each other, you're in deep trouble. Ignoring, for example, her feelings about a horrible experience at work while telling her to "tough it out" does little to advance your relationship.

- **Lack of communication:** Conflict often begins and ends with a lack of communication. The negative effects of failing to engage with your partner about a given issue can quickly snowball.

These are just a few of the many distressing but common issues that often arise in relationships. Many combinations of these issues will emerge as you, your partner, and your baby grow together. As you all grow, remember that issues, conflicts, and problems tend to arise gradually rather than appearing spontaneously. How can you prevent the buildup of conflict? Sometimes just raising the issues can be helpful.

These questions can be used as a springboard for a deeper discussion of other issues. Without blame or accusation, ask each other . . .

Are we helping each other?

Are we fulfilling each other's needs?

Do you know what I do at work?

When was the last time I told you how tedious or horrible the worst day of this week was?

What's the emotional or symbolic significance of the baby in our lives?

What impact does the baby have on our daily routines?

Do we still talk with each other?

How can we become better at listening to each other?

Are there things I'm doing that really bother you?

Are we taking each other seriously?

When was the last time we laughed together?

How can we improve our sex lives together?

What can we do to improve our relationship?

Like anything else, the substance of a relationship is usually not all negative. You and your partner should meet from time to time to discuss how your lives have been inexorably changed for the better. Do your best to facilitate communication with your partner, try not to lose your collective sense of humor, go out on a date with each other, and don't take yourselves too seriously—you're both still learning and growing together.

Safety-Proofing the Outside

The "art" of safety-proofing, while labor intensive, is really a labor of love. As a dad, you should always be thinking, "What's the little dickens going to be getting into next?" The ongoing nature of the job should keep everyone on their toes. Safety-proofing the outdoors is really no different than safety-proofing the inside of your house, except that it's pretty hard to round up all the bees and wasps. Try to stay a step or two ahead of your baby. You can start by reviewing the four tips I introduced in the previous chapter:

- **Don't put it off.** Your baby may be initially overwhelmed and thus hesitant out of doors, but this won't last long. The sand that terrified her yesterday she'll be eating today.

- **Think like a baby.** Babies want to touch everything they see, and everything they touch, they want to put in their mouths. Your baby will lunge for and try to ingest snails, broken glass, and other equally horrifying things. Stay one step ahead of her.

- **Plan.** Be familiar with the lay of the land. Stroll around the outside of your house and try to anticipate what your baby would want to do, touch, pull, push, and insert in each particular area of the yard. Look up, down, and around. Look for objects that could fall or tip over. Your goal is to try to obtain some control over the environment through which your baby journeys.

- **Pace yourself.** Although there's a lot to be done, start with the absolute necessary measures.

Play Update

You've probably noticed an intensification in your baby's desire to interact and play. Try the following games. They're designed to enhance motor, sensory, and emotional skills and are fun besides.

"Release" Games: These games, albeit simple, help your baby learn how to let go of objects—perhaps even helping him to start learning how to share or give. Get out a big pot, mixing bowl, or metal pan and some blocks. Hold the blocks over the pot and release them. Your baby will like the sound produced by the objects hitting the pot and will mimic you.

Mirror Games: Babies love to look at themselves in the mirror. Show your baby her facial features and how cute they are. Point in the mirror to your baby's mouth and encourage her to touch the mirror and her own mouth. This game helps develop your baby's self-image, motor skills, and abstract thinking.

Peek-a-Boo: Every time you play this game with your baby, you'll help him develop a sense of object constancy—the notion that although you're temporarily out of view, you haven't and won't go away.

Singing: Most babies love to be sung to. Singing also helps you brush up on your near perfect operatic voice.

And for extra fun . . .

Put Your Baby on Your Shoulders: Hold her upper arms or shoulders tightly. She'll love it! Make sure to walk in front of a mirror. If you can possibly help it, don't smash her head on the door frame.

Bonding with Baby

If you haven't already begun, now is the time to start reading to your baby. Before he may not have sat still enough on your lap to be able to read a book. However, now his concentration should be improved. Choose an appropriate book. *War and Peace* is not one. Instead select one with a high ratio of pictures to words. Reading picture books will build on the name games you started last month. Be sure to point out something from each picture, such as a dog or a car, to teach him more names. Some books will only list names and not tell a story. While those are fine on occasion, you should read at least one storybook a day to your baby. You will be not only teaching him names but also to speak in a conversational tone with complete sentences, as babies need to hear the structure of a sentence. By this stage, your baby may like to look at books on his own. Just make sure you give him a board book with the thick cardboard pages so he doesn't tear the book or eat it. While not always possible for busy fathers, a scheduled story time is a tradition you should start now, and is one that will last for years and your child will look forward to.

FOCUS: HOW TO MAKE THE OUTSIDE SAFE FOR YOUR BABY

Perhaps the most important safety step you can take is to deny your baby independent access to the outside. Many nine-month-olds have a way of leaning against doors and gates and actually getting them to open. Make sure all doors leading outside are secured.

Weather

Protect Your Baby from Harsh Weather Conditions: It doesn't take much for a baby's skin to burn. Make certain you use a sunscreen especially created for babies (a hat with a visor would be nice too).

Dress Your Baby Warm: In the winter, making certain to protect his fingers and toes from the cold.

The Driveway and the Street

Beware of Walkers: Walkers have received a less than favorable safety rating for good reason. Inside the house, babies ramble over to the stairs and plummet to certain injury. Outside, baby's scurrying little feet have a way of getting away from you quickly. Be sure to watch your baby carefully. Don't assume that she can't get too far. Before you know it, your baby's at the end of the driveway directing traffic.

Secure the Garage: There's no reason for your baby to be in the garage. Keep the doors closed. If your garage doors are electric, make sure they stop going down with the slightest bump.

Lock Your Baby's Stroller Wheels: When you're not pushing the baby, secure the stroller by locking the wheels. This will prevent embarrassing and potentially dangerous situations.

Beware of Cars: Common sense tells you not to be anywhere near cars, especially ones that are backing up. Avoid walking with your baby in heavily trafficked areas.

Water and Patio Safety

Secure the Pool: It must be fenced and secured with a locking gate. Consider a self-closing, self-locking gate—which can be installed by any fence company. Consider investing in a pool alarm that sounds an intense siren if the water in the pool is disturbed. If you own a kiddie pool, empty it every day. This not only will keep your baby safe but also will discourage wild animals from stopping by the house for a drink. Emptying the kiddie pool will also help to prevent bugs from hanging around your yard. Never, ever leave your baby unattended in a kiddie pool, not even for one second.

Never Leave Buckets or Cans Full of Water: Your baby can drown in these.

Secure Barbecues and Grills: These should be kept clean to discourage bugs and animals from congregating. Also, use common sense when cooking. Your baby should be nowhere near the grill.

Yard

Discourage Bugs: Bugs are unavoidable. However, consider using a nontoxic baby bug spray to protect your baby from discomfort and from the potentially serious infectious diseases associated with mosquito bites and ticks. Remember that bugs are drawn to water. Empty kiddie pools and any other standing water daily and clean your grill or barbecue frequently because bugs are drawn to greasy things. Bees and wasps like to live inside the covers of grills and on sunny surfaces.

Beware of Plants/Grass/Mushrooms: If given the opportunity, your crawling baby will try to eat grass, dirt, plants, and mushrooms. While you shouldn't raise your child to be fearful of nature or afraid of getting a little dirt in his mouth, remember that lawns are frequently treated with chemicals and plants and that mushrooms are often poisonous. Dirt can harbor parasites and insects.

Beware of Sandboxes: Unless the sandbox is covered when not being used, I tend to discourage young babies from playing in them. Cats frequently

(cont.)

FOCUS: HOW TO MAKE THE OUTSIDE SAFE FOR YOUR BABY

(continued)

use sandboxes as litter boxes, sometimes depositing parasite-infested feces in the sand, which can then be easily passed on to your baby.

Wash Up After Outdoor Play: Babies should be washed after playing in the grass and dirt, especially if you live in an area where ticks, which carry diseases, are common.

Park

Use the Appropriate Car Seat When Traveling: By this time, if your baby is around 20 pounds, she is likely in a larger car seat. Make certain it's properly installed and rests firmly against the seat of the car. Make sure the safety belt is snug against your baby. The safest place for the car seat is in the middle of the backseat of the car.

Never Leave Your Baby in a Car Alone: Not even for a minute.

Never Assume Your Baby Is Safe in a Swing: To prevent strangulation or falls, never leave your baby unattended.

Make Sure Your Baby Is Playing in an Age-Appropriate Area: Since bike-riding or running children can easily trample your baby, don't allow older children to play near your little all-terrain vehicle.

Never Leave Your Child: Especially with a stranger, for any reason.

Wash Your Baby's Hands Carefully After Every Play Session: Hand washing is the best way to prevent the spread of infection. There's no telling what they've gotten into. This holds true for petting zoos, feeding the ducks, or just playing in the dirt.

Never Allow Your Baby to Touch or Pet Unknown Animals.

And remember, with a bit of common sense and some good supervision, your baby can enjoy the outdoors safely.

In addition to reading, continue to play with your baby. He may enjoy playing with plastic building blocks. Several companies, such as LEGO, make big blocks suitable for this young age. Don't expect him to build a giant castle or a two-story house right off. In fact, to begin with, you may be building things so he can knock them down. Start by showing him how the blocks connect. Then help him to build towers straight up. After some practice, he'll begin putting blocks together himself.

Another fun activity for your baby is singing songs. While you may have already done this, now start adding actions to the songs to teach her coordination of words and actions. A good example of such a song is "The Itsy Bitsy Spider." Use your fingers to simulate a spider climbing a web as you sing, "The itsy, bitsy spider climbed up the water spout." Then use your hands and arms, starting straight up and lowering them slowly while wiggling your fingers to represent rain as you continue, "Down came the rain and washed the spider out." Put your arms arched in a bow over your head—"Out came the sun and dried up all the rain." Do the spider climbing again—"And the itsy bitsy spider climbed up the spout again." Other fun songs to sing with actions are "Ring Around the Rosie" and "Pop Goes the Weasel."

Growing Together

Being a dad is hard work! Obviously, there's far more to raising a child than sitting around and making silly faces. Along with all your other responsibilities, you need to remember to look after your own health. In the next chapter, along with a review of what your baby will be up to, I'll review things you can do to ensure your sanity and physical well-being. We'll also take a look at some inappropriate parental behaviors.

Raising children is a creative endeavor,

an art rather than a science.

—BRUNO BETTELHEIM

The Tenth Month

Get ready for the ride of a lifetime! Your 10-month-old baby—really more a child than an infant—might be characterized as a tiny tornado. Buzzing around the house, getting into all sorts of mischief, your little twister is probably crawling wildly. Get ready—he will soon be moving on to more mature forms of locomotion.

Don't count on your home being a very peaceful, laid-back place. Your baby will probably be into everything. Since he is better able to get around and may be exercising a fiercely independent attitude, don't plan on sitting down much; chasing after your baby will become a full-time job. Along with your baby's invigorated status, look for hints that he is beginning to understand you a bit better. To the extent a 10-month-old can use his limited comprehensive skills, look for your baby to "disobey" you on a regular basis. For some dads, this can set off a series of negative feelings and sometimes even inappropriate behaviors:

> "I know this sounds ridiculous, but babies are damned selfish. I know they don't mean to be, but no matter how hard I yell, 'No!' or something to that effect, my son just keeps on doing what he's doing. It's infuriating. I hate to babysit because I can never sit down. Sometimes I think I get way too angry."

In this chapter and the next, we'll take a look at a number of issues that can result in excess anger, domestic violence, and other inappropriate behaviors.

We'll also be taking a look at some things dads can do for themselves to stay fit and happy.

What's New with Your Baby?

In the tenth month, cruising around and exploring is the name of the game for your baby. Your baby will be anxious to see the rest of the world with little regard for your fatigue or previously made plans.

Developmental Milestones

While your baby may still insist on getting around by crawling, look for her to take bigger steps toward walking. With determination and unbelievable amounts of energy and coordination, your baby will likely surprise you with all the new things she can do. Improvements in your baby's ability to communicate will also be apparent.

Motor Strength: Not only will your baby probably be able to pull himself up to a standing position more readily, but he probably will be making serious attempts to walk. Your baby will spend a great deal of time in an upright position, grabbing furniture, your legs, or any other object that looks as if it might help him stand. By the end of the tenth month, a few babies may be able to walk on their own!

Your baby will also have far better control of his body and will probably be able to flip over readily, crawl quickly, stop, then turn around, and possibly get into a sitting position from lying on his belly. His enhanced coordination and refined motor skills will help your baby learn to pick up objects, clap hands, and do several things at once. Better control over virtually all aspects of his body will help him negotiate in an increasingly complex world.

Vocalization: Look for increasing amounts of two-syllable words or phrases. Your baby may be able to say (but not fully comprehend) "dada" or even "mama."

Sensory Perception: Your baby's hand-eye coordination will enable her to explore and examine items of different shapes, sizes, and consistencies. Your baby should eventually be able to bring two objects together in front of her body and drop them. She may be able to find objects hidden under clothing, blankets, or pillows and will likely be able to understand that just because something is hidden, it isn't necessarily gone forever. As usual, she will want to touch and be involved with everything around her. Name recognition is enhanced as well.

Psychological: The tenth month brings with it several new and important emotional developments. Fear and stranger anxiety may become more developed. Since he is continuing to develop a sense of individuality, look for intense howls of protest when you remove an object from your baby's hands. Although still distractible, look for a longer attention span. Your baby may cry if he sees you leaving the room.

What Is Your Baby's Day Like?

Let's track some of the highlights of a typical morning in the life of you and your 10-month-old baby:

5:30 A.M.: "It's 5:30 in the morning, I think. My wife is still in bed. I'm somewhere between in bed and getting out of bed. The baby started having a reasonably calm conversation with invisible people, in his crib, at about 4:45 A.M. He's not so calm now. He and the invisible people are having a huge argument. He's screaming at them. He wants out. I'm compelled to get up since my wife was up with him at around three—so she says. She's pretending to be asleep right now, so who knows what the truth really is."

5:34 A.M.: "I walk into the baby's room, only to find him teetering precariously over the crib rail. I guess it's time to put the mattress down a notch or two. He couldn't even reach the darned top of the rail just a few weeks ago. As I approach him, I also notice that sometime between eight last night, when he went to sleep, and now, he's managed to gnaw a sizable portion of nontoxic enamel off the headpiece of his crib. I know he's the culprit because there's a hunk of paint stuck to his cheek. I politely ask him why he chewed up his crib and point to the badly damaged area. He just smiles and mutters something completely unintelligible. It sounds like 'Motorola.'"

5:37 A.M.: "I lift him out of the crib and take him over to the changing table. I pull off his diaper, only to find a foul-smelling load. It's alive. It looks up at me. I believe, in my heart of hearts, that it is smiling sarcastically. I believe that this poop told my son not to cooperate with me. My son, who never listens to me, listened to that poop. He won't keep still for me. Poop is everywhere. I need a backhoe to clean him off."

5:41 A.M.: "I try to lift him up off the changing table, but he wriggles out of my arms and almost falls on his head. He's come a long way, but he still doesn't have the height thing down yet. Once firmly down, he moves quickly to the door and scurries down the hallway toward the stairs. By this time, I've been out of bed for seven minutes and am still hoping that I'm dreaming. I leap after him and catch up to him at the top of the stairs just as he's about to take the plunge. I scoop him up with one hand, catching him directly in his center of gravity. Not bad. I've been practicing. Within the first few minutes of this new day, I've already used the extra daily energy God has allocated for me today. It was supposed to have lasted the entire day. It's a bad sign. I will request more."

5:44 A.M.: "I've been out of bed for 10 minutes. Seems like longer. In the family room, he claws his way out of my arms and is again crawling around on the floor. I rush immediately to the exit I think he's most likely to head for, turn my back for an instant, and close the security gate. I turn around. He, of course, has already left the room, finding the other exit more interesting. But to what area of the state has he gone? I walk into the kitchen. 'Everything's in order,' I mutter to myself. He couldn't have been through here. I frantically look back in the family room to see if he's wedged himself under a chair or couch or if he's behind the TV set again. I notice that the TV set has been turned on. I look up toward the ceiling. He's not there."

5:47 A.M.: "I head back into the kitchen, where my ears pick up a faint distress call from a distant cupboard. I go to the sink and try to open the cabinets, but they're locked shut and I don't have the access code. I run back and open the pantry. My son, who's in far less distress than me, has become wedged between the folds of the pantry doors. He doesn't seem particularly disturbed by his inability to move since he's too busy tearing the tops off raisin boxes and stuffing the cardboard tops into his mouth."

5:49 A.M.: "I feel like calling 911 to have myself taken away. He's now screaming loudly, unhappy with the technique I employed to extract the wet cardboard chunks from his mouth. I bring him back into the family room and secure the doors—with a blowtorch. I put him down and hand him his bottle. He drinks some. I turn the TV on, turn around, and head for my comfortable chair. Just as I sit down, the TV goes off. Using a large toy bucket full of electronic toys that chirp, beep, sing, and scream all night long, my son has pulled himself up and is pushing the on-off button to the TV, repeatedly. I'd like to turn off *his* 'on' button. I get up, take him away from the TV, and turn it back on. I head for my chair. He crawls over to the toy bucket and punches it. The toy bucket starts chirping, beeping, singing, and screaming, making it nearly impossible for me to enjoy my morning workout—watching other people doing aerobics.

"I scan the room restlessly. 'What's this?' I ask myself, as I notice something on the floor. There's a surprise waiting for me. It's a two-day-old newspaper! I eagerly grab it, anxious to catch up on the news. My son wants it too."

5:53 A.M.: "My boy and I have finally reached an understanding with each other. The TV is between stations. I choose to leave it this way. He and I are sitting next to each other enjoying last week's news. We're both holding a section of the newspaper. I am reading it. He's eating it."

6 A.M.: "I've just gotten all the newsprint off his face and hands. I'm working on scrubbing it off the wall. This little cyclone of a boy seems to have unlimited energy, complete and utter disregard for me and my wishes, and excessive curiosity. Sometimes he drives me nuts."

What's New with Dad?

If you're like most dads, you've found the last 10 months to be a combination of wonder, pleasure, pain, and love. Having children triggers a variety of emotional responses not easily characterized, quantified, or otherwise measured. As a result of his nature, the way he was raised, his present circumstances, and a variety of other less identifiable factors, every father comes away with a different set of feelings. Unfortunately, sometimes anger and irritation can cause even the most well-meaning parents to act in inappropriate ways.

While men have made incredible gains over the past few decades—demonstrating improved devotion to their families, ability to nurture their children and support their partners, and generally acting in a manner becoming a dad, the plain truth is that some men are still responsible for a lot of what's wrong in the world. Young men sometimes act out violently or in socially inappropriate ways, commit the majority of violent crimes, and often express anger counterproductively.

For a young family, these frightening (and often deadly or damaging) behaviors can devastate a child's chances to grow and develop normally. While not unique to dads, these issues are found more commonly in men than women. While a fine line often exists between right and wrong, proper and improper, listed here are a few of the numerous behaviors that are just plain wrong.

Inappropriate Parental Behaviors

Assault: Strictly speaking, an assault, as defined by the law, is the threat of physical violence toward another person. For our purposes, however, we'll assume that assault means actual, direct, physical contact. Assaults come in numerous different forms—punching, kicking, slapping, shaking, spitting, twisting limbs, bruising, squeezing, burning, and scalding. As unbelievable as it seems, these behaviors do occur—they're called child abuse. There's simply no justification for using any of these brutal behaviors on your baby—at this age or any other. You'll be reported to your state's child protective service if anyone suspects that you've been engaging in these behaviors. Your child's pediatrician has a legal responsibility to report you as well.

> **TIP**
>
> The word "discipline" actually comes from the Latin word meaning "to teach." Use discipline to teach a child correct behavior, not to instill fear of punishment for incorrect behavior.

Threats: We all make constructive threats toward our children—if he doesn't clean his room, there won't be any TV, or not eating dinner will preclude eating dessert. There are a variety of other destructive threats, however. Threatening a child with physical violence, for example, can be a trauma and will induce fear and anger. Threats of abandonment can be equally destructive, making a child feel tenuous, rejected, and worthless. Threatening a child with loss of love can be devastating. Sometimes the threats are spoken aloud, "If you don't do this, I won't love you anymore," while often threats are transmitted through body language or through the withholding of affection. These threats can be very injurious to your child's self-esteem.

Ignoring Discomfort: Ignoring a child's obvious physical or emotional discomfort is a form of child abuse. Don't fail to soothe, treat, protect, and reassure your injured child.

Sexual Issues: There are really two distinct categories here. The first is your baby's natural curiosity about the human body. This is common, natural, and understandable. The second is the inappropriate sexual interest some men have for their babies, children, or other young kids.

Sexual abuse of minor children is an epidemic. Under no circumstances should you be examining or touching your child's genitals or anus unless your

TO SPANK OR NOT TO SPANK

The issue of spanking has been discussed for generations. Obviously, it's important to understand the difference between a savage beating and a limited spanking. The area, though, is a controversial one. There are those who feel that an episode of controlled spanking, born out of love and concern and when used judiciously, can be a deterrent against dangerous behaviors. Proponents claim that a spanking serves not only as a disciplinary measure but may also be appreciated by an out-of-control child.

On the other hand, opponents feel that spanking is simply a form of violence. Feeling that violence begets violence, those opposed to spanking find absolutely no need, ever, for the measure. Opponents of spanking maintain that spanking offers no deterrent value. They also feel that the act itself sends the wrong message—that violence is an effective way to solve problems.

The truth is that most parents, from time to time, will impulsively strike their child on the hands or bottom out of fear, anger, or concern, particularly when the child is engaged in dangerous behavior. Spanking should *never* be used to humiliate a child, should *never* be done with an object other than the palm of the hand, and should *never* be done on naked skin. Furthermore, spanking a child who doesn't yet possess the capacity to understand why she is being spanked (i.e., under two years old) is not appropriate. There's no reason to spank your 10-month-old.

child has been injured, has a complaint or a rash, or needs cleaning. If you feel uncomfortable examining your child or if such examination requires anything more than just a cursory glance, it's best to have the pediatrician do it.

A baby or child, like anyone else, is a sexual being. Baby boys—even infants—may from time to time have erections. This is completely normal.

TIP

Consistency in discipline is a must. If you want a child to stop doing a certain action or behavior, you must let him know it is wrong every time he does it. Responding only on occasion will confuse the child.

Babies and small children will be naturally curious about your "privates," particularly if you're bathing together, and may even grab your genitals. He should never be punished for his curiosity (although jumping up in the air out of surprise is not terribly uncommon). A small baby can be redirected easily, while an older child can be gently told that "Daddy's penis is private."

On occasion, usually while you are bathing your baby, the softness of the skin may be stimulating to you. This usually brings a degree of emotional discomfort. If this happens, it is time to end that night's bath.

Purposely showing or allowing a child to touch or examine your genitalia is also completely inappropriate. If you're having sexual feelings toward your baby or other small children, ask your primary care physician to recommend a therapist—you don't need to tell your physician the reason.

For the young child under three or four, casual nudity—getting dressed in the room while your child is present—seems reasonable to me. As your child grows older, it's probably best to dress in private.

Scolding or Humiliating for Soiling a Diaper: Regardless of your child's age, punishment for wetting or soiling is inappropriate and will fill your child with feelings of "badness," being "dirty," fear, failure, defeat, and low self-worth.

Abandonment: Leaving your child alone in a car, house, store, restaurant, park, and so on places your child in great psychological and physical danger.

Using Drugs or Alcohol: Appearing intoxicated before your child is inappropriate. The negative effects of drugs and alcohol—whether precipitating violence, impulsivity, unpredictability, or hypersexuality—will have lifelong implications for your family. Most sexual abuse occurs during times of intoxication. Giving your child drugs or alcohol is completely inappropriate and also constitutes child abuse.

Being There for Your Baby

Now that we've discussed what not to do, how about relaxing a bit and doing something nice for yourself? As is quite often the case, some dads, particularly those in the last few months of the first year, fall into a pattern of a mindless routine, which breeds boredom and inactivity:

> "Toward the end of the first year, I was really starting to feel down. I got depressed because, although my baby was thriving and it seemed to those around me that I was being a pretty good dad, I wasn't taking care of myself. For the first time in my life, I was overweight, wasn't really enjoying anything, hated my job, and felt like I had nothing that I could really call my own. I wasn't engaged in any activities and felt really unattractive. I felt like my wife didn't enjoy me sexually anymore because of my weight problem. My self-image was at an all-time low. I didn't understand it either. I had everything—a house, a great wife, a terrific baby!"

So what does it take to maintain your mental health? For the majority of dads, getting back on track is really just a matter of time and some structured activities.

Maintaining Your Mental Health

Overcoming Guilt: Sometimes, being good to yourself means having enough time to be *by* yourself. Being there for *yourself* is a crucial component of being and feeling healthy. For some dads, this can be difficult:

> "I can't help but feel guilty whenever I want to do something for myself. It sometimes means that I have to be without my baby and partner.

TIP

Always follow through. If the child does not stop an action after you say "No," get up and immediately move the child away from what she was doing, especially when the child may be in danger. Also, try to distract her by taking her into another room or giving her something to do or play with.

There have been times when I just have to get out of the house and away from everybody. Is this okay?"

There'll be times when you'll want to be alone—without your partner or baby. There's absolutely nothing wrong with this; in fact, it's essential to your mental health.

Finding Time: Carving out time to improve yourself or to relax is really a must. The best way to obtain some free time is to discuss the issue with your partner. Don't stonewall, threaten, or demand. She'll undoubtedly want some time too. Weekends and evenings are great times but may interfere with the care of your baby. Your partner may also want you around to help with the chores. Compromise with her. Trade babysitting or household chores. Work out a schedule so that you can each be free for a few hours every week.

Another way to find time is to get up an hour earlier in the morning. Since some dads either work late or help with a restless baby in the middle of the night, this is often not practical. Nonetheless, a lot of dads use this free time wisely:

> "When I'd start to feel out of shape or a bit down, I'd get up around 5 A.M., go into the basement, and do the treadmill. By the time everyone else was up, I had already gotten in an hour of exercise."

Likewise, some dads use the time for hobbies:

> "After dragging my sagging body out of bed at the crack of dawn, I'd go to my computer and do some writing or play some computer games. When else could I have found such complete peace and quiet?"

Eating: Many dads, who are otherwise concerned with how their partners look, tend to let themselves go—snacking on junk food, missing meals, or eating seven of them a day.

Having little energy for their kids and feeling poorly, these dads need help! Poor eating habits can also adversely affect appearance and self-esteem. You are what you eat, and a poor diet can sometimes turn even nice guys into snarling, irritable boars. There's another good reason for practicing good eating habits—being there for your baby, for a long time.

FOCUS: DIETS FOR DADS— QUICK AND HEALTHFUL EATING

You don't have time to prepare the meals right? Eating properly doesn't mean going to extremes. You don't need to spend tons of time cooking or preparing. Keep it simple. Listed below are just a few examples of the ordinary kinds of healthful foods you can prepare quickly. For the ordinary working dad, the prep time for the following foods is under 20 minutes per day! I've asked my good friend, "Physical Ed©"—bodybuilder, personal trainer, and former Mr. Massachusetts—for some tips and recommendations:

Physical Ed's and Emotional Marc's Basic Guidelines

• Avoid processed foods.

• Avoid foods high in fat and sugars.

• When eating out, beware of oils and fats in sauces.

• Keep alcohol consumption to a minimum.

• In order to avoid eating a huge dinner, eat four to five small meals a day.

• Snack on low-fat, sugar-free yogurt.

• Eat pretzels instead of potato chips.

• Instead of eating whole eggs, eat egg whites. Make egg-white omelets with low-fat cheese and vegetables.

• Eat turkey or chicken (take the skin off) instead of beef.

• Use jam on bread instead of butter or margarine.

Exercise: What challenging diet would be complete without the misery of exercise? You've heard it before. Many dads choose cardiovascular activities to help maintain or improve their overall health. Some prefer lifting weights. Some dads can't quite seem to find the time or motivation and get down on themselves:

> "I'm embarrassed. I want my daughter to grow up feeling proud of me and the way I look. I feel like a little runt. I'm weak and out of steam. What can I do?"

Exercise plays an important role in any overall health plan. It helps with self-esteem, offers a release of tension, builds a strong body, and helps create a healthy family environment. You'll sleep better and feel more invigorated. Don't think that you need to go to extremes either. Walking, in-line skating, tennis, swimming, jogging, using the treadmill, martial arts—all can be effective forms of exercise. Start slowly; put your headphones on or drag the treadmill to the TV. Do whatever you need to do to get into it or back into it.

Hobbies: Distractions, skills, and hobbies are all important ways of keeping yourself happy and fulfilled. Don't underestimate the power of doing something that pleases you to induce a sense of well-being and relaxation:

> "I used to love collecting coins. I haven't done it in a year. I forget what they look like. They're kind of round and shiny aren't they? I really miss it. In fact, I often used the time to collect my thoughts or to put the whole workweek into perspective. Now, without my hobby, I feel perspectiveless."

If you had a hobby, get back into it. If you don't, check with your local community college to see if there are any classes that interest you. Remember, there's more to being a dad than physically being there for your baby:

> "After being homebound for 10 months, I finally unlocked the door and let myself out. I started jogging again. Now I feel so much more alive. I enjoy my family more and appreciate getting back into an old hobby of mine—staying in shape."

Sex: If you and your partner are still not having sex on a regular basis, you need to ask yourselves why. The private intimacy offered by sex is as important to a couple's mental health as anything we've discussed so far. Make sure your sex lives are on track.

Laugh: The power of humor can get you through some pretty wild times. When I stop to think of all the unbelievably ridiculous things that have happened to me since the birth of my children, I can't help but feel better. Maintaining your sense of humor is something great you can do for yourself. I've often felt that my own (at times precarious) personal mental health has been steadied by laughter:

> "One day, when my wife was out, I was stuck at home with my son, who was carrying on terribly. He'd been teething and was inconsolable. He was miserable. I was miserable. I couldn't tell what it was he wanted. I tried everything. I rubbed his gums, I rubbed my gums, I gave him some magazines to chew up—you name it. He was totally uninterested in the things he so typically loved. I took him up to my study and unleashed him. I couldn't even get him to ruin any of my personal belongings!

> "I had actually begged my wife not to go out that day. I whined to her and volunteered to do all the things I never ever wanted to do in order to avoid taking care of the little critter. I confessed to my wife that I'd recently been rethinking our roles and had developed an intense craving to leave everyone behind and do the grocery shopping, go to the laundry, take the car and get it washed—even vacuum it! She's a bright woman and didn't buy any of it. I even implored her to let me do something I've never done before—go out and buy myself pants. She was impressed but said no.

> "So there I was with my 10-month-old. He was screaming wildly. I was screaming wildly. I needed to go to the bathroom in a major way. When I stopped to think about all the ways in which my BMs had been interrupted by a meddlesome, cabinet-slamming, toilet-paper-unrolling, crawl-a-holic, I decided to defer.

> "I was just about to place my baby in a safe place and drive myself into the local ravine for some relief, when he smiled at me lovingly, then pooped his shorts. I couldn't believe the mess. Quite frankly, I couldn't

FOCUS: PHYSICAL ED'S AND EMOTIONAL MARC'S DUMBBELLS FOR DADS

The following workout is designed to make dad a mean, lean, baby-playing machine.

Basic Guidelines

1. Consult your physician prior to any workout program.

2. Weight training should be done three times a week for 30 to 45 minutes per session. A day of rest between workouts is essential.

3. Don't attempt serious weight training unless instructed in the proper techniques by a qualified instructor.

4. Cardiovascular (aerobic) exercise should be done two to three times each week for 20 to 30 minutes.

5. If you smoke, try the "patch," acupuncture, hypnosis, or behavioral therapy. Do anything to stop.

First Session

Start with the following exercises for your first workout:

Abs for Dads

1. Sit-ups: Using proper technique, do 15 to 25 of each of the following, wait no longer than 60 seconds, and do another set. Do two to three sets.

2. Leg raises: Using proper technique, do 15 to 25 of each of the following, wait no longer than 60 seconds, and do another set. Do two to three sets.

Pecs for Little Perching Peanuts

1. Bench press: Using weight that allows you to do 15 repetitions (reps) comfortably, do 12 reps of each of the following. Wait 45 to 60 seconds between sets and do two to three sets.

2. Incline press: Using weight that allows you to do 15 reps comfortably, do 12 reps of each of the following. Wait 45 to 60 seconds between sets and do two to three sets.

Strong Shoulders for Sitting Babies

1. Shoulder press: Using weight that allows you to do 15 reps comfortably, do 12 reps for each of the following. Wait 45 to 60 seconds between sets and do two to three sets.

2. Lateral raises: Using weight that allows you to do 15 reps comfortably, do 12 reps. Wait 45 to 60 seconds between sets and do two to three sets.

Second Session

Do only these exercises during your second session:

Terrific Triceps for Teetering Tots

1. Dips: Do 12 to 15 reps. Wait no more than 60 seconds between sets and do two to three sets.

2. Push-downs: Using weight that allows you to do 15 reps comfortably, do 12 reps. Wait no more than 60 seconds between sets and do two to three sets.

Big Back for Bouncing Baby

1. One-arm rows: Using weight that allows you to do 15 reps comfortably, do 12 reps. Wait 45 to 60 seconds between sets and do two to three sets.

2. Pull-downs: As for one-arm rows, do two to three sets of 12 reps.

Bulging Biceps for Balancing Baby

1. Dumbbell curls: Using weight that allows you to do 15 reps comfortably, do 12 reps. Wait 45 to 60 seconds between sets and do two to three sets.

2. Standing curls: As for dumbbell curls, do two to three sets of 12 reps.

(cont.)

FOCUS: PHYSICAL ED'S AND EMOTIONAL MARC'S DUMBBELLS FOR DADS

(continued)

Third Session

Do only these exercises during the third session:

Pony-Ride Legs

1. Leg extensions: Using weight that allows you to do 15 reps comfortably, do 12 reps. Wait 45 to 60 seconds between sets and do two to three sets.

2. Leg presses: As for leg extensions, do two to three sets of 12 reps.

3. Leg curls: Again, do two to three sets of 12 reps.

Finally, don't forget that exercise and a proper diet will benefit everyone in your family. This small investment of time and energy will produce solid, long-term emotional and physical gains.

tell where the poop ended and he began. For an instant, I considered dropping the entire child, diaper and all, into the washing machine or dunking him and the diaper into the toilet. But I tested the water. It was just too darn cold. I changed him—but only after climbing into a wet suit.

"He was still screaming, and I thought maybe he'd like something to eat. I went over to the cabinet where the baby food lived. I had never been there before. I opened it. There were 600 jars of baby food. I stood there, staring at them in vacant disbelief. There were jars mashed to the brim with foods of different colors and textures. I could smell some of them through the glass. There was some stuff in those jars that was alive. These jars of baby food—foods I had never imagined existing—actually looked back at me. The carrots, an entire row of them, smiled at me, chuckling out loud because they knew full well that I hadn't been paying close attention to my baby's diet. I didn't know what foods would be safe to give him, and the baby food knew this. I was angry at my wife for leaving me without a map. I looked at my son. 'You're not hungry are you?' No answer. 'I didn't think so.' I snarled at the jars of carrots, corn, and mush as I closed the cabinet door.

"Discouraged, I felt the mush on the back of my arms that some people would call 'triceps.' Then I had a great idea! I could make my son happy and improve my physique at the same time. Baby dumbbells! Using my son as a dumbbell weight, I stood in front of the mirror like an idiot. With my son gleefully perched on my shoulders, I started with my triceps. I lifted him up and down behind my back to work the flapping skin on the backs of my arms. He loved it! I loved it! I went on to do baby biceps, curling him upward ever so gently. Then lying on the floor with him teetering over my chest, I did pecs. Back, legs, shoulders, I did it all. By the time my wife got home, my son was completely chuckled out and we were both in great moods. She looked at us suspiciously and said, 'Now about the grocery shopping . . . .'"

Reprinted with Special Permission of King Feature Syndicate

Spend Time by Yourself: Arrange to have some "by yourself" time or some time alone with your male friends. Go to the movies or eat out:

"Sometimes, when I'm by myself, I end up thinking about my family and come up with new ways to have fun with them."

If you're unable to do for yourself, you can all but forget about being a great dad. It just won't be possible. Remember your own needs: a good diet, regular exercise, and some fun and relaxation. Try to do the things you need to do to keep yourself sane and happy.

Bonding with Baby

Your little one is probably getting ready to walk soon. At this stage he can probably walk while you hold his hand or while holding on to furniture. He has the leg motion down, just not the balancing act. There are several things you can do to help him learn to balance and walk on his own.

Begin by holding both of your baby's hands and walking with him. From holding his hands tightly, you can progress to just holding out your hands flat to him and letting him hold on to you as he follows you around the room. After he has mastered that step, use just one of your hands to support one of his hands. You're still able to help him stay up, but he must rely on himself for a greater part of balance.

Once he's going pretty good with only a little help from you, it's time to take off the training wheels. For the next exercise, you should do it along with your partner. Start by sitting on the floor, facing one another, with your legs slightly spread and feet touching. While holding your baby's hands, have him walk from one parent to the other. After he understands what's going on, support him by holding his waist and eventually letting go. Your partner and you are close enough to catch him if he begins to fall. If he doesn't want to walk on his own, the parent toward which he's walking should hold out his or her hand and give the baby something to walk toward. As he's able to walk from one of you to the other, slowly begin scooting away from each other. This will require him to walk further and further on his own. After lots of practice and exercise, your partner and you can be on opposite sides of the room.

Balance is achieved as a result of the equilibrium in the inner ear. If your baby seems to have a hard time standing or walking because of the balancing part of the activity, he may have something affecting his equilibrium, such as an ear infection. He may act like he is dizzy while upright. Be sure to let your pediatrician know of his balancing problem. She can then check to see if it is caused by an illness or something else. However, it may just be that your baby is still developing.

Growing Together

So far, you and your baby have had 10 months to be together. Although you've grown accustomed to the concept of togetherness, you're still discovering new things about each other every day. That's the way it should be. Living, growing things are full of surprises. In the next chapter, I'll continue my discussion of inappropriate parental behaviors and take a close look at traveling with your baby.

Being a parent is unlike any previous job—the results of any one action are not clearly visible for a long time, if at all.

—Anonymous

12

The Eleventh Month

Y ou're in the home stretch! Can you believe the first year is almost over? For some dads, the entire year will have passed by at the speed of light:

> "I swear, I just blinked and in that fraction of a second, my daughter, this little beanpole of a girl, just recently so incapable of moving or doing anything on her own, is walking, smiling, cooing, and loving. I'd do it again in a second!"

While for others, the first year dragged on just a bit:

> "I kept blinking but nothing ever happened. At times, it seemed like we were all ants crawling through molasses. Taken on their own individual merits, each one of my daughter's misadventures—her refusal to sleep, *ever,* her yelling and shrieking, not to mention her poor table manners, seemed so reasonable, so . . . 'baby-like.' But I finally caught onto the conspiracy. These behaviors constituted an entire chunk of rudeness—a freestanding, independent, malicious mass of nastiness, spaced over the entire year so as not to appear too obvious, screeching itself down the chalkboard of my life. What a nightmare. I stabbed myself with a big nail, twice, just to make sure I was really awake. I kept asking my wife, 'Darling, is there a return policy on this child?'"

Regardless of your point of view or belief in conspiracy theories, the year is winding down. Hopefully, nobody's gotten hurt, you still have most of your teeth, and you've learned something about living together with your new family. Still, some dads find fatherhood to be a complex struggle that seems to get more difficult as the months go by. In this chapter, we'll take a last look at some of the angry emotions that can interfere with family life. On the lighter side, we'll also explore ways in which traveling with your family can be made a little easier.

What's New with Your Baby?

In the eleventh month, your baby, almost a toddler, will be interested in two things only: cruising around and ignoring your pleas to stop ruining important family heirlooms. Always delighting you, your baby will seek the most interesting and destructive routes as he shuffles from one piece of furniture to the next. You'll likely be uttering gentle words of encouragement: "Hey, slow down!" "Be careful!" "Oh my gosh, don't eat that!" "Put that down!" "Get off the TV!" "Don't lick the dog!"

Developmental Milestones

You'll probably notice a broad range of behaviors during this stage. Don't forget, these "stages" or "milestones" are simply convenient ways to categorize your baby's progress. All babies develop at their own pace. Try not to be too alarmed if you're not noticing some of these milestones.

If you do have serious concerns, it's advisable to contact your child's pediatrician. She will probably offer reassurance or may choose to perform some diagnostic tests to make sure your child's development is progressing normally. Rarely, if a problem is detected, your doctor may recommend various early interventions or refer your child to a specialist.

Motor Strength: With confidence, your baby will be pulling herself up with relative ease. Starting to spend more time upright than crawling on the floor, she may even be able to stand alone, without support, for brief periods. Some babies may be able to walk unassisted. Look for your baby to take some interest in using a cup and feeding herself.

Your baby's body control will be markedly improved. Using muscle tone not previously available, look for your baby to get in and out of tight spots on her own.

Language Skills: Jabbering on and on about who knows what, your baby will seem to be holding conversations with you, invisible people, your pets, and so on. This new command of language will also be accompanied by greater comprehension skills. Your baby may start to understand some basic commands and requests—and will promptly ignore them.

Sensory Perception: Problem solving, manipulating toys and objects, and improved memory are commonly found during this stage. Since your baby is now better able to get around, he will learn more about the sizes or dimensions of the world. Hand-eye coordination continues to improve, allowing your baby to stack things or place smaller objects within larger ones.

Psychological: Your baby's improved coordination and refined motor skills will help you both learn more about mutuality. That is, you and your baby will soon be able to play together in ways not previously possible. Playing patty-cake or rolling a ball back and forth to each other will be evidence that your baby is more in tune with you. The eleventh month also brings with it updated issues in emotional development. Stranger anxiety and tears when you leave the room may continue. Your baby may also change moods rapidly. Since she is continuing to develop a sense of individuality and naturally wants the world to conform to her wishes, look for shows of intense anger during times of frustration.

What Is Your Baby's Day Like?

Let's rejoin our exhausted dad from the previous chapter, as he prepares lunch for 11-month-old Hurricane Henry:

10:45 A.M.: "It's never too early to start preparing lunch. At last glance, my little genius was sitting in the family room watching the TV—just watching the TV; it wasn't turned on. He seems content though, sitting there babbling to himself. It sounds like he's chatting with someone in Russian or some mysterious coded language. I watch him for some time. He's very busy these days. I don't need to literally sit next to him every second, which is nice, but I can't take my eyes off him for more than a minute. For reasons I still don't fully understand, much of my hard work in safety-proofing has largely gone unnoticed by my little Houdini, who seems to be able to unlock the unlockable. Whenever I need my vitamins opened, under strict supervision, I give him the bottle and he chews the cover off. I wish I could safety-proof the dogs. He loves them. He's always gnawing on them, climbing over them, or pulling on their lips. They're nice dogs, but every mammal has its breaking point."

11 A.M.: "If he's on schedule, soon he'll be screaming for something to eat. It's my job to find something suitable. I turn and head toward the baby food cabinet. I'm not afraid of it anymore. 'I'm not afraid, I'm not afraid,' I repeat to myself. Gone are the nightmares of falling into and being devoured by huge jars of thick, slimy, multicolored baby food. Gone are the frightening thoughts of feeding the baby purple slop he's allergic to and having to carry him, gasping for air, to the emergency room. Gone are the fears of having every precariously perched jar, all 600 of them, tumble over on top of me. No longer do I fear lying there crushed under all that glass, being slowly devoured and absorbed by baby food.

"I've made progress. I've made peace with that baby food living there in that cabinet, and we've all become moderately good friends. I respect them. I understand that this is their home too. I also know that they no more look forward to being ingested by my son or smeared all over his face than I look forward to cleaning up the mess afterward. I think they have a new respect for me too.

"I boldly put my hand into the cabinet and work my way through my wife's elaborate food-filing system. The jars yield to me easily. Sensing my enthusiasm and confidence, they step aside. I'm heading straight for the good stuff and grasp a jar. Making no sudden moves, I gracefully begin my withdrawal from the closet. On my way out, a jar of squash snaps at me. I ignore it, and it leaves me alone. I triumphantly pull out an age-appropriate food—yellowish green stuff."

11:07 A.M.: "I glance over my shoulder into the family room and find my son using one of the dogs to steady himself. He's pulled himself up by grasping the thick skin around the dog's neck ever so gently between the tip of his thumb and forefinger—a new skill for him. 'Nice doggy,' I say calmly and reassuringly. If the dog perceives even for one second that what is happening to him is anything but normal, the entire structure of the family will collapse. 'Nice doggy,' I say again, smiling at him. The dog starts to walk toward me. The baby falls on his face, pulling with him a clump of dog fur. I pick the baby up and carry him into the kitchen."

11:15 A.M.: "As I place him in the high chair, he starts to scream. He always does that. I've always maintained that he screams in anticipation of being forced to eat yellowish green baby food, but I'm assured by my wife that, like Pavlov's dogs, the thought of eating has conditioned within him an excited response. I think I'm right. I unclench the baby's fist and extract the dog's hair. It's a fairly substantial clump. If this were my hair, I would want this back.

"I start the mealtime chant of distraction and start to shovel it in: 'Daddy loves you. Daddy's proud of you . . . Here, eat this . . . open your mouth . . . don't touch your hair . . .' The chant culminates when he poops. Now daddy is unhappy."

11:17 A.M.: "I try to efficiently change the baby, but he's kicking and hissing at me. He's hungry. I ask him if he'd rather sit in a poop all day. I think he would. I wish the poops would treat me with the same kind of respect the baby food has recently shown me. I finish up and transport him back to the high chair, where I bolt him in."

11:20 A.M.: "I pull my chair up to his. We smile at each other. He has two teeth on the top and two on the bottom, and when he smiles, he looks like a beaver. This must be why the food ends up everywhere but in his oral cavity—it's scared. The food refuses to go into the beaver mouth. The boy probably sees my unshaven face and bizarre smile and thinks I look like a beaver. I open the jar and pour some more of the substance into his little dish. He's grabbing for the spoon. I pull the spoon away, then reconsider. It's odd, but my sense is that he really wants to feed himself. 'OK,' I say, 'feed yourself.'"

11:30 A.M.: "Having fed the middle of his chest all by himself, the baby is covered with yellowish green stuff. He seems very happy. Who am I to interfere with his pleasure? Another meal survived."

What's New with Dad?

All parents become angry. After all, you often make enormous sacrifices for your baby and are sometimes rewarded by oppositional behavior and lack of sleep. Most of us, however, have the capacity to move beyond our anger. That is, we have a clear view of our lives with our families, which enables us to see the good and bad, the fun and not so fun. We're able to merge all of these experiences and come away from a given situation with a healthy outlook and constructive way of interacting.

While most dads enter fatherhood with the best intentions, not all dads successfully work to control their anger. Some dads choose to raise children in an atmosphere of fear. Although the courts would likely disagree with me, to my way of thinking, being a dad should be seen as an honor or a privilege— not a right. Of course, not all anger is harmful or pointless. In this section, we'll take a look at the spectrum of anger—from being slightly "pissed off" to reasoned anger to destructive, harmful rage.

Anger

Few, if any, dads can honestly say they've never gotten angry:

> "I admit it. Every now and then, I feel like I am just going to blow and totally lose control."

Anger is particularly common during the initial stages of infancy when everyone in the house is run down. As your baby grows older, you may find yourself tempted to swat him every so often, particularly when he defies you or places himself in danger. There's a big difference, of course, between an impulsive yell or swat and egregious anger that results in real violence. There are also many different kinds and degrees of anger. Episodic, situational anger is very different from a chronic, persistently angry way of perceiving and interacting with one's environment. Violent, impulsive anger is different from normal feelings of frustration and irritability.

Commonly, men who have a history of anger or a "short fuse" have a strong chance of becoming even less tolerant of changes in their environment when they become dads. These dads may be more likely to respond with anger, whereas dads with histories of tolerance and patience will have less trouble adapting to fatherhood. The Focus on page 250 lists some of the more common manifestations, causes, and treatments of different kinds of anger.

Being There for Your Baby

Ah, the family vacation! Who could ever doubt the peace of mind the family journey brings:

"I'll never forget our first big vacation with our daughter. She was four months old. We went all the way to the tropics and stayed in a nice hotel. Our baby screamed all night. The people next to us knocked on the walls and screamed at us to stop beating our kid. We never even had the chance to swim. It was awful."

But not all travel experiences with baby are bad:

"We took our baby to Disney World. It worked out well. He carried on a bit on the airplane, but in general, we had a relaxing time."

Vacationing with Your Baby

All vacations with young children take solid planning and preparation as well as patience.

Planning Your Trip

Traveling with your baby can introduce her to an enormous new world and can acclimate her to adventure. It can be terrific. However, ask yourself why you're doing this. Are you going away to impress your friends or yourself? Are you a masochist? Remember, unless you plan on ditching your baby with some tropical day care for the duration of the trip, you're going to be spending most of your time together. Make sure you understand the limitations, advantages, and disadvantages of traveling with your baby. If you have a very difficult baby, it might make sense to delay the big vacation or take several shorter, more local excursions.

TIP

If you're traveling, your will should be completed (see page 173).

Choosing a Destination: If you decide to go away, be sure to select a place that's baby friendly. That is, choose a location that's used to catering to families with small kids and has a high tolerance for baby behaviors. Restaurants, hotels, and entertainment should be accustomed to kids' needs, messes, and behaviors.

Avoid going to places that are excessively cold or unbelievably hot. Between changing outfits and sweating, you'll be wiped out before the trip even begins.

FOCUS: WHAT CAUSES ANGER
AND WHAT TO DO ABOUT IT

Regardless of the cause of your anger, it's you and only you who bears the responsibility to express your anger in an appropriate fashion. "Causes" are not excuses for bad behavior.

Some Common Causes of Parental Anger

Lack of Privacy: Something seems to happen to the concept of privacy once a baby comes into your life. Going to the bathroom and bringing a crying child with you, leaving your bedroom door ajar at night so that you can hear your baby's cry, having your belongings sucked on, having to hold or play with your baby during previously sacred personal time, listening to your baby's snorts and snores invade your bedroom at night by way of the baby monitor—these are just some of the many ways in which your private life has changed.

Socioeconomic Pressures: Babies are expensive to feed, clothe, and care for. When you're faced with financial problems or trouble at work, coping with additional expense can take its toll:

"My baby is intolerant of most formulas. The pediatrician put him on this formula that costs almost six dollars a can! He drinks two cans each day and has to be on it for six months. I have enough money trouble. I'll do it because I love my baby, but man, it infuriates me."

Problems with Your Spouse: Anger often appears in the context of the relationship. If you and your partner have had trouble in the past and it's led to unresolved or continuing anger, you have work to do. You may, for example, be feeling jealous of her abilities as a mother, competitive with her for the love of your child, or unhappy with the way she looks:

"My wife called me a bum the other day because I was just sitting around relaxing. The truth was that I wasn't just sitting around. I was thinking. She's the bum. All

she does is sit around the house. I have to go to work and then come home and
work some more.”

Envy: Dads may feel (or may even be) neglected at times. Some dads may feel their partners are giving their babies preferential treatment:

“My wife thinks everything our baby does is just ‘darling.’ It must be nice to be
able to fart freely and not be called a disgusting pig.”

Situational: Getting angry over situational problems is quite common in fatherhood:

“I was picking my daughter up off the floor when she grabbed the hair on my arm
and twisted it so hard that I impulsively screamed at her and firmly pried her hand
off. She didn’t understand why I was so upset and started to cry.”

Personality Problems: For some dads, being angry, not just at their family or baby but at the world, is a way of life. This sort of anger is often associated with a personality disorder. A personality disorder describes a set of behaviors or attitudes that adversely affect the ways in which some people interact with the world. These dads tend to see the world, and everyone in it, as hostile forces to be reckoned with. They may be rigid, controlling, and uncompromising and tend to see things in terms of black or white, right or wrong. They may also feel as if everyone else is “wrong” and they’re “right” and may respond with rage to any suggestion that they’re at all to blame for a given problem. People with certain kinds of personality disorders don’t feel responsible for their own actions or behaviors. They’ll rarely apologize—an essential gesture in all healthy relationships—unless it’s self-serving to do so.

Mental Illness: While people suffering from mental illnesses are generally not angry or violent, those who fail to take their prescribed medication or who are in denial of their illnesses may be particularly vulnerable to rage.

“Short Fuse”: For lack of a better term, there are some dads who, while otherwise seemingly “normal,” may explode at the slightest provocation. Of

(cont.)

FOCUS: WHAT CAUSES ANGER
AND WHAT TO DO ABOUT IT

(continued)

course, there's a broad range of displays of anger or impulse behavior—some harmless and others destructive.

Depression: Depression—sadness, the blues—can lead to irritability and anger:

"When I'm depressed, I become completely disinterested in anything around me. I isolate myself and become very intolerant and nasty. My wife gets like that too. We're charming to be around. We sometimes wrestle with each other for the last Prozac in the box."

Sleep Deprivation: For those of you whose babies are still not sleeping through the night, I feel your pain. None of my kids were good sleepers and awakened at all hours of the night, most every night, for years:

"The torture of sleep deprivation is unlike anything I've ever experienced. I'd rather be torn apart by weasels than have to sleep in a house where my kid wakes up 15 times a night for no good reason. I've actually wept from anger and fatigue."

Angry with the Wicked Things Babies Do: Being chewed on, sucked on, thrown-up on, peed on, pooped on, having your belongings eaten—how much can a man take?

"There have been times when I have considered my daughter to be little more than a thankless bag full of puke, poop, and pee. I then have to stop and remind myself that there is also saliva, blood, and ear wax."

Drugs and Alcohol: Just about the worst thing you can do to yourself and your family is to indulge in illicit drug use or abuse prescription drugs or alcohol. The characteristics of these substances will have devastating effects on your baby and family:

"I used to be a happy drunk. Now, when I'm intoxicated, I punch doors and yell and scream. There's no telling what I might do if someone gets in my way."

Family History: Angry dads tend to have angry kids—not always of course, but it's not atypical:

"My dad was an angry man. He'd shriek, yell, slam doors, and scare the hell out of me. Sometimes, when my baby does something I don't like, I get this feeling— something that I automatically have to respond to. It just sort of bubbles up. I'm scared I'll be like him in that way."

How Does Anger Manifest Itself?

Does anger always reveal itself through slamming doors or yelling and screaming? Not typically. Anger can manifest itself in just about any way.

Withdrawal: Withdrawal is a common way to show anger. Isolation and diminished sociability can be a sign of tension, displeasure, or anger.

Passive Anger: Being chronically late for meetings, procrastinating, and "forgetting" to do something important are some of the ways in which anger is expressed indirectly.

Irritability: Having a short fuse or reduced threshold for tolerating perceived problems often leads to irritability, which can be a harbinger of angry feelings.

Increasingly Punitive Discipline: Watch out for feelings of wanting to be more of a disciplinarian. Unless your baby has recently held up a bank, this is likely a sure sign of anger. Your first-year disciplinary measures should consist of gentle redirection, a firm but polite "no," and consistency.

Aggression: Slamming doors, yelling, and throwing things are obvious signs that your anger has gotten out of control.

Poor Work Performance: Poor performance on the job can be a sign of increasing anger toward your job, your boss, or your life in general.

(cont.)

FOCUS: WHAT CAUSES ANGER
AND WHAT TO DO ABOUT IT

(continued)

Poor Family Skills: Inability to relate well to your family can be a sign of anger.

Depression: Sometimes, anger and depression go hand in hand.

Sexual Acting Out: Having affairs can signal, among other things, intense hostility and rage.

Domestic Violence: The anger responsible for violence toward your partner affects everyone in your family—and will for generations. Not only will this destructive form of violence impact your spouse, but it will have serious implications for your children. Here are some disturbing facts: Over three million children witness spousal abuse every year; and around 20 percent of all homicides (some of which are the result of domestic violence) are witnessed by children. You should also know that your children will carry the sounds, images, and fears of your assaults for the rest of their lives.

Child Abuse: There are many different forms of child abuse—physical abuse, sexual abuse, emotional abuse, and physical neglect. Consider the following facts:

- The most common form of abuse is physical neglect.

- Physical and sexual abuse are increasing.

- Twenty to 40 percent of adult women and 10 percent of adult men have been sexually abused during childhood.

- More than one million children are abused and have suffered observable harm from abuse or neglect each year.

- Two thousand children die each year as a result of abuse.

- The abuse will likely be transmitted down through the family tree. Violence begets violence.

What to Do About Anger

Some anger is appropriate and needs no "treatment," while anger that is unrelenting, overly reactive, frightening, physical, or otherwise destructive is cause for concern.

Avoid the "Black or White," "All or Nothing" Approach to Anger: Accept and rejoice in the dichotomy of feelings that healthy dads experience. That is, you can feel angry with your partner and baby but still be in love with them.

Identify Whether a Problem Exists: If you've ever tried to reduce your expressions of anger, felt angry when those around you mentioned your anger, or experienced significant guilt feelings about your anger, you may need to examine treatment options more carefully. If you have trouble saying you're sorry or if you feel as though you're never wrong, it's time to take a look at yourself more closely. If your anger frightens those around you, would wake up a slumbering baby, leads to physical assaults or destruction, or interferes with your or (your partner's) functioning, get help now.

Solve Problems Together: Enlist the support of your partner, even if you feel she's part of the problem.

Consider Individual and/or Couples Therapy: Ask your primary care physician or trusted friend for the names of a few different therapists. Therapy need not be excessively time consuming or expensive. Behaviorally oriented therapists have been trained to quickly focus on a specific set of problems. Through certain therapeutic interventions, they can help you better control your anger.

A Variety of Medications That Treat Impulsive Behavior, Anger, and Depression Are Readily Available: Check with your primary care physician. Since they may exacerbate the problem, avoid long-term use of sedatives, sleeping pills, or hypnotics and ask instead for information on mood stabilizers, antidepressants, or agents used to treat impulsivity.

(cont.)

FOCUS: WHAT CAUSES ANGER
AND WHAT TO DO ABOUT IT

(continued)

Develop Healthy Outlets: You should have personal time, space, hobbies, friends, and the opportunity to exercise vigorously. These activities need not be expensive or time consuming, and they are essential for the maintenance of your mental health.

Develop Your Own Traditions: Make your own traditions with your baby. If you're feeling left out of the intimacy between your baby and partner, develop your own special closeness. Sing to your baby, take her to the park, or bring her along when you go out for coffee.

Keep Your Sense of Humor: In previous chapters, we've seen some of the ways in which humor can be used to help stabilize an unpleasant situation. While it's not always easy to laugh instead of yell, I can only tell you that a good part of your family's health depends on *your* health. Substituting a good line of gentle sarcasm or playful self-criticism rather than a yell or scream can make a big difference.

Comfortable Accommodations: Request, through your travel agent (or call the hotel directly), a microwave oven, small refrigerator, and crib for your hotel room. Call the hotel again the day prior to departure and make certain they haven't forgotten.

If your baby doesn't sleep well, request a room on a lower floor.

Being Comfortable on the Airplane: Very young babies can be held on your lap in an airplane for no charge. If your child is very squirmy, be prepared to cross time zones walking up and down the aisles. Infant car seats can be strapped to purchased seats and can be helpful in containing a restless baby. They seem to be fooled by being in a car seat and tend to be less fussy.

Traveling first class is great, but unless you and your baby are very well behaved, it's not worth the dirty looks of first-class passengers, who won't be willing to tolerate your baby's screaming, pooping, or puking. It's better to fly coach with the masses. They're more understanding. Regardless, wherever you sit on the plane, you'll always sit near a guy who says he always gets stuck sitting near people like you.

Request two aisle seats across from each other. Your baby can then be passed back and forth across the aisle. You'll have more freedom of movement. Your partner can rest without being bothered by you or the baby and vice versa.

Try to keep all your stuff—diaper bag, jackets, and so on—as close to you as possible. It's much easier getting everything and everyone together upon landing if all your things are centrally located. It removes one or two steps in trading your baby back and forth.

Equalize Pressure in Baby's Ears: Be sure to give your baby a bottle or pacifier or feed him age-appropriate food both when taking off and landing. This will greatly aid in equalizing the pressure in his ears and avoid a screaming baby and a painful flight.

Play Update

The following activities are designed to strengthen your baby's muscles, improve her sensory and expressive skills, and hone her emotional development.

- Roll a ball back and forth with your baby.

- Show your baby how to drop an object, like a ball, toy, or stuffed animal, into a pail. Now let your baby try.

- Quiz your baby by asking him where his tummy is or where mommy is.

- Continue reading regularly to your baby.

 **TIPS**

- Anticipate being thrown-up on, perhaps by your baby. Always carry plenty of wipes or a cloth diaper in the diaper bag.
- It's nearly impossible to find a good place to change your baby on an airplane. One way is to cram yourself into the so-called bathroom with your partner and baby. Sit on the covered toilet with your baby's legs pointed toward your partner while she changes the diaper. Not easy. Smells bad.

- Be sure to always replace a dangerous object that you've removed from your baby's hands with another, more appropriate one. Don't simply take things away without replacing them.

- Lie on your back with your baby standing on your chest. Hold her arms and help her bounce up and down. This will not only make her laugh but will also improve her muscle tone.

Bonding with Baby

As your baby approaches her first birthday, she is getting ready to begin talking. It will begin with just a word here or there and over the course of the next

PACKING AND OTHER PREPARATIONS

- Consider hiring a transport agency or limo service to pick you up at your home and take you to and from the airport. You'll avoid airport parking headaches, and your family's walk will be shorter.

- If your baby is on formula, don't pack it. Buy a box or case of the stuff and check it through as luggage at the terminal. You can do the same thing with diapers, juice, and baby food. It's too bad you can't do it with the baby.

- Pack light for yourselves but don't skimp when it comes to your baby. Have lots of options for clothing and extras of everything for messes.

- Take a portable, lightweight stroller—they're more durable than they look. Hang carry-on luggage over the handles.

- Strap "fanny packs" onto your collective fannies. These can take the place of a purse. You can keep your wallet, camera, film, and a pacifier in it.

- Carry a backpack full of baby toys, the video camera, snacks, distractions, and other essentials.

- If you or your baby are poor sleepers, consider packing a white-noise maker for the hotel room.

year will develop into complete thoughts and sentences. Following are a few tips and exercises you can do to help develop your baby's speech.

One of the most important things you can do to encourage your baby to talk is to listen to her. When she finishes, respond with something like, "Is that so," or "That's a good story," to let her know you were listening and are encouraging her to talk more. The more you listen, the more words you will be able to pick up. If she's saying the name of an object, reinforce it by picking up the object and giving it to her or at least pointing to it if it's too big to move. Some words will be too garbled to understand. Try giving her things until you find the right object to go with what she's saying. Don't worry—she'll let you know when you're right and when you're wrong.

Another concept to work on is opposites. These can include big and small, hot and cold, in and out, up and down, and so on. Illustrate each with an example. For big and small, use two similar toys of opposite sizes. For hot and cold, you can use ice and warm water. Much of this we take for granted. However, we had to learn it, and so does your baby. In addition to this, start

AT THE AIRPORT

- Never turn your back on your stroller-bound baby.

- Let the skycaps check your luggage for you. They'll greet you at the car. The cost of the tip is well worth avoiding the headaches of dragging everything inside.

- Don't check your baby's diaper bag. Carry it with you. This bag should contain essentials for traveling—change of clothing, diapers, wipes, and enough food, formula, and bottles to get you to your destination.

- Don't check your baby. You'll need to take her on the plane with you.

- Ask for a gate check and attach it to the stroller.

- Take advantage of the early boarding call and stroll your baby right up to the plane.

- Remove your baby, fold up the stroller, and leave it on the floor in front of the door to the plane with the gate check attached. Upon deplaning, it will, in theory, be waiting for you.

mentioning the color of objects: the blue ball or the red block. Just by doing this, you will teach her the names of different colors.

Begin to use simplified adult talk instead of baby talk. This encourages her to speak with real words. You can also combine this with double-speak, where you speak in the adult talk, then rephrase with baby talk so she sees you mean the same thing but are just saying it differently. Slowly start introducing pronouns like "I" and "you" back into your speech. While she may not start using them for some time, she will be able to understand other people when they use them.

In the same way you introduce colors by just mentioning them during speaking with your baby, you can teach her the basics of numbers as well. Mention the number of things when you point them out: "See the two cats." Playing games with fingers, such as "Ten Little Indians," also furthers the concept.

Growing Together

As the eleventh month winds down and the twelfth begins, consider that your baby has matured and developed at an unbelievable pace. With your help, love, and guidance, she has taken in and integrated an astounding amount of knowledge and experiences that will help form the basis of future behaviors and attitudes. What responsibility!

AND SOME FINAL VACATION HINTS

- Keeping everyone well hydrated will reduce fatigue.
- When your baby naps, take a nap too.
- Trade off with your partner. Babysit for an hour or two so she can lie on the beach or shop and vice versa.

The final month of your baby's first year should be celebrated by everyone as an enormously important milestone. Don't forget, however, the contributions you, as a loving dad, have made to the quality of your child's life. Enjoy your time together.

Being a father
Is quite a bother,
But I like it, rather

—OGDEN NASH

13

The Twelfth Month

For your baby, now standing on the threshold of a far bigger and more accessible world, the twelfth month signals the end of the first year of developmental challenges—the essence of which forms the foundation on which your baby will continue to grow and flourish. For you—well, what does it signal?

> "Whew! It's over, but I know it's really just the beginning."

If your experience has been a largely positive one, perhaps it signals your acceptance of yourself as a dad. Perhaps you've found that being a father gives your life more meaning:

> "Before I became a father, I searched for a meaningful way to understand who I was and why I was here. I mean, I was happy with my wife, but I felt as though something was missing. My daughter brings me a happiness, even in tough times, that I never felt before. Fatherhood fills a large void for me."

If, however, you've experienced fatherhood as painful, unpleasant, or horrible, it's time to assess what went wrong:

> "It's taken me an entire year to admit this to myself, and I haven't mentioned it to anyone else yet; I really don't like my new 'job' as a dad. I don't think I'm very good at it, and nobody seems to benefit from me. No matter how hard I try, I can't bring myself to tell my child that I love

her. I feel worthless—like an unneeded appendage. I think I've always felt like this—even before my baby was born. It's very possible that my displeasure with my own fatherhood has more to do with my own sense of who I am and where I came from than with who my baby is. I feel so guilty. I don't want my child to grow up feeling rejected or unloved. I decided to get into therapy to prevent this from happening."

If your first year of fatherhood has brought up unresolved emotional issues, you may want to consider therapy. On the other hand, try not to feel too disappointed with yourself. Some dads don't particularly enjoy the first year but nonetheless go on to find the next stage of their child's life to be fantastic!

Whether you're a completely content dad, a dad in crisis, or a dad somewhere in the middle, as the first year winds to a close, one thing is clear—you aren't the same person you were one year ago.

What's New with Your Baby?

While you're busy trying to sort out who you are, where you are, how you got there, and what you're going to do about it, your baby is pretty darn certain who he is. By this time, many babies are novice toddlers and will be having a great time going from place to place, touching everything, tearing up things, and racing around. These behaviors form the core of your baby's personality at this particular time—and there's nothing you can do about it other than enjoy it!

Developmental Milestones

The end of the twelfth month sets the stage for a burst of new and creative energies. Look for vast improvements in a variety of previously difficult maneuvers. As usual, though, try to remember that your baby will advance on her own terms and that "milestones" are just convenient ways to group your baby's progress. Don't be overly alarmed if, when comparing your baby to her peers, she can't accomplish all of the same skills.

Motor Strength: Look for your babbling, jabbering baby to be better able to walk with assistance, stand momentarily, and have better control of his body.

Some babies will be able to walk well unassisted, while others may only now be starting to pull up and creep or cruise along the furniture. Climbing, twisting, turning with ease, and squatting will be easier for your baby. Manual dexterity will show marked improvement, and your baby will be better able to feed himself.

Language Skills: Language skills are progressing, and your baby will be particularly responsive to words that end in an "E" sound, like "doggy," "daddy," and "mommy."

Sensory Perception: Your baby's problem-solving abilities and memory continue to improve. Your baby may also be starting to learn to connect an object with its function. For example, your child may be able to comprehend that a spoon is associated with eating.

Psychological: "Mutuality," the inclusion of you in her world, will continue to develop. Since she is continuing to develop a sense of individuality, look for shows of intense anger during times of frustration. Your baby will take pleasure in her accomplishments. Searching for a hidden or desired object and capturing it will be an emotional triumph for your baby. These feelings should be greeted with your applause and smiles.

What Is Your Baby's Day Like?

Let's rejoin our exhausted dad as he helps to get Hurricane Henry ready for bed:

6 P.M.: "Well, it's never too early to start getting the baby ready for bed. We've almost finished dinner. I'm eating it, he's wearing it. The baby's in a particularly good mood tonight, which means that the pressure's on me to be in a good mood too. Dinner, while always eventful, is particularly satisfying tonight. The baby's much better able to feed himself when he feels so inclined. I'm so proud of him that I lean down to kiss him on the nose and am rewarded by a sneeze right in my mouth, spraying me with some kind of white, baby-food slime. You know, for months now, I've been making fun of his baby food. To be perfectly honest, it isn't so bad. I could do without the snot, though. After I wipe myself down and extract him from the high chair, we all go upstairs to get washed up for bed."

6:30 P.M.: "I put the baby on the bed and am desperately trying to remove his clothing. It displeases him, and he has, unwittingly I'm sure, kicked me in the crotch. He's screaming and cursing at me in some kind of language that sounds like a Korean-Dutch hybrid. As I struggle with him, I talk to him and tell him that he's a good baby, a nice baby, and a fun baby to be with. It doesn't seem to matter. I can't hold him still. As he wriggles away from me and heads toward the edge of the bed, teetering precariously close to the edge, I dive after him, fearful that he'll plunge off the bed into the abyss that is the floor, suffer a spine-crushing injury, and it'll have been all my fault. My groin still hurts me, though, and I'm moving pretty slow. I just miss his body as he slips off the edge of the bed. As luck would have it, I grab his foot. He's suspended upside down. He loves it. I gently put him on the ground, crawl backward across the bed, and head around the other side for him."

6:39 P.M.: "By the time I've reached him, he's standing up, holding onto the side of the bed. He's making his way toward my night table, upon which is meticulously piled a dozen or so important documents and a glass of water. I can't get to him in time. For an instant, just to show me how cool he is, he lets go of the bed and stands for a second or two, wobbling around like a Fabulous Walenda, then turns and looks at me, smiling broadly. I smile back, hoping that he'll interpret my gesture of friendliness and goodwill as a subliminal message not to mess with the stuff piled on my bedside table. He doesn't care about goodwill. He falls toward the night table and grabs my papers, pulling them off the table and onto the floor. The glass of water is spared, but it, like me, is perched precariously close to the edge. Holding my groin, I crawl over to him and pull the papers out of his mouth. He's angry at me for this, even though I give him something more appropriate to chew on (a pair of socks), and hisses at me. He stands and turns toward the night table again, where my water glass is sitting. The water beckons him."

6:42 P.M.: "I use a cloth diaper to mop up but there's too much water—I need a towel. No matter. I run into the bathroom to get a towel. I come out. He's gone. My wife comes into the room. 'Where's the baby?' she asks. 'What baby?' I respond. 'You know, the one you've been hanging out with for the past year.' 'Oh, *that* baby. I was just looking for the little pisher myself.'"

6:46 P.M.: "He crawls out from under the bed—a mysterious place full of dog hair, dust balls, and old sneakers. 'I must explore this place,' he seems to say, 'I will return to it again one day.' 'Bring Indiana Jones over here,' I say to my wife, who scoops him up skillfully without dislocating any part of his body. I am impressed. My wife and I both hold him down to remove his clothing. I grab hold of the sleeve of his outfit and shake him a bit to get the arm out. He laughs. He thinks it's funny. Meanwhile, I'm worried that I might tear his shoulder off. His arms are now encased in the outfit. Rolling around on the bed like that, he looks like a mummy. I like him like this, for an instant or two. I sit back, winded, and take a break. My wife removes the rest of his clothes until he's naked and places him on the rug. He pulls himself up and pees on the floor right next to the large water stain on the rug where the glass fell."

7 P.M.: "We put the baby on the bed and prepare for washing and getting him into pajamas. We know full well that this will be a two-person job tonight. I hold him down ever so gently while my wife gets the washcloth. The little monster kicks me in the groin again. I don't flinch—I've built up calluses."

7:15 P.M.: "He's washed and dressed. My wife asks me if I want to put him to bed tonight. I feign excitement, 'Oh, yes please, can I? I was hoping you'd offer. How'd you know that I didn't want to have any time to myself at all today?' She gets mad, understandably. I look at him. He's wearing fuzzy blue pajamas. He's the cutest thing I've ever seen in my life. 'Yeah, give him to me,' I say to my wife."

7:22 P.M.: "I'm rocking my boy and giving him a bottle. We're looking at each other. I can't believe he's a year old. Sometimes I get confused and can't remember, for an instant, whether he's six weeks or a year old. I'm sure it's wishful thinking. I'm so glad he's growing up, but I'm afraid it'll be all over too soon. I'm full of a thousand feelings."

7:30 P.M.: "Time has passed quickly. I stare at my baby. I look at the little bits and pieces of myself and my wife in his face. My distress and anguish, my rude awakenings and sleepless nights, my mouth full of his food, his mouth full of lint and dirt and sneakers, all seem worth it now. He closes his eyes and goes to sleep."

Health Issues: Twelfth-Month Pediatric Visit

The last checkup of your baby's first year will include a history, a physical, and perhaps a routine pinprick blood test. Your pediatrician will spend some time assessing your baby's developmental milestones. If you have any concerns, be sure to ask questions.

Measuring Height, Weight, and Head Circumference: As is typical for these visits, the doctor or nurse will check your baby's height, weight, and head circumference. The doctor will assign a percentile to the figures, comparing the measurements to other same-age babies. All children develop and grow at different rates. Feel free, however, to ask the doctor what the measurements are and whether she has any concerns.

History: After the measurements, you'll be asked how things have been going and whether there have been any noticeable problems with your baby. Your pediatrician will also want to know how your baby is feeding, sleeping, and acting. Feel free to join your partner in describing how home life has been. It's important for your pediatrician to obtain your perspective as well.

Physical Examination: As usual, you can expect your pediatrician to perform a thorough examination, checking your baby carefully to make sure her body is functioning as it should be.

In order to assess your baby's development, your pediatrician may also spend some time playing with your baby—testing responsiveness, coordination, hearing, speech, and strength.

What's New with Mom?

Don't forget to congratulate your partner! After all, she's made it! Look for some of these feelings to emerge during the last month of the first year.

She May Feel . . .

Joy with Baby: Despite all the challenges she's faced and even though she may be exhausted, your partner is probably very much in love with her baby.

Like a Mother: Try to remember that she has her own doubts, concerns, and issues. While she may not necessarily feel like *her* mother, after all the sleepless nights, baths, feedings, sore breasts, trips to the doctor, and so on, your partner will definitely feel like a mom.

Ready for Another Baby: Soon after the end of the first year, some moms feel ready for another child. Many, on the other hand, feel as though they don't yet know the first one well enough or don't want to split their time between two. Some moms are perfectly nauseated by the very idea.

Proud of Her Accomplishments: Deeply satisfied with her ability to mother, your partner may feel enormous pride at having created, nurtured, and cared for a baby.

Like Weaning: If she hasn't yet weaned the baby, your partner may decide that now is the time. When she does wean, look for feelings of both relief and loss.

TIPS

• As the year ends, consider meeting with your partner to discuss the year and make plans for the next.

• As usual, the best way to celebrate your partner's accomplishments and understand her frustrations, concerns, or conflicts is through open dialogue.

Exhausted: Chasing a one-year-old around the house all day is no easy task. This is especially true if your baby is still not sleeping well at night or is a high-maintenance baby.

Conflicted About Her Role: Some moms feel conflicted about their roles. Some are completely content to stay home and raise babies, while others are anxious to return to their careers out of the house or start new ones. Moms who must return to work may be experiencing stress and grief over having to leave their baby in the hands of another. Many moms express the hope that they can accomplish both paying work and involved mothering by working part time. Your partner may be confused about these issues, particularly as the first year winds down.

Stir Crazy: Feeling sensory deprived by caring for your baby, your partner may express frustration, anger, or sadness over her current role.

What's New with Dad?

If you're like most dads, there's a pretty good chance you're looking back at the blur that was the first year with some disorientation. While you may or may not be ready to do it again, one thing's for certain—the upcoming year will delight you and present you with unimaginable challenges. Get ready! Meanwhile, as this year winds down, what are you feeling?

You May Feel . . .

Like a Dad: Despite your own initial concerns about your ability to father, the first year has come and gone, and you've done it. By now, most dads have accepted the concept and settled in to their roles.

Delighted with the Prospect of a Second Child: Drawing on their success and accomplishments over the past year, some dads are wild about the idea of another baby. Others, however, are slightly less enthusiastic:

> "When my partner suggested that we start trying to have another baby, I felt like crawling under a rock and dying. I'm still not ready for the one I have!"

Confused About Your Role: Just as your partner has doubts, worries, and concerns, you also may be having ambivalent feelings about being a dad. You may feel overwhelmed and frustrated with your responsibilities.

Conscious of Your Own Mortality: The life cycle is in full swing! For some dads, having children, while meaningful and joyous, also reinforces the notion of their "temporariness."

Proud of Your Accomplishments: Most dads, when they think about it, pat themselves on the back a bit. Having given up time previously spent on hobbies or other activities that they loved in order to be there for their babies, dads should feel good about their accomplishments:

> "I had numerous concerns when I first started, and I know full well that there will be many challenges ahead. But you know what? I'm making it as a dad!"

In Love with Your Baby: This is what it's really all about:

"I've made many sacrifices—both social and financial—for my baby and family. But that's what you do when you're in love!"

Being There for Your Baby

Hopefully, you've been there for your baby this past year and are working on new ways to continue your involvement in her life. Of course, the "new" ways are really the old standards—helping, listening, talking, and loving! Page 272 lists some tips and suggestions you can employ as your baby's first year comes to a close.

Bonding with Baby

It's time for your baby's first birthday party. However, while your partner and you may want a big gala for your little one, chances are she will care less whether there is a party at all. Since at this age she'll feel uncomfortable around unfamiliar faces and may even cry, invite only family and a few close friends. Most babies won't have a lot of friends their own age; however, if she's in a play group, go ahead and invite a few of the babies she seems to get along with best.

When decorating the room, do so with a very light touch. Maybe have a theme based on a character your little one likes, such as Disney or Sesame Street. But avoid lots of streamers and don't spread confetti all around. Balloons are fine as long as you keep a close eye on the little ones. If they pop, the scraps from a broken balloon can choke a baby if put into her mouth.

Go ahead and let her have a little cake of her own. Since it will be demolished, make a cake for the rest of the guests. When selecting a cake for her, remember to pick one without chocolate, nuts, or honey. Also, be careful with ice cream. Don't give her any if it contains eggs. Party snacks should be placed out of the reach of the babies, or they may choke on things such as nuts or pretzels.

Try to time the party so she's well rested and fed. Otherwise, she may be cranky or fall asleep during the festivities. Be sure to record the event with photographs and a video camera if you own or have access to one. Watching her with her first cake is priceless.

TIPS FOR THE LAST MONTH AND ON . . .

- Enjoy your time together. The next year zooms by even quicker.

- Smile and laugh together with your partner and baby as much as possible.

- Hold, kiss, and hug your baby frequently.

- Tell your baby how much you love him and how important it is that he is a part of your family. Talk to your baby as much as possible.

- Give your partner the afternoon off once in a while.

- Take as many photos as possible. Put a picture of you hugging your baby in her room and talk about it with your baby.

- If grandma and grandpa are too intrusive, set gentle limits. Explain to them that "now" is not the best time to visit and offer them an alternative.

- Keep your baby occupied by showering him with a dozen balled-up pairs of socks.

- In order to head off sleep problems later on, avoid bringing your baby into bed with you unless she is sick or frightened.

- Babies are easily overwhelmed. To avoid tears, keep your baby's first birthday party small and "underwhelming" but get every bit on video.

- Now that your baby is walking, be especially aware of safety issues. Animals and small kids can be confused by the apparent "maturity" of your standing, walking baby. Watch out for rough play.

- Learn to listen. When you listen to your child and your partner, make them feel as if they're the only ones in the world at that moment.

- Get used to taking your baby out with you.

- Don't worry about making ordinary mistakes. Nobody appreciates perfection—it's boring, and you'll never learn anything.

- Work through the hard times with your partner through dialogue, humor, and compromise.

- Every once in a while, just to check up on yourself, take a step backward and watch yourself interacting with your family.

- Watch what you say and how you say it. Speak to your baby as if she can understand every word you're saying. Don't wait until she is old enough to understand your every word before you cease using obscene language. Old habits die hard. At about four months, your baby will start to remember language she has heard!

- Always carry a bunch of Kleenex in your pockets. You never know what's going to happen.

Keep Playing Together

Your baby's development continues on past the twelfth month, as should your bonding with him. If he's not yet walking, he will be soon. Encourage your baby to walk as often as possible. Since it's difficult at first, he may crawl because he can move around faster. To help bring him upright, place enticing items up out of his reach as an incentive to stand and walk. This also works well for babies who haven't decided they want to walk yet. With the development of walking and standing comes climbing. Little indoor slides are fun for this stage. However, you must supervise him so he doesn't fall off and get hurt.

Your little one needs variety. Get him out of the house and take him to new places. Let him walk, holding your hand if near dangerous areas such as streets or on hard, rough surfaces that can trip him or really hurt if he falls. Pet shops, museums, shopping malls—anywhere with something to look at, whether it be people, animals, even paintings and statues.

Another activity that will be popular is drawing and coloring. Give your baby a nontoxic crayon and some paper and teach her to draw. You must closely watch her, or she may end up chewing on the crayon. While a green mouth may be entertaining to you, especially when it freaks out your partner, it is not a good behavior to allow to develop. There are many toys that are rated for 12 months and up. You will have fun going to the toy store and picking them out. However, as before, just because it is rated for the correct age-group does not always mean it is safe. You should still watch for choking or other hazards. Pushing and pulling toys encourage your baby to walk during play. However, closely supervise your baby with these toys, especially if they have a cord for pulling. It could get wrapped around your baby's neck and cause strangulation.

Your bonding with baby should continue on, though she is no longer a baby. The key is to be involved and fun to be around. Do you want to be remembered as the father who worked hard to support your family or the dad who always took time to play and love and care for your child? The choice is up to you, and you must make that decision every day when choosing how you should spend your time.

Growing Together

About a year ago, you embarked on a bold new adventure. During this time, you've probably learned more than you realize, or at the very least refined what you already knew. You've gotten much better at helping, living with less sleep, teaching, compromising, playing, learning, being there, loving, working as a team, protecting, saving, assessing, worrying, dressing, undressing, cleaning, feeding, burping, wiping, eating quickly, driving while holding a bottle in someone's mouth, laughing, yelling, apologizing, holding, and carrying. Who would have thought that one little baby could be such a powerful force in your life?

As you continue on your way through the wonders of your baby's life, remember that he looks at you with awe, wonder, and admiration. To your baby, you're a timeless hero, and he wants to be with you. One of the nicest things you can do for your baby is to have a dialogue with yourself from time to time. Take stock of the past, present, and future. Ask yourself where you've been, where you're going, and how you can best get there. Remember, you're making history:

> "I remember the day my newborn baby 'spoke' to me in the birthing room and symbolically called me 'Dad,' setting off in me a barrage of conflicting emotions. That day, thousands of newborns around the world were having their first conversations with their fathers. As I sit with my one-year-old baby on my lap, I consider, for a moment, my own dad. I used to think he would have made a great president. Now, to my baby, I'm presidential material. In this fabulous Möbius strip of fatherhood, where one point twists impossibly around, seeing all sides of everything, only to meet itself again, the laws of physics and psychology merge, allowing this glorious ritual of learning to be fathers to come full circle. I don't think I'd make a very good president but what lovely and joyous pressure!"

APPENDIX A

Common Childhood Ailments

There's little that arouses such concern, fear, and anxiety as having to deal with a sick child by yourself. Perhaps you've been depending on your partner to handle your baby when he's sick. One of these days, though, chances are you'll need to administer medications or make some important decisions without your partner. Fortunately, most ailments that occur during the first year of life aren't serious and, with your doctor's help, can be treated at home. Regardless, it's vital that you familiarize yourself with the basics of medical treatment.

Taking Care of Your Sick Baby

Once you've determined that your baby is ill, what do you do to make your sick child more comfortable?

Never Worry Alone: When in doubt, phone it out. If you're at all uncomfortable with a given situation, call your pediatrician. If your pediatrician, or her designated on-call substitute, seems uncomfortable with the idea of receiving phone calls during off hours, find another doctor. Have a low threshold for using the emergency room.

Keep a List of Emergency Phone Numbers: Have a list of important phone numbers easily visible, among them your pediatrician, the local emergency room, fire and police (911), a poison control center, and a friend or neighbor who can watch your other children if you need to leave the house quickly. Review these numbers with babysitters and other family members.

Comfort Your Suffering Child: Sometimes, comforting, holding, or rocking your baby will be enough to diminish the pain or fear that often accompanies injury.

Observe Your Child Carefully: You're not your child's doctor and shouldn't be making life-or-death decisions, but you can help by being observant. While most illnesses aren't serious, there are several childhood ailments that if left untreated can progress rapidly to severe injury or even death. You have nothing to lose by using your local emergency room—even employing an ambulance—if you're feeling strong discomfort about your child's appearance or clinical condition.

Essentials for Your Medicine Chest

There are a variety of medical supplies that every home with kids should have. Most are inexpensive. As a general rule, it's always best to check first with your pediatrician before using any medication on your baby. Make certain you not only have the following items in your house but also are familiar with their use. Make sure they're locked up.

Medicines

Analgesics: Analgesics are pain-relieving medications. Aspirin, acetaminophen, and ibuprofen are but a few. As a rule, you should be able to do without aspirin, which should never be given to children (including teenagers) because it can induce Reye's syndrome (see the following discussion). You may want to purchase an over-the-counter ointment for your baby's teething gums that contains a local anesthetic and can provide temporary relief. The concentrations of medication in infant, child, and adult medicines are very different. Therefore, be sure to use the appropriate form for your baby.

Antipyretics: Antipyretics are medicines that are used to bring down a fever. The analgesics listed previously are also used in this capacity.

Anti-Inflammatories: These are medications, such as ibuprofen and aspirin, that are used to help relieve the swelling and irritation that can accompany a variety of clinical conditions. Acetaminophen is not an anti-inflammatory drug.

Cold and Flu Medications: Not to be used unless cleared by your pediatrician, these over-the-counter medications can help relieve stuffy or runny noses, coughs, and other cold symptoms. A number of different compounds exist. Ask your doctor.

Antifungals: You've probably always wanted to know how to treat that mushroom growing out of your baby's armpit. Antifungal creams and ointments can be helpful in treating somewhat more serious diaper or groin rashes. Babies can develop fungal rashes under their arms and necks as well. However, before using antifungals, consult your doctor to make sure the rash is caused by a fungus. It could just be eczema.

Antibiotics: Antibiotics must never be administered to your baby unless prescribed by your pediatrician. Over-the-counter antibiotic ointments, on the other hand, may be helpful in the treatment of cuts and scrapes. Antibiotic ear- or eyedrops may be prescribed by your pediatrician to fight local infections.

Emetic: An emetic, like syrup of ipecac, is a liquid that induces vomiting and is used in certain cases of poisoning. It can be purchased over the counter. The induction of vomiting with certain toxins can make matters worse, however, so you must call your pediatrician or local poison control center prior to the administration of an emetic.

Bee Sting Kit: Very rarely, a young child can suffer a serious reaction to a sting. A bee sting kit is a syringe containing epinephrine, which is to be used only in cases of dire emergency; for example, when your baby develops severely labored breathing. Your pediatrician will prescribe it for your baby and educate you as to its use if your baby is allergic. After the first sting, if he develops any of the previously mentioned symptoms, immediately go to the emergency room at the closest hospital.

Ointments: Petroleum jelly for chapped lips and diaper rash creams are a necessity. Get your pediatrician's professional opinion on the best products and how to use them before you purchase any of these.

Hydrocortisone: This ointment is good for taking care of nonfungal rashes. Again, check with your physician before using.

When to Go to the Emergency Room

There are many clinical conditions that require immediate medical intervention. Hopefully, you and your baby will never be faced with such an emergency.

However, the following clinical conditions must not be ignored. If your baby is experiencing any of the following, phone your doctor or 911 immediately.

High Fever: Fever greater than 104 degrees. Phone your doctor for advice.

No Food or Liquid Intake: Most babies will have times when they choose not to eat or drink much in a given day. When lack of appetite is accompanied by a perpetually dry diaper or very dark smelly urine and a pale appearance, dehydration must be considered. Phone your doctor.

Changes in Mental Status: Your baby's mental status is a good measure of her physical condition. A sudden change in the way your baby does these things could signal an important medical problem. Daytime lethargy, a confused or dazed appearance, disorientation, inability to respond normally to you, constant tearfulness, or any other behavior that didn't exist before should set off an alarm. Phone your doctor immediately.

Uncontrollable Diarrhea or Vomiting: Don't let this go on too long. Severe fluid loss from vomiting or diarrhea can put a young child at serious risk of dehydration, electrolyte imbalance, and even death. Call your doctor if vomiting or diarrhea persists for more than 24 hours.

Rash or Spots: A quickly appearing rash, particularly when combined with wheezing or another impairment in breathing, can lead to a life-threatening condition. Spots—purple, blue, or red—that develop rapidly on your baby's body could signal a virulent form of infection and constitute a medical emergency. Phone your doctor or 911 immediately.

Blue Appearance: This condition, known as cyanosis, means that your baby's body is not getting enough oxygen. When it occurs in a baby, cyanosis may indicate heart or lung problems or poisoning. You can sometimes detect it by looking at the area around your baby's mouth. A choking baby (see the following discussion) will also be blue in the face.

Choking: A choking baby is a terrifying sight. Described here is a brief summary of some of the measures you can take to aid your choking baby. It isn't, however, a substitute for a course in lifesaving. As a parent, it's your responsibility to stay current with lifesaving techniques.

As long as the baby is actively coughing, just stand by. If she is laboring greatly to breathe or isn't moving any air in and out at all, call 911 immediately. After you've done this, place the baby on her stomach, over your out-stretched arm with her head lower than her body. Hit the baby's back firmly between the shoulder blades four times with the heel of your hand.

TIP

Learn CPR—Contact your local Red Cross Chapter.

If this isn't effective, with her head still lower than her body, turn the baby over onto her back. Place two to three fingers of your free hand (the other hand should be supporting the baby's back, neck, and head) just below where a line drawn from nipple to nipple would intersect the bony sternum (chest bone). Push firmly and quickly and release, four times (one and two and three and four), depressing the chest by an inch or so each time (chest thrusts).

If the baby is still conscious, continue to alternate between back blows and chest thrusts. If the baby has lost consciousness, put your thumb in the baby's mouth to open it and hold the tongue and jaw between your thumb and fore-finger. Check the mouth and throat for any object. If you see a foreign object, try to sweep it out with one finger, making certain not to push it farther back (do not place more fingers in the baby's mouth).

If this isn't effective, place the baby on a flat surface and tilt her head back to open the breathing passage. With your mouth sealed firmly over the baby's nose and mouth, give two slow breaths. Look to see if the baby's chest rises and falls with your breaths. If so, the air passage is open. Make sure the baby is breathing on her own before you stop breathing air into her. If the air doesn't move in or out, continue the back blows and chest thrusts and breaths. Help will arrive shortly.

There are other finer points to these techniques that you need to be familiar with. Please register for a CPR course immediately.

Stiff Neck: A baby who appears uncomfortable when moving his head or whose neck seems rigid or stiff to the touch may have something as innocuous as a pinched nerve (not serious) but may possibly have an infection of the central nervous system. This is often accompanied by changes in mental status and fever. This is a medical emergency. Go to the emergency room immediately.

Seizure: Some babies can have a seizure (fit or convulsion) in response to a high fever. These seizures, if brief, usually have no serious long-lasting effects.

There are, however, other more serious conditions that can present themselves by way of a seizure. Unless your pediatrician has indicated otherwise, a trip to the emergency room is essential after a seizure of any kind.

Head Injury: All babies bump their heads. However, a blow to the head that results in immobility, seizure, unconsciousness, lethargy, a dazed or confused look, excessive sleep, vomiting, bleeding from the ears or nose, an obvious pushed-in area on the head, unequal pupil sizes, or bruising around the eyes or behind the ears must be evaluated by a physician immediately.

Electric Shock: Shocks that result in a loss of consciousness and/or cessation of breathing require emergency intervention.

Severe Cuts or Lacerations: Cuts or lacerations with bleeding that can't be stopped with pressure or bandages require emergency treatment.

Common Childhood Ailments

The following list is a brief overview of some of the common ailments that can affect your baby. As always, if you have questions or concerns, be sure to discuss them with your pediatrician. Remember, your goal is to feel somewhat familiar with these terms so you can effectively communicate with your partner and the pediatrician:

> "The first time my son got sick, my wife took him to the doctor. When she got back, she seemed to be speaking a different language. I had no idea what she was talking about, so I pretended not to care. I wish that I had the ability to talk about my son's clinical condition."

Respiratory Ailments

Lung (respiratory) problems can adversely affect breathing. The respiratory system starts with the mouth and nose. Air then passes through the trachea, or windpipe, and breathing tubes, or bronchi, which branch off into the lungs. Breathing problems may be the result of environmental irritants, allergies, infectious diseases, or other illnesses. Most of the time, respiratory illnesses aren't serious. However, when they do become severe, they may be life threatening. Look for fever, irritability, diminished appetite, nausea and vomiting, coughing, labored breathing, a change in color, and fatigue.

Common Cold (Rhinitis): Typically affecting the nasal passages, the common cold is caused by viruses. Often fluid from the nose drips down the throat, causing irritation and coughing. Colds in children, like in adults, generally disappear on their own.

Colds and nasal congestion are so common in young children that everyone should know how to treat the condition:

"What do I do with these boogers? My kid is whistling like a freight train!"

If your child is finding it difficult to sleep at night and is uncomfortable during the day, a gentle over-the-counter decongestant may be given with the approval of your doctor.

Suctioning out your baby's nose, although an unpleasant task for the entire family, can be accomplished with a nasal aspirator and saline drops. If your baby is coughing and you suspect she is suffering from postnasal drip, elevating the head of the crib (or lowering the end of the crib) is often useful. Cool mist humidity (or a steamy shower) can be effective as well. Don't forget to wash your hands after wiping your baby's nose.

Sore Throat (Pharyngitis): Pharyngitis can result from any number of clinical conditions. The blood vessels in the throat will be bright red. The throat itself may be red and possibly full of lesions and pus, which could signal a more serious infection. Your doctor may perform a throat culture to check for strep throat. If the culture tests positive, your baby will receive antibiotics. Your doctor may also suggest an analgesic medication.

Croup and Other Coughing: Croup results from inflammation from deep in the back of the throat, near the trachea (windpipe). Your baby may have trouble moving air and will labor to breathe. A honking sound when coughing is common. This can be very frightening. Your doctor will likely prescribe medications. You can also take a croupy baby outside into the cool night air.

The coughing baby can be made more comfortable by the use of a cool mist humidifier. Taking your baby into a steamy shower with you can also help to loosen a cough. Call your pediatrician, who may recommend a cough medicine and/or expectorant to help rid the lungs of secretions.

Epiglottitis: This rare but life-threatening closure of the respiratory passage in back of the throat may lead to suffocation or asphyxiation and is usually caused by infectious bacteria. Epiglottitis is characterized by severely labored breathing and a blue color to the skin. Epiglottitis is a medical emergency.

Bronchitis: This is an infection of the bronchial system—the network of breathing tubes in the lungs. When inflamed or infected, coughing is common. Your doctor may prescribe antibiotics if the infection is bacterial. A steamy shower or cool mist will help.

Bronchiolitis: An infectious process (see Bronchitis) may creep deeper into the lungs, causing an irritation of the small branches of the breathing tubes. Bronchiolitis causes wheezing and labored breathing and can be very serious if not treated.

Pneumonia: Pneumonia is a serious infection of a part of the lung tissue itself. Many viral and bacterial causes are known. Pneumonia in infants can be serious but is generally easily treated.

Allergies: Allergies to medications, certain foods, and the environment are found even in young children. Some allergies can cause minor irritation, itching, and hives; some can result in life-threatening medical problems, including an inability to breathe.

Ailments of the Eyes

Conjunctivitis (Pinkeye): This is an infection or irritation of the outermost covering of the eyeball. Its causes include bacterial or viral infection and environmental or chemical irritants. Infectious conjunctivitis is highly contagious, so remember to wash your hands. It may be treated with an antibiotic ointment prescribed by your doctor.

Strabismus: Lazy eye, or "squint," may be tough to diagnose for the first five to six months of your baby's life since his eyes won't fully function as a team for a while. Once diagnosed, early treatment is essential to preserve "stereo" vision. Your pediatrician will refer your baby to a pediatric ophthalmologist.

Ailments of the Ears

Otitis Media: Otitis media is an infection of the middle ear, otherwise known as a garden-variety ear infection. Ear infections can occur at any age and for a variety of reasons. Since a very young baby isn't yet able to articulate his distress in a meaningful way, and since he doesn't yet possess the ability to pull on his ear, detecting an ear infection can be a challenge. Typically, your baby will eventually develop a fever or may have a cold or the sniffles. Irritability, vomiting, and diarrhea can accompany an ear infection. Your baby's sleep or feeding schedule may be off. Your baby may want to be held all the time or may want to feed or nurse constantly.

Ear infections are diagnosed via an otoscope—an instrument inserted into the ear canal that, under the best of conditions, will be perceived by your child as an instrument of torture. Your baby will be treated with a course of antibiotics and possibly an analgesic. If caught soon enough, most typical ear infections have no long-lasting ill effects.

Sometimes, if your baby has had multiple episodes of ear infections over a given time period, your doctor may recommend a minor surgical procedure. The procedure, which involves placing tiny tubes in the ear, is designed to prevent repeated infections by relieving pressure in the ear and allowing the infectious material to drain. This procedure will provide pain relief to your child and will usually stop the seemingly endless cycle of infection. Also, a child that has constant ear infections may have difficulty developing his speech.

Foreign Body in the Ear or Nose: Although more common in older children, once your baby starts to motor around a bit, anything is possible. If you notice a foreign body inside your baby's ear (or nose), it will need to be removed by the doctor.

Unless the object is easily reachable with your fingers, don't attempt to remove it yourself. Never insert swabs or anything else into the ear canal or nostrils. It is important you see the doctor as soon as possible so the object does not cause an infection.

Gastrointestinal Illnesses

Nausea and Vomiting: Most babies spit up on a regular basis. Vomiting is another matter. The reason for your baby's vomiting must be found, so be observant and call your doctor. Treatment with fluids, such as sips of water or electrolyte solutions as well as bland foods in small quantities, will help.

Diarrhea: Certain foods, formulas, medicines, infections, flu, and other illnesses can cause diarrhea—loose, sometimes watery stools. Since any fluid that babies lose constitutes a large proportion of their already small fluid volume, diarrhea needs to be taken very seriously. Your doctor will probably recommend a special diet and fluids to prevent dehydration (not fruit juice) and may sometimes treat it with medications for more severe cases. In order to fully treat this condition, it's important to determine the underlying cause, especially if the diarrhea persists.

Dehydration: Dehydration, or fluid loss, can have a variety of causes— diarrhea, vomiting, and lack of appetite are but a few. Dehydration can be life threatening in an infant or young child. Like all medical problems, the origins of your baby's dehydration need to be discovered in order for your child to receive proper treatment. If your baby can be treated at home, your doctor will likely tell you to push clear fluids, like water and juices. Like adults, babies lose essential substances, called electrolytes, from their bodies. Your pediatrician may recommend that you purchase a special electrolyte solution designed to help replace these lost substances.

Constipation: As with diarrhea, many factors can cause hard, painful, infrequent bowel movements. Your doctor may advise a change in diet and will sometimes recommend a gentle laxative.

Constipation can often prevent your baby from feeling well enough to sleep soundly or eat normally. Depending on the age of your baby and his stage of food intake, routine constipation can be treated by increasing his consumption of fruits, fruit juices, and vegetables.

Environmental Ailments

Poisoning: Poisoning can occur with any number of substances. Once your baby is rolling around, grabbing everything in sight, accidental poisonings are more likely. Beware of poisonous plants, lead paint, medicines, and alcohol.

Suspected poisoning is cause for great alarm. Any of the following near your baby—pills on the floor, an open or empty pill bottle or liquid medicine on the floor, open detergents or alcohol, cosmetics or perfume, and plants and flowers—are cause for concern. You must assume your baby has ingested a substance unless you know for certain she hasn't. Whether your baby may have consumed medicine, plants, or "white-out," as my baby once did, try to remain calm. Call poison control immediately. Worry about your guilt later. As calmly as possible, give them your phone number and remain on the line. They'll tell you what to do. Have an emetic, like syrup of ipecac, ready, but don't administer it unless told to do so by poison control. Certain poisons do more harm coming back up than they do going down.

Fractures and Dislocations: An obvious fracture is generally easy to diagnose. Your baby will be in great pain and will be unable to move the limb. In severe cases, the bone may be protruding from the skin. Call your doctor, who may instruct you to immobilize the bone, use an ice pack, stop the bleeding, and give your baby an analgesic. Take your baby to the emergency room.

A dislocation of the elbow or shoulder is common in babies and is generally easy to repair. Your baby will be in pain and will be unable to move the affected area. Call your doctor.

Animal and Insect Bites: Animal bites can lead to skin, muscle, or bone infections and can also cause rabies, a potentially fatal disease. Watch insect bites for systemic (body-wide) or severe localized allergic reactions.

Childhood Infectious Diseases

Chicken Pox (Varicella): This is a common, infectious viral illness characterized by blistery red skin eruptions that scab over. Fever and itching are common. Your baby will want to scratch the lesions. To prevent scarring and local infection, cut her fingernails and consider putting soft socks or mittens on her hands. Treat the itch with an oatmeal paste or tepid bath. Don't give your child aspirin.

Chicken pox can be deadly to newborns. Therefore, keep your baby away from anyone suspected of having the disease (or shingles—it is the same virus) or having come in contact with an infected person. After 12 months, your pediatrician may suggest the varicella vaccine.

Fifth Disease: This illness is characterized by rashes on the body and generally has no serious complications. The facial rash resembles the result of a slap of a hand.

Flu: Common flu is caused by a virus and may lead to a variety of complaints—cold-like symptoms, fever, gastrointestinal distress, and aches and pains. The flu can be treated symptomatically. If you use an analgesic, be certain to avoid aspirin.

German Measles (Rubella): Rashes on the face and body are common in this infectious viral illness. If your baby has received the MMR vaccine, he should be immune to it.

TIP

Never treat your baby's medical illness with alcoholic beverages. Alcohol is a poison and can adversely affect your baby's nervous system.

Lyme Disease: Increasingly common, this disease is transmitted through tick bites and can cause a variety of serious symptoms, such as joint pain, changes in mental status, fever, and arthritis. It's treatable if discovered early.

Measles (Rubeola): This serious infectious viral disease, generally prevented by immunization, can cause a red rash all over the body.

Mumps: This viral illness causes swollen glands on the face and may result in serious neurological problems. It's prevented through immunization.

Pertussis (Whooping Cough): Cold symptoms, fever, severe coughing, and cessation of breathing can be the result of pertussis, a bacterial infection. Immunization will prevent this disorder.

Reye's Syndrome: Following a viral infection, Reye's syndrome may result in mental impairment and coma. The use of aspirin or aspirin-containing products around the time of certain viral illnesses seems to precipitate this disease.

RSV (Respiratory Syncytial Virus): RSV is characterized by coughing, a sore throat, and breathing difficulties. Treatment is symptomatic, and most babies recover. Preterm babies are at a higher risk for RSV.

Roseola: Fever, malaise, a rash, and no interest in eating characterize this illness. Roseola is usually not serious.

Scarlet Fever (Scarlatina): This disease, caused by the same organism that causes strep throat, can cause a rash and sore throat. If left untreated, it can lead to serious body-wide complications. Your doctor will prescribe antibiotics.

Tetanus: Caused by the poison produced by a bacteria, tetanus can cause muscle spasms, fever, seizures, and death. Immunization will prevent the illness.

Neurological Illnesses

Encephalitis: This potentially fatal illness is characterized by brain inflammation. It can be caused by any one of a variety of infectious agents. It can result in changes in mental status, seizures, coma, and permanent brain damage.

Meningitis: This is an inflammation of the lining of the brain and spinal cord. It can be caused by any one of a variety of infectious agents and, like encephalitis, can result in changes in mental status, seizures, coma, and permanent brain damage.

Seizures: A seizure, fit, or convulsion occurs during an insult to the baby's brain. This insult can result from a variety of illnesses, accidents, and clinical conditions—some serious and others benign. A febrile seizure, a typically nonserious but frightening event, can occur during an episode of high fever.

Bringing Down a Fever

Eventually, you'll learn to tell when a fever is rearing its ugly head. While you should learn to use a rectal thermometer, I'd encourage you to invest in an electronic ear thermometer. It isn't as accurate as a rectal temperature, but it's far less intrusive, and I think dads are more likely to use it.

Fevers can be caused by numerous ailments—some serious, most not. Whether simply due to a cold or something more serious, the reason for the fever must always be investigated. To bring down a fever, use infants' liquid acetaminophen (Tylenol) or infants' ibuprofen (Advil), as directed by your doctor. Don't exceed the recommended doses of medications. Doing so can severely injure your baby's internal organs. A nice way to bring the fever down quickly is to place your baby in a tepid (not too warm, not too cool) bath. Cool drinks can be helpful, so encourage your baby to drink.

OTHER FIRST-AID SUPPLIES

- Medicine dropper: You'll need this to administer medications to your baby.

- Nasal aspirator: This can come in handy for the little tyke who doesn't yet know how to blow his own nose.

- Thermometer: Although you should have a rectal thermometer on hand, an electronic ear thermometer, while slightly less accurate and substantially more expensive, is more convenient and easier to use.

- Bandages: Even little babies get boo-boos.

A Word About Medications and Alcohol

This information, discussed in chapter nine, bears repeating. Common, every-day items can pose a serious threat to the health and welfare of your baby. Here are a few:

TIPS

• Since an old filter left soaking in a humidifier can breed bacteria and viruses, which will then be shot out into the air and taken into your baby's lungs, be sure to periodically change the filter.

• Don't use unlabeled medicines or give out-of-date medications to your baby.

• To your baby, alcohol—any type—is a poisonous drug that can cause convulsions, coma, and death. Don't give your baby alcoholic beverages and don't allow him any access to them whatsoever. However, not only does alcohol come in the form of adult beverages, it's also found in many items around the house—cosmetics, rubbing alcohol, various elixirs, and mouthwash.

• Most antidepressant medications can be extremely hazardous to your baby. In overdose, they can cause cardiac arrhythmias, coma, convulsions, hallucinations, and death by cardiac arrest.

• Acetaminophen, a commonly used analgesic, is a particularly toxic drug when taken in high doses. Liver failure may result.

Be careful when giving several different medications at once to your baby. Inform your doctor of all the medications your baby is taking and call the pharmacist to check on any possible drug interactions.

Resource Guide

This resource guide has been included to provide some additional sources to help you become a better father. I have include various Web sites, books and publications, and even some movies for entertainment. The amount of material out in the world increases every day as more and more fathers are taking a more active role in the lives of their children.

Internet Web Sites

With the increasing popularity of the Internet, many sites covering the topic of fatherhood are springing up. Several are included here that provide good information and/or allow for fathers from around the world to chat and share the experiences of their joys and trials as fathers.

Dads Can

Address: www.dadscan.org
Description: This site is based in Canada and is written in both English and French. While limited in scope, it does contain a section of fathering tools and a chat room where fathers can meet and discuss the ups and downs of fatherhood.

National Fatherhood Initiative

Address: www.fatherhood.org
Description: This is the official site for the National Fatherhood Initiative (NFI). Its mission is to improve the well-being of children by increasing the number of children growing up with loving, committed, and responsible

fathers. A nonprofit, nonsectarian, nonpartisan organization, NFI conducts public awareness campaigns promoting responsible fatherhood, organizes conferences and community fatherhood forums, provides resource material to organizations seeking to establish support programs for fathers, publishes a quarterly newsletter, and disseminates informational material to men seeking to become more effective fathers.

The site contains a number of articles on fatherhood as well as advice and tips from other fathers. It also includes a message board where fathers can post questions and answers to each other. Finally, a catalog of materials that can be ordered from NFI provides a good source for purchasing publications.

The Fatherhood Project

Address: www.fatherhoodproject.org
Description: The official site for the Fatherhood Project. It is a national research and education project that is examining the future of fatherhood and developing ways to support men's involvement in child rearing. Its books, films, consultation, seminars, and training all present practical strategies to support fathers and mothers in their parenting roles.

The site consists mainly of a catalog of publications that can be ordered from the Fatherhood Project. Currently, there are no on-line articles or other information.

Bay Area Male Involvement Network

Address: www.bamin.org
Description: The Bay Area Male Involvement Network (BAMIN) is a partnership of several Bay Area child-serving agencies who are working to increase the involvement of fathers and other significant men in the lives of children in the San Francisco Bay Area.

While this site primarily addresses local issues, it is also a good source for articles on fathers' involvement in the lives of their children as well as other male involvement issues, such as education.

Families and Work Institute

Address: www.familiesandwork.org

Description: The Families and Work Institute is a nonprofit organization that addresses the changing nature of work and family life. It is committed to finding research-based strategies that foster mutually supportive connections among workplaces, families, and communities.

This is a place to go for fathers who have to work out of the home as well as for families with both parents working. While it includes some articles and on-line information, it is useful mostly for ordering publications on the subject.

FatherNet

Address: www.cyfc.umn.edu/FatherNet

Description: FatherNet produces information on the importance of fathers, fathering, and how fathers can be good parents and parent educators. It includes research, policy, and opinion documents to inform users about the factors that support and hinder men's involvement in the lives of children. FatherNet is also the official home of Father to Father, an organization dedicated to the importance of fathers in the lives of their children.

In addition to articles, this site also has an extensive listing of links to other related sites.

The Institute for Responsible Fatherhood and Family Revitalization

Address: www.responsiblefatherhood.org

Description: The Institute for Responsible Fatherhood and Family Revitalization is a home-based grassroots nonprofit organization dedicated to encouraging fathers to become involved in the lives of their children in a loving, compassionate, and nurturing way.

While the purpose of this organization is to get fathers back into the lives of their children, it contains some interesting statistics about children growing up in homes without fathers and the importance of a father's role in the family.

National Center for Fathering

Address: www.fathers.com

Description: The mission of the National Center for Fathering (NCF) is to inspire and equip men to be better fathers. In response to the dramatic trend toward fatherlessness in America, the Center was founded in 1990 by Dr. Ken Canfield to conduct research on fathers and fathering and to develop practical resources for dads in nearly every fathering situation.

This is a good site with articles on various topics and tips for fathering, a humor section, chat room, bulletin board, and links to other fathering sites. This is one site worth checking out.

The National Center on Fathers and Families

Address: www.ncoff.gse.upenn.edu

Description: The mission of the National Center on Fathers and Families (NCOFF) is to improve the life chances of children and the efficacy of families and to support the conduct and dissemination of research that advances the understanding of father involvement. Developed in the spirit of the Philadelphia Children's Network's (PCN) motto, *Help the children. Fix the system,* NCOFF seeks to increase and enrich the possibilities for children, ensuring that children are helped and that the system allows for the participation of fathers in their children's lives. NCOFF shares with PCN the premises that children need loving, nurturing families; that families need to be supported in providing nurturance; and that family support efforts should increase the ability of mothers, fathers, and other adults within and outside the biological family to contribute to the child's development.

The key attraction to this site is that it contains the FatherLit database. This database contains a great wealth of on-line literature concerning fathers and families on a large number of topics.

The Father's Network

Address: www.fathersnetwork.org

Description: This site celebrates and supports fathers and families raising children with special health care needs and developmental disabilities.

While limited in scope, it contains news, resources, articles by dads, and other areas for fathers of children with special needs.

Father Work

Address: fatherwork.byu.edu/birth.htm

Description: FatherWork contains over 300 pages of information, including stories from fathers illustrating "fatherwork" across various contexts (across the life span, in challenging circumstances, and so on); ideas on generative fathering, including their theory; numerous metaphors of fathering in many contexts; and hundreds of activities that fathers can do with children of various ages.

This site is developed and edited by David C. Dollahite, Ph.D.; Alan J Hawkins, Ph.D.; and family science students at Brigham Young University. It is a very good site for fathers with all ages of children. Unlike many sites, it has an area specifically geared to fathers of infants.

Father's Forum Online

Address: www.fathersforum.com

Description: This is a great site for both expectant and new fathers. While based in the San Francisco Bay Area, it contains some good information on fatherhood and the development of your child. It also encourages fathers outside of Northern California to organize their own father's forums and lists activities for local fathers.

Fathermag.com

Address: www.fathermag.com

Description: Fathermag.com is the on-line magazine for men with families. It is a great site with articles on a variety of fatherhood issues. Since it is an on-line periodical, there are always new articles. Some of the topics include health, the importance of fathers, the joy of fathering, single fathers, fathers and sons, fathers and daughters, and fathering news. Take a look at this site and return to it regularly.

Books and Publications

Here is a list of some good books full of information for new fathers and fa-thers-to-be. I have also thrown in a couple written by comedians to give you a laugh and help break up the tension of fatherhood.

At-Home Dad (Newsletter)

The *At-Home Dad* newsletter is devoted to providing connections and re-sources for the two million fathers who stay home with their children. The journal was created by Peter Baylies, also the editor, who has been a stay-at-home father since December 1992. A subscription to *At-Home Dad* costs $15 a year. For more information, contact:

Peter Baylies, Editor
At-Home Dad
61 Brightwood Ave.
North Andover, MA 01845-1702
By e-mail: athomedad@aol.com

The Gift of Fatherhood: How Men's Lives Are Transformed by Their Children

Aaron Hass, Ph.D.
Simon & Schuster
May 1994
Dr. Hass writes about parenthood as an opportunity for the father. He shows how taking an active role in children's care can have a positive effect on a man's self-esteem and self-confidence, making him happier and more fulfilled.

The New Father's Panic Book: Everything a Dad Needs to Know to Welcome His Bundle of Joy

Gene B. Williams
Avon Books
May 1997

This book will tell Dad everything he needs to know about pregnancy, delivery, and infant care and give him the confidence to experience all the joys of getting to know his new baby.

Fatherhood

Bill Cosby
Berkley Publishing Group
April 1987
Bill Cosby's bestselling, warm, and humorous look at fatherhood. Very entertaining. It helps fathers to laugh at some of the trials of fatherhood and enjoy the experience.

Seven Secrets of Effective Fathers

Ken R. Canfield
Tyndale House Publishers
August 1993
This book analyzes the habits and characteristics of fathers across America. It gives a good breadth of view from different perspectives.

Fathers and Babies: How Babies Grow and What They Need from You from Birth to 18 Months

Jean Marzallo
HarperTrade
March 1993
A comforting and vastly perceptive guide for fathers or soon-to-be fathers who want to learn how to enjoy the first months of their babies' lives.

Finding Time for Fatherhood: The Important Considerations Men Face When They Become Parents

Bruce Linton
Fathers' Forum Press
May 1998

The 20 essays in this volume run the gamut of men's concerns with fatherhood, including sex and parenthood, a mate's pregnancy, educating children, sports and gender roles, and relationships with one's own father.

Babyhood

Paul Reiser
William Morrow & Co.
August 1997
This is a humorous look at fatherhood by the star of *Mad About You*. It is great for helping to laugh at the situations you find yourself in as a father.

Movies and Videos

While the movies and videos listed here are not necessarily educational, they offer a good break and often a laugh at the job of being a father. It may also make you feel like you don't have it so bad. Though not listed, there are also a great many videos covering the topic of fatherhood and parenting.

Parenthood, 1989

Steve Martin plays a dedicated husband and father trying (and inevitably failing, as do most of us) to balance the demands of his kids and his job. Very funny, especially now that you have a child.

Baby Geniuses, 1999

When babies babble or draw, adults jokingly say they know what the baby is trying to communicate. What if a clinic found that these babblings and doodles were actually very intelligent responses or scribbling of an ancient form of communication? This movie stars Kathleen Turner and Christopher Lloyd.

Look Who's Talking, 1989

This is a classic baby movie starring John Travolta and Kirstie Alley with Bruce Willis as the voice of the baby. The things the baby is thinking are often hilarious.

She's Having a Baby, 1988

Kevin Bacon and Elizabeth McGovern are newlyweds struggling through the tribulations of a youthful marriage and pregnancy. The fears that Bacon has about being a father can easily be related to.

Three Men and a Baby, 1988

Three confirmed bachelors find a baby on their doorstep, and they have to cope with providing the little girl's basic necessities. Watching these professional men become entirely discombobulated by the child provides the most humorous moments, but as they warm to her presence and their foster-paternal instincts, the film reaches a level of sincerity not often encountered. Stars Tom Selleck, Ted Danson, and Steve Guttenberg.

Index

About the Author

Marcus J. Goldman, M.D., trained in general psychiatry at Harvard Medical School. He is board certified in general, forensic, geriatric, and addiction psychiatry, and is an associate professor of psychiatry at Tufts Medical School. He has taught psychiatry at Harvard, has published numerous articles on a wide variety of mental health issues, and is the author of *Kleptomania: The Compulsion to Steal*, and *What to Do After You Say "I Do"*, which he co-authored with his wife, Lori. Dr. Goldman is currently the medical director of New England Geriatrics. He lives in Massachusetts with his wife, four children, a Great Dane named Riker, and an Old English Mastiff, Zoe.

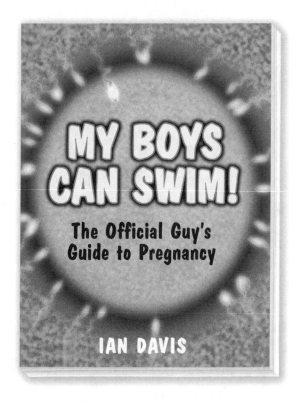